He'll Be
OK

CELIA LASHLIE

He'll Be OK

OK

Helping
Adolescent
Boys
Become
Good Men

Collins

First published in 2008 by Collins, an imprint of
HarperCollins Publishers Ltd.
77-85 Fulham Palace Road
London
w6 8jb

www.collins.co.uk
Collins is a registered trademark of
HarperCollins Publishers Ltd.

First published in 2005

A catalogue record for this book is available
from the British Library.

ISBN   978-0-00-727880-0

For the many good men I met on the journey:
know how special you are.

For the many gorgeous boys I met on the journey:
know that magic lies within you.

For Bek and Gene
and all who continue to walk with me
on the journey of life:
know it is you who give my life meaning.

Contents

Introduction:
The Beginning of the Journey

While I was still considering whether there was any real merit in writing a book about what I'd learnt as a result of my participation in the Good Man Project, I sat in a café and watched the interaction between a man and his three young sons, aged between four and eight. As I unashamedly eavesdropped on their conversation, it became apparent that the boys' mother had passed responsibility to Dad for the morning.

What drew my attention was the very calm approach of the father as he dealt with three extremely energetic boys. He allowed them time to clamber up onto the seats they'd selected and spoke clearly and slowly to them about what they might like to eat and drink. He gave them plenty of time to make their choices and didn't appear to get at all agitated when, more than once, they became distracted by something else in the busy café. When the youngest boy got down off his chair to investigate something he'd seen on the floor, his father just quietly asked him to sit down again, which the child did in his own time; no harm was done in the meantime.

When the food arrived, the father helped where necessary, but generally left the boys to manage it themselves and didn't become upset when, as was inevitable, things got a bit messy. He let them wander from the table once they'd finished eating, never rushing to stop them doing whatever they were focused on, but always keeping an eye on them and pulling them back within his reach whenever he deemed it necessary. The boys seemed to relax into their father's calmness, knowing intuitively how far they could go before he would call them back. His voice was their boundary: he knew it and so did the boys. As I watched, I couldn't help but wonder just how different things might have been if the boys had been in the company of their mother or another woman.

A week or two later I boarded a plane and found myself sitting across the aisle from a man and his son, a boy of about ten. The boy's mother and the younger brother, aged about four, were seated behind me.

The father and son were talking in low tones about the plane and what was happening outside on the tarmac and as we prepared to take off, I noticed the father reach for his son's hand and cradle it within his, presumably to reassure him. Once the plane was in the air, a commentary from the seat behind me began as the mother checked continually on the wellbeing of her elder son. At least every two or three minutes, or so it seemed, she asked the father whether the boy was 'alright', while at the same time working to keep an energetic four-year-old under control.

Perhaps I'm being a bit hard on the woman, but she appeared to be undermining the father's attempts to relate positively and reassuringly to his son. Having made several enquiries and comments about the boy's welfare, she then went on to contradict her husband. When he asked the flight attendant for coffee, from across the aisle (and one seat back!), she said, 'But wouldn't you prefer tea?' She seemed to have decided that she needed to be involved in everything that was happening with both her sons, while at the same time trying to manage what their father was choosing to drink.

In a way, the comparison between these two incidents has pushed me to write this book. I consider myself a feminist: I see feminism as the right of women to pursue whatever path they choose without in any way being restricted by their gender. My chosen direction in life has been strongly influenced by a desire to be free, while working to ensure that same freedom for everyone with whom I come in contact. I consider it extremely important that my freedom should not come at the cost of anyone else's. Unfortunately, my experience within the Good Man Project has left me with the impression that women's quest for freedom has perhaps taken its toll on our perception of men and manhood.

> 'I lost my jacket in the pavilion yesterday. If anyone picked it up I'd be grateful to have it back. Of course my wife says it isn't lost until she's had a look for it.'

In 2002 I published *The Journey to Prison: Who Goes and Why*, a book I was persuaded to write because of a growing interest, within various communities, in imprisonment and the issues associated with it. The opinions about crime and punishment I'd heard being expressed over a number of years in the media and in general conversation often seemed short on facts and I considered there might be value in sharing some of what I'd discovered while working inside the world of prisons.

Since writing that first book, I've been on another journey, one that has taken me away from the world of prisons and into the world of boys' schools, one that has allowed me to revel fully in the delight that is adolescent boys. The journey has involved working in a number of boys' schools on the Good Man Project, which was undertaken in the hope it would facilitate discussion within and between boys' schools about what makes a good man in the 21st century.

It was intended to be a small piece of work that would involve 'just a few' boys' schools and take 'just a few' months, but the project grew and in the 18 months between September 2002 and March 2004 I worked in 25 boys' schools across New Zealand. It was an amazing experience, one that taught me a great deal both about myself and about adolescent boys and the world they occupy. It proved to be a wonderful contrast to the time I'd spent in prison wings where I'd often grieved for the lost potential of the young men I was meeting.

During the Good Man Project, discussions about the concept of contemporary manhood flourished among teachers, parents and the students themselves, and it began to seem that this was an idea whose time had come.

When the project was being mooted, I was looking through the eyes of a woman who, in her role as the single parent of two children, had coped reasonably well with her daughter's sometimes rough journey through adolescence, but who had regularly lost her way when accompanying her son on the same journey. With that experience still very much alive in my mind, I was keen to be involved for both personal and professional reasons.

Following my visits to the 25 schools, I completed a report to the headteachers that summarised my findings, identifying what their schools do really well in their quest to educate young men, and setting out some ideas about what they might do better. Their response to the report has been extremely positive and a number of initiatives under way within the schools are a direct result of their involvement in the project.

What neither the heads nor I anticipated was the level of interest that would be shown in the project and its findings by the parents, both mothers and fathers, of the students involved. In the course of each school visit, it became usual practice to invite parents to a meeting to hear about the project, including the process being followed and why the school was spending money in this way. Attendances were always good, in some cases significantly beyond what had been hoped for. What I was saying about their sons struck a real chord with the parents: laughter and many 'aha' moments were a regular feature of the discussions.

And so I agreed to write a second book, in order to bring the findings of the project and the stories of the students out into the wider community, and to explore a little further how we might all work together more effectively to keep our young men safe as they ride the roller-coaster that is male adolescence.

I've also written the book to honour men, their skill, their intuition, their pragmatism and their humour and their extraordinary ability to become boys again at a moment's notice, whatever their age. I also want to suggest mothers, that, consciously or unconsciously, they're preventing men from using their talents in raising their boys. The answer to the things that worry us most about our boys lies in recognising who they are rather than in trying to make them who they're not.

We seem to lose far too many of our young men to suicide, to prison and to death on the roads. In preparing this UK edition of *He'll be OK*, I've been struck by the horrifying similarity in our countries' statistics. Prison numbers are at an all-time high with a significant proportion of this prison population made up of young men – young men with enormous potential who have made stupid decisions as part of their quest for manhood. These decisions have taken them to the prison gates and created pain and suffering for numerous others, including their victims and their own families.

'How is it, do you think, that young men like you sometimes get into so much trouble?'

'Some nights are really boring and you just want to go out and create some carnage. You don't think of the consequences at the beginning, but you do once you're in the middle of the act and usually that's too late.'

Although the experience that underpins this book was gained in New Zealand, the lessons and conclusions are universal ones. In our increasingly global community the pressures exerted by drink, by drugs, or by joy-riding and all the myriad other ways that young men find of getting into trouble are pretty similar whether you're in Wellington, in Washington DC or Welwyn Garden City. Go into a mixed inner-city comprehensive, or a single-sex fee-paying institution, and you'll hear exactly the kind of conversations I report in the pages that follow. The good news that the solutions are universal too.

I can only hope that this book may add to the discussion already occurring within families and communities about how to reduce the negative statistics and enable more of our gorgeous boys to grow into good men.

I'm able to write this book because of the graciousness of the headteachers who, having shown remarkable insight by becoming involved in the project in the first place, have been willing to share with a larger audience information that rightly belongs to their schools.

Above all else, I've written this book in an attempt to share the magic I encountered inside the world of boys' schools and inside the minds of adolescent boys. They're gorgeous creatures, full of potential. They may drive us to distraction as they hurtle recklessly towards adulthood, then decide they want to remain boys for just a little longer and turn back to play, and we may often wonder whether they, and we, will make it to their 20th birthday. But they're also insightful individuals who carry in their heads the answers to many of the questions we have about them and who can show us the way forward if we will only pause long enough to ask the question . . . and then wait graciously (and silently) for the answer.

Chapter 1
What Was the Good Man Project?

The Good Man Project grew out of an energetic discussion that took place at a Heads of Boys' Schools Conference hosted by Nelson College, in New Zealand, in September 2001. The talk had focused on such questions as 'What is the definition of a good man?', 'What is the essence of being male?' and 'What does it mean to be a young man in today's world?'

As I've mentioned, the aim of the project was to develop a working definition of what makes a good man in the 21st century, a definition it was hoped would influence the schools' education of their students.

After working in male prisons for a number of years I'd concluded that, for many young men, prison becomes a rite of passage, the place where they end up as a result of their misguided attempts to prove to the adults around them, and to themselves, that they're men. They don't go to prison deliberately; rather, they go almost accidentally, having chosen to indulge in behaviour they see as manly without pausing to consider the likely consequences. That behaviour includes drinking alcohol in significant quantities, fighting to defend their own or their mates' honour and driving cars too fast.

After 15 years in the prison system, I began to work a little more closely with at-risk adolescents and became increasingly interested in investigating the rites of passage that might be used to stem the flow of young men into our prisons. One project I became involved in took me into Nelson College, a boys-only state secondary school with a long and esteemed history. As I wandered the halls for the first time I wondered how a traditional boys' school like this managed its at-risk students. As such boys became problematic, did they just move them down the road to the local co-ed school, turn their backs on them and concentrate on those students whose progress reflected well on the school? Or did they make genuine attempts to meet the needs of these students even when the going got tough?

In the course of the regular visits I was making to the school, I began to debate this issue with the head, Salvi Gargiulo, who, it was easy to see, was passionate about boys and their education. During one of our conversations I talked about prison, linking it to male rites of passage. I could practically see Salvi's brain stretching as I put the words 'Nelson College' and 'prison' into the same sentence. His response to the idea that there could be any connection between the two things was to comment on the long and esteemed history of the school. My immediate response was that, long history notwithstanding, I had met a number of the school's old boys in my previous life. That focused the conversation a little, and we continued to talk and laugh.

At one stage in the discussion, I found myself talking about how silent, in my view, men had become: we don't seem to hear their voices in debates about boys and manhood as much as we used to. Salvi's response: 'We really need a men's revolution, don't we?' I looked back at him and said, 'Yeah, you do.' Then he did a very bloke-ish thing: he grinned at me and said, 'I don't suppose we could get you to do it for us?' The women reading this will understand that as a typical male response in those circumstances, that is, something needs doing and if I wait long enough and apply a little psychological pressure, she just might do it for me.

My response to the suggestion that I lead a male revolution was an immediate 'No', something that seemed to surprise Salvi. I then made the point that it was a men's revolution we were talking about. 'I'm a woman – we women have had our revolution and we won. We're actually running the country now.' Completely unfazed by this slight glitch in his plan, he then looked at me and said, 'Well, if you won't run the revolution, will you at least come to the Heads of Boys' Schools Conference I'm hosting?'

This question drew a second 'No' from me. 'They'll be stuffy, boring old farts. They'll only want to talk about rugby and I've had enough time in the prison service to have done my bit in terms of talking about rugby. And anyway, they won't be interested in anything I have to say. From the moment I walk in, they'll have me classified as a radical feminist lesbian and that will be that.' The look on Salvi's face at that point suggested he was wondering exactly which part of any such classification might be wrong. After a bit more discussion on the topic, Salvi persuaded me there would be merit in meeting his colleagues so I agreed to spend an hour with them.

I went for an hour, I stayed for the day and I had a great time. They didn't want to talk only about rugby and they didn't appear to classify me as a radical feminist lesbian – well, not that I could detect anyway. Nor were they stuffy, boring old farts. They were intelligent, articulate men with a clearly discernible interest in and passion for boys' education. They demonstrated highly developed senses of humour and showed themselves well able to debate new and challenging ideas.

In the course of the discussion with the 14 heads present at that meeting, I drew a link between the world of boys' schools and the world of prisons and challenged those present to lead the debate today's society must have about manhood in the 21st century. What does manhood involve? How does a boy become a man? What role do/should men such as themselves, in positions of leadership within a male environment, play in bringing boys across the bridge of adolescence?

It seemed to me that the heads were (and continue to be) very well placed to identify and provide more positive rites of passage, rites of passage that celebrate manhood and maleness rather than denigrating it, while increasing the chances of young men making it safely into adulthood.

During the discussion of the concept of manhood in today's world, someone in the group said the words 'good man'. Straight away I asked what the definition of a good man was and in that moment I received my first lesson about the real difference between the genders: 14 men sat looking at one another around the table in complete silence. Being a woman, I naturally assumed that the silence meant they didn't know the answer to the question. After all, if I'd asked 14 women for the definition of a good woman, I'm reasonably confident the answers would have begun almost immediately and a vigorous debate would have followed. But it wasn't that the men didn't know the answer to the question; they were silent because they were thinking.

The basic difference between men and women? Forget

biology and whatever else you might think constitutes the major difference between the genders. I learned in that moment, and continued to learn throughout the project, that the foremost difference between men and women is that we women think and talk at the same time. We learn what we think about something by talking about it. We start in one place on an issue, keep talking it through with someone, usually another woman, and often end up in a completely different place (with the men in our lives frequently lamenting silently that we're continually changing our minds). In fact we aren't changing our minds: we're simply establishing what we think – out loud. Men, on the other hand, think, then talk and there's often a gap, sometimes an enormous gap, between the two processes. In terms of effective inter-gender communication, this is often where the problem starts. We women sense the existence of the gap and immediately move to fill it in by talking to the man and interrupting his thinking processes.

This isn't about intelligence. Don't be tempted to take offence because I'm suggesting one gender is naturally more intelligent than the other. This is all about process. We just think differently.

So there was a long pause, and then all of a sudden the conversation took off and they were away. 'Wouldn't it be great to have a definition of a good man? What do you think might be in there?' The debate raged. As a woman, I was somewhat nonplussed that there wasn't already a definition they could immediately call on and I said so. 'Hey guys, thousands of women all over the country are giving you their boys in the hope you'll help raise them to manhood and turn them into good men and you've got no bloody idea what you're doing.' 'Oh no, no,' they replied, 'we've got *some* idea.' I have to say I wasn't reassured.

Salvi recognised the value of the conversation and as the day drew to a close, those present agreed that I would return in the not too distant future to continue talking with him about this topic to see what, if anything, might be done to take the idea further. And so the Good Man Project was born. In subsequent discussions we agreed there was a conversation to be had and that it was worthwhile exploring further the idea of manhood and rites of passage within the laboratory that is boys' schools. How that conversation might take place was something we trusted would unfold in time. All we had to do was to work out the first steps to be taken and the rest would follow. And so it proved.

The plan was that all boys' secondary schools in New Zealand would be invited to take part in what we were classifying as loose (very loose) action research. I would spend three days at each school that wished to take part in the project, this being seen as a reasonable amount of time in which to immerse myself in the culture of the school. I would then see where the discussions about manhood led me. Initially six schools were willing to take a risk with this idea (and willing to try to find some funding) and it was with their backing the project got under way.

As the visits to the first half-dozen schools continued across the fourth term of that year and word about the project began to spread, another eight schools enrolled, then another ten. Finally, once the newly appointed headteacher of Christchurch Boys' High School had settled into his role, he joined the project, bringing the final number of participating schools to 25. Among them were 18 state-funded schools, three private schools, and four others.

The project involved no government funding. The heads and I agreed that we would operate outside the bureaucracy because that would mean fewer boundaries and no red tape. We wouldn't need to concern ourselves with political correctness and we could follow whatever leads presented themselves in terms of gaining admission to the world of adolescent boys. My only concern in terms of how I worked was to ensure I was on side with the school heads as they were in effect my employers. The complete absence of bureaucracy meant there were no restrictions on what I could discuss with the boys, a freedom I came to appreciate and value.

Each of the schools taking part did so on the understanding that they would have to find the necessary funds within their already stretched budgets. This I thought extraordinary: it showed their commitment to their students and their staff, and their belief that everyone within their school community would benefit from being involved.

This was a project undertaken with a great deal of enthusiasm and very limited financial resources. Schools taking part covered the entire spectrum from privileged to those drawing their pupils from low socio-economic communities.

The project was never about whether boys' schools are 'better' for boys than co-educational schools. Rather it was about identifying the points of difference within boys' schools, including what they do well. It was hoped this information would then help parents to decide whether a co-educational school or a single-sex school might best suit their son.

The project meant we could explore ideas about manhood in an all-male environment without having to pause and ask, 'What about the girls?' There are and always will be boys who'll do well in an all-male environment while others will flourish in a co-educational setting. It's entirely possible that two boys from one family could suit the two different types of school available to them.

As I've said, each school visit lasted three days. During that time, I held conversations with staff and management and with as wide and diverse a range of students as possible.

On some occasions I finished my introduction of the project by challenging the male teachers in the room to think about when they'd become men. The silence was often deafening until they realised I didn't want them to disclose the information then and there, but just to think about it and perhaps, once they'd worked out the answer to the question, to share it with their sons, their male colleagues and maybe even their partners.

The conversations with individual staff usually started with me asking 'Why are you working/teaching in a boys' school?' and led on to discussion of a wide range of issues associated with boys and their education. In the course of the project I talked with approximately 110 individual staff members and took part in a number of delightfully energetic group discussions in various school staffrooms.

I was impressed by the degree of enthusiasm staff had for their work, and for boys' education in general, and by their willingness to be exposed to, and openly discuss, new ideas. Many of these discussions had us all in fits of laughter as we explored the reality of working in the presence of large numbers of adolescent boys.

I was often amused and entertained by the men present in the staffrooms, their humour, their quick wit and the way in which they communicated non-verbally but very clearly and succinctly with one another. As the men revelled in being in each other's company, I noted that insults were regularly traded, one-liners were the norm and laughter abounded.

In the discussions with students, I deliberately focused on keeping things as relaxed and informal as possible, so there were no set questions to work through, just a series of topics I was keen to explore, including sex, alcohol, drugs, peer relationships, parental control and future pathways. The students were seen in classroom groups and the discussions lasted for the duration of the set period I'd been allocated, usually between 45 and 60 minutes. I talked with approximately 180 classes of boys ranging from Year 7 to Sixth Formers, the majority of the discussions being held with more senior students.

It quickly became apparent that if I was to get the best from the boys, I could neither write down nor record the discussion. In the first few classroom meetings, whenever I paused to scribble down a particularly humorous quote (of which there were many), I immediately noticed that I'd just lost my audience and it always took a few minutes to get them back. In time I learned to hold the quote in my head until the bell rang and the students plunged noisily from the room. Fortunately the quotes were so memorable that it wasn't hard to keep them within mental range until pen and paper were available. This was in fact my first lesson within the project: the boys responded best to roving eye contact, which reassured them that what they were saying mattered and was OK, acceptable, even important.

I enjoyed my time in the classrooms immensely. The students handed me some amazing information, though they often had no real awareness of the importance and value of what they were communicating. On occasion they were so candid in expressing their views that I'd be almost paralytic with laughter; they had no idea why this middle-aged woman was standing in front of them, laughing her head off, but I can definitely recall struggling to get my breath, they were so funny. The junior students were insightful and their humour and approach to life shed a great deal of light on the maturation process of boys. The Year 10 students presented major challenges in terms of maintaining any semblance of control of the discussion and the classroom, but also provided extraordinary insights. But it was the discussions with senior students that had the real potential to produce answers to the questions that had prompted the project. It was in these classes I struck gold and understood just what potential lies within young men making their way towards adulthood.

After an introduction to the reasons behind the project, I usually initiated discussion by asking the students why they were at a boys' school and what they saw as the main differences between themselves and girls of their age – other than the obvious physical ones, I was always quick to add.

On a few occasions some of the students tried to check just how many of the basic biological differences between men and women I was aware of. When that happened, I was always quick to assure them that I'd done my own research in that regard over a number of years and didn't need their help to clarify matters. Their reaction at that point was usually to put their hands over their faces and groan: the idea of a woman of my age having been involved in such research was obviously a little too hard to digest.

Discussion tended to flow within a very short time of my arrival, going off on a number of tangents, but always coming back to their relationships with their parents, with girls and with their peers, the alcohol and drug scene, their ideas about what makes a good man and who in their lives they considered to be good men.

Rather than attempting to lead the conversation in any one particular direction, I let it take its own course, usually with delightful results. The discussion would often amble around the room without much apparent focus until a wonderful one-liner would emerge, usually from a student who hadn't appeared to be particularly connected to the discussion. As the session drew to a close, I would attempt to pick up the threads of the discussion and plug the gaps in the information they'd given me by asking some slightly more focused questions. This wasn't always successful though. They were having such a good time exploring the issues I'd raised that they often resisted any attempt to tie the conversation down.

In the course of their introduction to the project, I spoke to the students about the time I'd spent working inside prisons and raised with them the idea that many young men, young men just like them, seem to enter prison as part of proving their manhood. The mention of the word 'prison' guaranteed the students' immediate attention and they were always very keen to hear any prison stories I was willing to tell.

I didn't hold back in my descriptions of prison life and often pondered what the conversations over the dinner table at home that night might have been like and whether parents wondered just what their sons had been learning at school that day. Of course this fleeting concern applied only to the more junior students, boys who were still in the habit of telling their parents about their day. I had no doubt that little or nothing would be discussed by the older students, given that adolescent boys and talk at the dinner table very rarely go together, especially when the boy is in the Year 10 and 11 monosyllabic grunting stage. I was pretty safe really.

One of the trade-offs (aka bribes) I used in the classrooms was to suggest that if the students answered my questions, and talked about what I wanted to talk about, then just before the end of the time available, I was willing to stop the discussion and allow them to ask any question they had about prison and what happens there. This technique proved very useful in terms of focusing the boys' attention on the conversation I wanted to have.

In about 90, if not 99, per cent of the classroom discussions, the first question a student asked about prison was, 'Is it dangerous to bend over for the soap in the shower?' Although I'd said that the questions about prison would come at the end of the session, on some occasions, especially when working with Year 10 boys, I had to answer one question up front to prove that I intended to keep my promise and that this wasn't just another piece of conning by an adult. And sometimes in the more prestigious schools, where there's a strong emphasis on what does and does not constitute polite behaviour, I would have to both ask and answer the question in order to put the boys out of their misery and move the discussion on. 'Is this the question you would like to know the answer to . . . ?' 'Oh, yes please' would be the response, followed by a sigh of relief that the dilemma was over.

> In about 90, if not 99, per cent of the classroom discussions, the first question a student asked about prison was, 'Is it dangerous to bend over for the soap in the shower?'

I always answered a very emphatic 'Yes' to the soap question – in my view, any deterrent to prison is a good deterrent – but then went on to explain the facts about life in prison a little more realistically than most American prison movies do. It isn't as common an occurrence as the movies suggest, staff don't watch, it doesn't only happen in the shower – these were the sorts of issues we explored once the topic was up for discussion. Separate to the matter of possible sexual assault, I wanted the students to understand that ultimately it would be their choice whether they ever saw the inside of a prison cell; my work experience suggested they shouldn't want to.

Was there any potential conflict in a woman spending time in boys' schools discussing the concept of a good man and what might constitute legitimate and effective male rites of passage? It is, after all, men's business and should remain so. This aspect of the project was canvassed fully with the heads in the initial discussions as the project brief took shape and I was fully aware of it as I began the school visits. At each opening staff briefing I explained that I was there not to talk but to *listen* to both the students and the staff as they described the world of boys' schools. I then had to place what I was told and what I was able to observe within the context of the alternative rite of passage, the journey to prison, and to hold up a mirror so that the teachers and parents of adolescent boys could see, as I had, the potential of boys' schools to positively affect the choices made by boys in their quest for manhood.

My job was only to collect the stories and hold up the mirror. It was not then, and nor is it now, to translate for men what they're seeing in the mirror or to tell them what to do next. I can describe what the world of men looks like from my perspective, but it must always be remembered and acknowledged that my perspective is that of a woman looking into the world of men.

Because I've been a single parent who brought up a son, I have no qualms telling women what they might like to consider doing differently in raising their boys as a result of my experience with the Good Man Project. That, in fact, is the primary reason for this book. I'm also very clear, however, that having held up the mirror for both men and women to see what I was lucky enough to see, my job is almost over. The bulk of what now needs to be done is men's work and men must be allowed to get on with it. And get on with it they will, if we women have the courage and the willingness to stand back and allow them to do so.

The Good Man Project was a gift, a very special gift, that allowed me entry to, and changed forever my perception of, the world of boys' schools and the world of men. Before I move on to describe what I learned, I want to pause and say a heartfelt thank you to all those involved. It was a memorable time and I owe an enormous debt of gratitude to those who travelled the road with me.

Chapter 2
The Wonderful World of Boys' Schools

Before the Good Man Project, I thought, as many people appear to, that most boys' schools were part of the 'old school tie' network, focused primarily on ensuring that their students gained the necessary business and social connections to smooth their path through life. I also considered it likely that the more prestigious the school, the more any incoming student would have to fit the school rather than vice versa.

I was willing to concede that there was some potential value in single-sex education for boys: I had, after all, sent my own son to a Catholic boys' secondary school for what I thought at the time were a number of well-considered reasons. Interestingly, those reasons are now more than a little unclear. But although I saw enough advantages in single-sex education to trust my son to it, I remained unconvinced that boys' schools were reaching their full potential in exploring the reality of manhood in today's world. I'd been impressed with what I saw when I spent some time at Nelson College as part of the project about the management of behaviourally challenging students in the classroom, but that visit didn't substantially alter my generally negative view.

When I attended the meeting of Heads of Boys' Schools with Salvi Gargiulo in September 2001, I was certain that these men, the guardians of the bastions of traditional boys' schools, were unlikely to have anything to say that I would find at all interesting or challenging. How wrong I was. At that point I began a journey that has taught me much, unravelled my prejudices and left me with a strong sense of magic about the schools where boys can just be boys and where the business of boys is the sole focus.

This isn't to say there's no room for improvement in the way boys' schools prepare their students for the world – that was why the project was born – but they do a great number of things exceptionally well.

By their very existence boys' schools encourage the building of a sense of pride in being male. In a world where there's a great deal of discussion about the absence of positive male role models and where much of the media focus is on the more negative aspects of young men, the ability of boys' schools to provide an alternative view cannot be underestimated.

For many boys who choose to attend a boys' school – or, as many of them would have it, have that choice forced upon them – the initial school assembly will be the first time they've encountered their own gender in such numbers and in a totally male-focused environment. When I talked to Year 9 students I could discern their pride in entering a man's world, a world that would offer them a sense of belonging and validation. The message in these schools was clear: to be male is to be OK.

For many students, too, entering such a school means they'll be taught by a man for the first time. Male teachers appear to be a rare commodity in primary schools and it was encouraging to see the numbers and diversity of male teachers in the staffrooms of these secondary schools.

Entry to an all-boys' secondary school appears to be very much a case of 'welcome to the world of men'. At the beginning of the project I struggled a great deal with the sense of history and tradition visible in the schools, but in time I came to understand its significance in the eyes of the boys themselves. For reasons related to my personal experience, I don't tend to attach a great deal of importance to such things, but there could be no denying how much it was valued by most of the students I met.

At one school I was urged by an obviously proud teacher to visit the library and I wondered at his enthusiastic insistence that I do so. It was in fact a museum containing mementos from the lives of many of the school's old boys. On one wall hung photos of those who had become judges or taken other high-profile positions in the community; on another were sporting trophies obtained at world events, including the replica of a gold medal won at the Olympic Games by an old boy. It was as I stood in this room and took in the sense of tradition surrounding me that I began to understand more about the essence of maleness. It's about connection, about linkages to the past that show the pathways to the future and it's about excellence, striving to be successful in order to honour those who have gone before. It's about loyalty and hard work and belonging.

As a woman who has spent much of her life wondering what might be around the next corner, I've often rebelled against a system that emphasises clear and strong links to a past I struggle to understand, but I was unable to ignore the sense of pride and anticipation discernible among junior students as we discussed what it meant to be a member of their school. Although many of them had come to the school at the behest of their parents, if offered the chance to be elsewhere, all but a very few wanted to stay and continue the journey they'd begun.

It became apparent very early on in the project that one of the inherent strengths of boys' schools is their ability to revel in and celebrate the business of boys. In a world that's becoming increasingly hamstrung by political correctness and the reluctance of many in positions of power and influence to call a spade a spade, the freedom available within boys' schools to focus completely on boys' issues is extremely valuable. There's a kind of purity involved when boys can concentrate solely on what matters and is relevant to them at this stage of their lives.

It's important to reiterate at this point that the project was never about comparing the merits of single-sex versus co-educational schools. On the contrary, it was intended to stimulate discussion about the needs of boys in today's world and to see how we can improve the delivery of appropriate life skills to all boys making their way through the education system. Boys' schools and those working in them are extremely well positioned to lead this discussion and all those involved in the lives of adolescent boys, including those working in co-educational secondary schools, can and should make a contribution. I have no doubt whatsoever that the results of any such discussion will be equally applicable to boys attending co-educational and single-sex secondary schools.

Being able to revel in the business of boys isn't only about the absence of girls. The boys' schools I visited showed themselves well able to identify and address the issues of concern to boys, to pursue their specific interests and to provide a setting within which it was safe to explore emotions in a male context. Put simply, there was overt support for being male.

On a number of occasions I observed a course of action being undertaken, usually in relation to the disciplining of a student, and thought to myself, 'I would have done that differently.' If I'm honest, what I really meant was 'I would have done that better'. It took me a while to realise that what I was seeing was men attending to men's business and that I was looking through the eyes of a woman. There's nothing wrong with that, but once I paused long enough to recognise the judgements I was making, I began to develop a keen sense of delight about what happens when men are given this opportunity. The main thing to realise is that it just doesn't look as it would if women were involved – and nor does it need to.

There's no doubt in my mind that men do things differently – this was apparent over and over again throughout the project – but differently doesn't automatically mean either better or worse. This is the trick: to learn to suspend the need for judgement that usually follows any such acknowledgement of difference. As a result of the time spent in boys' schools, I've learnt that silence on a woman's part can often allow the communication channel between an adult man and an adolescent boy to operate more effectively than it does when a woman interrupts the transmission, as we are often wont to do.

In time I came to understand the value in schools where the boys didn't have to concern themselves with their appearance beyond wearing the correct clothing, tucking their shirts in and pulling their socks up. The absence of jewellery, hair gel and piercings was one of the first things I noticed.

Students at all levels talked about the freedom of not having to worry about appearance – because there were no girls – and seemed to consider it a major benefit of being at a boys' school. Demonstrating their innate pragmatism, as they often did, the boys regularly commented that one of the main benefits of not having to worry about, for example, applying hair gel each morning was being able to spend an additional ten minutes in bed. 'No girls to impress, no need for hair gel.' They agreed that they paid considerable attention to their appearance outside school hours and didn't see themselves as any different in that regard from their peers attending co-educational schools, but they left me with the impression that the absence of pressure about their appearance at school made life a whole lot simpler and allowed them to stay longer in the moment of being boys.

'No girls to impress, no need for hair gel.'

Given this, I found it interesting to watch the debate that ensued when, not long after I'd spent some time at his school, one boys' school head came to public notice for enforcing the school rule of no hair gel. A number of people expressed their opinion via the media and many were critical of the school's stand, some going so far as to make an assumption about what sort of man the head was. One newspaper description had him cast as a pipe-smoking, tweed-jacketed chap of advanced years clinging to tradition, unable and/or unwilling to enter the modern world. Nothing could be further from the truth. He's in his thirties and is, I think, the youngest person ever appointed as the head of a boys' school in New Zealand. In my view, and in the view of many, he's a passionate and dedicated leader who possesses a great deal of insight about what boys' schools should be delivering to their students. His is one of the voices I implicitly trust when it comes to the reality of adolescent boys.

It seemed to me that most students didn't care about the restriction on the use of hair products and usually objected only in their often-quoted context of 'Yeah, I know it's a rule, but I'm going to have a go at breaking it anyway', before turning back and getting on with the things they considered really mattered.

Many of the students I spoke to, including those at this particular school, talked openly and without ridicule from their classmates of the freedom the school stand on hair and jewellery gave them and on one occasion when I asked a group of Sixth Form students how long it had taken them to get used to following the rules in this regard, they replied 'about a week'. Some students I spoke to, particularly in Years 11 and 12, did struggle with their

> 'Yeah, I know it's a rule, but I'm going to have a go at breaking it anyway.'

inability to register their individuality through their appearance and some of my classroom discussions with them did focus on what might be done to allow them a little more leeway, but even these boys also seemed to value the clarity and simplicity of those rules.

It also occurred to me as I monitored the media debate on this issue how many women were condemning the school for its stand, mothers standing up for what they perceived to be the rights of their sons, and how silent the men were. Where were the male voices? And were the mothers taking the issue on face value as presented by their sons, as I'd done many times with my son when arguing with the school, rather than looking beyond the matter at hand to the wider issues of adolescent boys and what they actually need rather than what they want?

The physicality of boys proved to be one of the absolute delights of the project. Standing in a school assembly of 1400 students very quickly grounded me in the reality that is testosterone-driven young men. The noise, the smell, the energy levels and the sheer size of some of the students meant there was never any doubt that I was in a male environment, albeit with some women present.

I'm not an educationalist and many will no doubt have a different view, but it seems to me that anyone who maintains there's little or no difference between boys and girls in terms of their educational requirements need only stand in an all-boy assembly to have their attitude challenged. The differences are palpable and no amount of politically correct analysis will alter them.

On numerous occasions I watched large numbers of boys stream into a school hall and felt a sense of joy at the positive nature of what I was seeing. In previous years I'd watched male inmates gather in prison wings, in work parties and/or on prison parade grounds and had wondered about and grieved for the extraordinary loss of potential I was witnessing. To see the boys' delight in being who and where they were, to feel their exuberance about life itself, was a glimpse of magic.

The boys' entry to the school halls also made me laugh. They appeared to have no real sense of their bodies and no awareness of the world around them. With shirts hanging out, socks down around their ankles, sandals or shoes flapping loosely, they lumbered around or over chairs, jostled one another and, in what appeared to be a totally unfocused way, eventually found their way to their allocated seat. They often had food in their hands (and mouths) – I've found there's never much distance between adolescent boys and food – and while they seemed able to eat and walk at the same time, they appeared incapable of doing much else or of doing anything at all at speed.

As always with boys, time was the main ingredient, time to allow them to reach their ultimate destination with just the occasional bit of prodding along the way. Hurrying them simply didn't work and an attempt to do so often made things worse since it seemed to lift energy levels and encourage their playful assaults on other students. Rather than explaining to the boys where they needed to be, something the female teachers present repeatedly tried to do, the male teachers seemed to instinctively know that the best plan was to position themselves like sheep dogs, guarding the boundaries and nudging the boys slowly and gently forward towards their allocated seats.

The physicality of the boys regularly overwhelmed me, as I'm sure it does their teachers from time to time. It was most evident in Year 10 and when talking to teachers involved with students at this level, I often commented that the most effective technique for controlling them, while trying to get at least a few scraps of information into their heads, might be to allow them to stand up every ten minutes and put someone in a headlock before sitting down again.

I have to admit that as a result of spending several school periods trying to engage in a meaningful way with Year 10 boys, I also began to wonder about the potential benefits of reintroducing the cane just for that year. The value of grounding them with a physical experience took on definite appeal in the face of their exuberance and inability to concentrate for more than 30 seconds – and that only if the subject fell within their somewhat limited classification of interesting.

In a class of Year 10 students, it was possible to actually see the levels of testosterone begin to rise and, as they did, to realise how impossible it was becoming for the boys to sit still. It was like watching a wave build from the back of the room and I sometimes felt the need to pause, duck and let the water roll over my head before carrying on with the conversation. Boys at this level, and to a lesser degree in the years either side, appeared completely unable to resist the temptation to flick anyone who came within arm's reach with a ruler or to move past a fellow student without hitting him. Asking them why they behaved this way often led to a look that suggested I'd questioned their need to inhale oxygen.

If they're ever going to learn anything, boys do need to learn to behave less boisterously on occasion, to be able to control themselves for at least part of their time in the classroom. Teachers and I often discussed possible ways of achieving this. Although this remains an ongoing challenge for those involved in the teaching of boys, I came to appreciate that the all-male environment was somehow able to provide both the space and the opportunity for boys to get the rough and tumble out of their system and move on rather than simply suppressing it in order to meet the expectations of the adults around them. While on occasion I struggled with the physicality of the boys, I frequently observed them being positively and actively managed through their exuberance and into moments of quiet reflection by very skilled teaching staff.

In my previous life, I'd noted that sport appeared to play

a major part in the lives of adolescent boys, but in the initial stages of the project I wasn't willing to consider it as anything other than a side issue. My time in boys' schools significantly challenged my views in this regard and led me to realise that sport is something boys' schools both do exceedingly well and use very effectively in their management of the students. In my discussions with the boys themselves, I came to understand that, for the vast majority of boys, sport is an integral part of the journey to manhood both because of its competitive nature and because it can give them a sense of being a part of something bigger than themselves. Most boys' schools can provide a wide range of sporting opportunities that allow their students to experience success and develop a sense of pride. Sport also means they can continue to build a positive relationship with their body and use their high energy levels in a positive way.

I particularly liked the way one teacher explained it: 'Young men have to have a regular adrenaline fix. If they don't get it in the right way, they'll get it in the wrong way. Boys' schools have the capacity to and do provide heaps of the right type of adrenaline.'

In addition to the formal sporting opportunities available, I noted the freedom students at boys' schools appeared to have to play and as the project progressed I became increasingly intrigued by what I saw occurring during morning interval and lunchtime breaks on the school campuses.

When the bell signalling a break in the teaching regime rang, the students would swarm out onto the school grounds and all manner of games would begin. Some were the more traditional games of football and rugby, but there were also numerous games that appeared to be made up on the spot, depending on the number of students wanting to play, the range of equipment at hand and the space available.

The atmosphere seemed to encourage the students to play regardless of their year level and through the mechanism of play the schools appeared able to accommodate and support the frequent dashes maturing students make between the gateway of childhood they're moving away from and the gateway to manhood they're inexorably approaching.

I've often encountered the negative view that boys' schools produce men who are unable to relate to women and who, because of their arrogance about being male – encouraged by the school – carry negative perceptions about the place of women in today's society. At the very least, it has been suggested, the boys leaving such schools are emotionally bereft and incapable of establishing and maintaining effective personal relationships with women. As one former head of a co-educational school put it, he'd grown sick of having to be a 'finishing school' for those boys who had been educated for four years at a single-sex school, but who then came to him for their final year to learn how to socialise with girls.

Although I didn't necessarily hold quite that view before I embarked on the project, I did have some reservations about the ability of boys' schools to produce emotionally confident young men. My son hadn't appeared to suffer any form of emotional or social retardation as a result of his time at a boys' school – quite the contrary – but I told myself that he'd developed his emotional confidence in spite of the school rather than because of it. He was who he was because of the excellent work done by his mother!

It was common for the fathers of some students, men who had themselves been educated at boys' schools, to reflect that they'd been unable to understand or communicate effectively with members of the opposite sex when they left school. Some of them went on to concede that the workings of the female brain remained a mystery to this day and I have no doubt they're not alone in holding that view.

Their adolescent sons didn't, however, appear to share their experience of not being able to communicate effectively with adolescent girls. Partly due no doubt to the greater degree of social freedom that is available to girls today, the boys appeared to understand their female counterparts much better than their fathers had. Almost all the boys I spoke to had close female friends within their immediate peer group – whom they often referred to as 'girl-mates' – and many spoke of the value of the conversations they had with these girl friends about the 'real' stuff, the stuff they could not or would not talk about with their male peers.

It's true that the boys expressed considerable nervousness about approaching a girl they considered to be 'hot' and were clear in their assertions that the thinking processes of girls were sometimes too hard to follow, but I saw and heard nothing that led me to believe they were any different in this regard from their peers attending co-educational schools.

The conversations I had about the likely impact of having girls in the classroom, or in some cases, the reality of actually having girls in the classroom, as happened at the senior levels of some schools, provoked a great deal of discussion and thought about the socialising process that occurs between adolescent boys and girls.

Many teachers who had also taught in co-educational

schools commented on the way adolescent boys appeared to modify their behaviour in the face of scorn or criticism from female classmates. At Years 9 and 10 in particular, when a boy often races between acting like a child and acting like a young adult, the censure or potential censure of a female student would cause him to curb his behaviour. 'Sit down and stop being a dick' is apparently a common cry from the girls in co-educational classrooms at the more junior levels.

The boys themselves often spoke of not wanting to appear a fool in front of girls and of how the concern that they might do just that made them quieter in the presence of girls. 'Better to be thought a fool than to open your mouth and remove all doubt' was a concept they seemed to have fully grasped, even if they couldn't express it as clearly as that. When we talked about alcohol they often expressed their anxiety about appearing a fool in front of a girl and explained that one reason for drinking to excess was to gain the necessary confidence to talk in an uninhibited fashion to the 'really hot chicks'.

Almost all Year 9, 10 and 11 students I spoke to felt the presence of girls would make them much less willing to participate in classroom discussions and that in such circumstances their behaviour would 'tone down' and become less boisterous.

Given this, I found myself wondering whether what actually occurs in the classrooms of co-educational schools is an education of boys about girls' expectations of their behaviour, rather than a gender-neutral socialising process. It seemed to me entirely possible that the value judgement of the girls about what does and doesn't constitute OK behaviour might be the major benchmark in the socialising that was taking place. When we talk about the boys at co-educational schools being more socially adept, more 'mature', are we in fact saying that they've learnt earlier than boys educated in single-sex schools just what expectations women have of them? Have they simply learnt to do what we women want of them and is this what we're classifying as maturity? It's an interesting question.

Whether or not that's the case, the more senior students in the boys' schools demonstrated a clear ability to get on with their work and to behave in socially appropriate ways and there was no hint of a lack of socialisation because they hadn't spent time in classrooms with girls. The boisterous behaviour, the inability to concentrate, the ebb and flow of testosterone clearly visible among Year 10 students, regardless of their academic ability and/or socio-economic background, had disappeared. In its place were groups of delightful and seemingly mature young men exhibiting well-developed social skills and leading what appeared to be very active social lives. There was no hint of the need for a year at 'finishing school'.

Many of the discussions held in the course of the Good Man Project focused on what boys need most as they make their way across the bridge of adolescence. On the basis of what I have observed, whatever else we might include in there, the essential element is time.

They need time to think, time to process newly found emotions and time to make decisions about their future. They need time to just be, to move freely between boyhood and manhood, returning several times, in the initial flush of adolescence, to a state of boyhood where they'll spend time playing while reflecting at a deeper (and often completely invisible) level on the fact that they're in the process of leaving that boyhood behind.

This is what boys' schools do best of all. They give their students the time they need to come fully into the adolescent experience at their own pace, time to adjust to the fact that life is moving on and taking them with it. And while this process is under way, the schools continue to put positive images of manhood before the boys which tell them and build a sense of anticipation about the world of men.

Having outlined what boys' schools do extremely well, I need to emphasise that there's definitely room for improvement and development in a number of areas. I'm not describing a perfect world. The commitment of the heads involved in the Good Man Project and their willingness to let me loose in their schools – a sign of courage, some would say – showed their willingness to learn new things and to listen to suggestions.

The aim isn't perfection; the focus is challenge and investigation and debate, and within the corridors of the boys' schools I visited, I found all these things. I found laughter and sorrow, movement and noise, reflection and discussion. Above all else I found places where my views about the world of men and what adolescent boys need to make it safely across the bridge of adolescence were challenged and where my faith in the inherent goodness and strength of men was restored.

The journey I was fortunate enough to be able to take into the world of boys' schools has left me with a strong sense of optimism about the future of the young men *if* we can make the most of the opportunities these schools present to learn more about what works for boys.

✦ By their very existence boys' schools encourage the building of a sense of pride in being male.

✦ Maleness is about connection, about linkages to the past that show the pathways to the future, and it's about excellence, striving to be successful in order to honour those who have gone before. It's about loyalty and hard work and belonging.

✦ Boys' schools and those working in them are extremely well positioned to lead this discussion and all those involved in the lives of adolescent boys, including those working in co-educational secondary schools, can and should make a contribution.

✦ Boys can eat and walk at the same time, but they appear incapable of doing much else or of doing anything at all at speed.

✦ For the vast majority of boys, sport is an integral part of the journey to manhood both because of its competitive nature and because it can give them a sense of being a part of something bigger than themselves.

✦ Boys appear to understand their female counterparts much better than their fathers did.

✦ When we talk about the boys at co-educational schools being more socially adept, more 'mature', are we in fact saying that they've learnt earlier than boys educated in single-sex schools just what expectations women have of them?

✦ Adolescent boys need time to think, time to process newfound emotions and time to make decisions about their future.

Chapter 3
About a Boy: Inside Their Heads

Having talked about the world of boys' schools, perhaps the next step is to talk about the world of boys and to begin to share what I've learnt about how their minds work – because work they certainly do, even if, from the outside, nothing much seems to be happening.

It's important to note that I'm offering my interpretation of what I saw while interacting with some 180 classes of boys over an 18-month period. The boys themselves may disagree with my interpretation, as may the men who read this book, and I'll be entirely comfortable should they do so. This is a woman's take on the world of adolescent boys, a take coloured by my experiences and natural bias. I'm not trying to in any way prove that I know how it is: rather my aim is to initiate further discussion about how men and women can work together to raise good men and what we might do to ensure we have as much fun as possible with our sons and grandsons, and with each other, along the way.

As a result of my involvement in the Good Man Project I am very clear about one thing: if I'd known at the time I was raising my son what I know now about adolescent boys and the way they view the world, I'd have done a number of things differently. And even if that had meant adjustments to my way of being and acting that only I knew about, I'm sure it would have made my son's passage through adolescence a little easier on us both. He's grown into a fine man, a good man, but as his mother I suffered moments of extreme angst while he negotiated his adolescent years and I lay awake for more nights than I care to remember wondering whether he would survive long enough to become a man. I'd like to think there wouldn't have been quite so many sleepless nights if I'd understood more clearly just how he viewed the world and what was driving his behaviour.

> 'Girls are always wanting you to commit. Boys like to live in the moment.'

In the discussions I had with students a number of themes emerged that allowed me to get a glimpse into the way boys think and how they process information. These themes can be grouped around three main concepts – their pragmatism, their intuition and their desire to live in the moment. Later chapters will address the impact of their inherent pragmatism and their well-developed intuition on the way they live their lives, but let's take our first step into the world of adolescent boys by considering their love of living in the moment and their inability and/or unwillingness to plan in order to better manage their lives. This facet of the adolescent male psyche led to some very humorous conversations. (In fact most of the discussions held during the project were very funny.)

Whenever I asked the boys about planning, their immediate response was to assert that they don't plan. 'We don't plan because plans never work out anyway.' 'Life's a roller-coaster, so there's no point in planning.'

'Do you ever plan?'

'Nah, not really.'

'Oh yeah Miss, we plan the weekends.'

'When do you start planning the weekend?'

'Oh about Wednesday.'

'So you know how to plan?'

'Yeah.'

'But you just don't do it?'

'Nah.'

'Girls plan a lot, don't they?'

'Yeah, but they change their minds, don't they?'

'Yes, I guess they do.'

'See, waste of time making the decision in the first place!'

One question I always asked as we moved towards a discussion about how they managed their academic workloads: if they were given an assignment that was due to be handed in on, say, Tuesday morning, when would they do it? Regardless of academic ability and/or socio-economic status, the answer at this point was invariably 'Monday night', with the occasional 'Tuesday morning' thrown in. When I went on to ask if there was anything the adults in their lives could do to persuade them to do it any earlier, they replied without hesitation, 'Yeah, money'.

'Do you think you'll ever have a life plan?

'No'.

'So how will your life sort itself out?'

'Oh that's easy. I'll be about 25 and some gorgeous-looking girl will walk past. She'll have a great plan, so I'll just hook onto her.'

When I made it clear that payment for assignments was not an option anyone was going to take seriously, we went on to discuss whether they ever considered doing the assignment any earlier than the night before it was due. At this point they were usually at pains to point out that yes, they definitely thought about doing it earlier, sometimes even going so far as to 'pick it up'. When I then asked what stopped them from actually doing some work on it in that moment, the answer was always quite clear: 'There's always something better to do.' The something better included a game to play, a video to watch and/or a mate to hang out with – none of these alternatives particularly pressing, but all more appealing than the waiting assignment. As I eventually came to understand it, the moment to do the assignment had simply not yet arrived.

It was a source of great amusement to me when, on some occasions, I pushed a little harder with the students and suggested that if they only did the assignment the night before anyway, regardless of when it was handed out, perhaps the best idea would be to ask their teachers to adopt the practice of giving out assignments overnight, working to the idea that they would have only the one night to get it done. It seemed a very logical step to me and one that would mean a significant reduction in levels of stress for those parents who spend their lives trying to compel their sons to start work on the assignment due next week.

Whenever I suggested this idea, however, looks of absolute consternation would cross the faces of the boys. 'No you can't do that.'

'Why not?'

'Because we need time to think about it!'

The boys seemed to survive this stage in their lives by combining their ever-present pragmatism with a touch of fatalism – 'no point in making the decision twice', 'who cares, it will happen anyway' – which allowed them to hold off doing the assignment in the hope that it might yet prove unnecessary. Maybe there would be a flood, an earthquake and/or a major fire overnight so the assignment would never need to be finished and any effort expended up until then would have been a complete waste of time.

'Thinking is boring. Who cares? It will happen anyway.'

This unwillingness to plan isn't all bad news, however. A story told to me by one teacher challenges the view that adolescent males will reach their potential in the classroom only through planning and organised work. This teacher described the time when he'd explained to a group of senior students that they had only five days left in which to complete their art portfolios and that if they didn't manage to do so within that timeframe, they would lose the opportunity to take art the following year. For many of the boys this would have been a major blow as the career paths they were considering required them to continue with their study of art and, perhaps more importantly, it was a subject they both enjoyed and were good at.

These were boys who were quite academically capable, but who had shown themselves to be fairly normal adolescent males by working at about 5 per cent of their potential throughout the year. The teacher had previously taught adolescent girls who, in his view, tended to work at about 90 per cent of their potential throughout the school year.

Once the teacher had delivered the news of the impending deadline, the boys seemed to accept the challenge and immediately got to work. They literally lived and breathed their art portfolios for the following five days, spending every hour at the school, taking only occasional breaks to eat and sleep while getting on with the work. In the teacher's words they went from their previous 5 per cent effort to about 250 per cent. Everything else in their lives fell away and nothing else mattered until their portfolios were complete. Although it is possible to imagine the chaos that might have been building in other areas of their lives during this period, the fact remains that they met the deadline and the work they turned out was of a very high standard. The moment had arrived, they responded and the results were excellent.

The boys also seemed to have been changed for the better and to have become more confident as a result of the experience. They'd been tempered by the challenge and had learnt a bit more about who they were and what they were capable of. So, here's a thought worthy of consideration at this point: is it possible that this learning might not have occurred and the high standard of work not been reached had they chosen instead to work steadily throughout the year?

Is it possible that the inertia frequently displayed by adolescent boys occurs because the challenges being put in front of them aren't of sufficient depth to merit a real response? That only when the challenge is significant in their eyes, rather than in ours, do they respond to it? Have we made education a series of relatively small steps because we think that's what works, when what boys actually want and need are fewer, much bigger steps? There are many far more qualified than me to answer that question, and no doubt many would disagree with the idea, but several times throughout the project it seemed to me that it's challenge boys are looking for and need if they're to be fully involved.

As a result of the education I received during the Good Man Project I've decided that the ability to cut to the chase, to focus on the actual issue rather than on all the associated matters we women might be aware of and seek to consider and manage, is an inherent male trait. We women seem to move in a circle, expanding its edges as we move and drawing in more and more 'stuff'. Men move in a straight line, often ignoring everything that's off to the sides as they focus on what needs to be done. Isn't this in fact what the boys working on their art portfolios did, pushing aside what needed to be pushed aside so they had the time and space to do what needed to be done? They were motivated because the moment had arrived, the deadline was in sight.

The fatalism evident in boys seems to be an adolescent trait, a sign that they don't yet feel any real control over their lives. The world still seems a bit too big and their place in it isn't clear, so they continue to evaluate which adult wants them to do what by when and act accordingly, always mindful of the consequences of non-compliance and playing their own game of chance. It's a way of making their world manageable (and more interesting) during a period when they still believe it doesn't really matter what they do, despite what those around them are saying.

Wherever I looked in my discussions with adolescent boys, linked to their ability to focus only on what needed to be done and their sense that there was no point in planning anything other than the next weekend's social activities, was their clearly discernible desire to live completely in the moment. Again and again they demonstrated, by both their actions and their words, that being fully in the moment is what matters; in fact it's often the only thing that matters.

At one school a group of senior students led the discussion around to the topic of death and grief and from there on to the issue of youth suicide. I suggested that in my experience many young men decided to end their lives because they were trapped in a phase of despair and could see no way out: in such cases it was living in the moment, as so many young men do, that had proven fatal. One student agreed, adding 'but we like living in the moment'. I confirmed that this was part of what made boys gorgeous, but then went on to ask whether he could understand how frightening we adults find the implications of some of the decisions made by the young men we love in their more vulnerable moments.

> 'You just have to keep telling us there'll be more moments.'

He acknowledged that he could understand our fear so I then asked him what he would tell despairing young men if he was one of us, the concerned adults. Without hesitation, and with extraordinary wisdom, he replied, 'You just have to keep telling us there'll be more moments.'

From the discussions I had with the students I concluded that fear of failure is one of the things that keeps them living in the moment longer than those of us who love them might wish. Fear of failure featured regularly in the conversations and was often given as a reason for not trying. Notably, it was raised most often in the context of competition with girls.

In the words of one teacher, 'Boys often won't have a go unless their success or a return is guaranteed. They constantly analyse the risk in terms of being made to look silly and won't put their heads above the parapet if there's the slightest chance of it being shot off.'

If there was any suggestion that they'd come second to a girl in something they were about to do, the boys admitted they would simply not try rather than risk failure. On a number of occasions, I gained the impression that they felt the world was stacked against them: girls were perceived to be better students because they were tidier in their work and paid more attention to detail, and the external world favoured women over men. This wasn't a perception held by all the students I spoke to, but it was common enough to give some cause for concern about the message we're giving adolescent boys. There's a fine line between the perception that girls learn differently from boys and the perception that they learn better. The boys often appeared to be receiving the latter message.

As discussions continued, I began to connect their fear of failure not only to their desire to live in the moment, but also to their unwillingness to plan. It seems to me now that all three are inextricably linked. Consider this discussion with 20 academically capable senior students just a few months before they were due to leave school:

'How many of you know what you're going to do next year?'

Twenty hands went up.

'How many of you are going on to further education?'

Twenty hands went up.

'How many of you know what course you're going to do?'

Twenty hands went up.

'How many of you know what jobs you want?'

Three hands went up.

Surprised by the sudden change in numbers, I backtracked

and asked how it was that they knew what course they were going to do, but didn't know what job they wanted. The answer came back immediately: 'You've got to keep your options open.'

Is it about keeping their options open or is it about avoiding the possibility of failure? As one student said in the ensuing discussion, 'The job you want mightn't be there when you've finished studying, so it's best not to think too far ahead.' If, for example, he wants to be a pilot and he's open about that and then doesn't make it, for whatever reason, he's deemed both by himself and others, possibly more particularly by himself, to have failed and his self-esteem takes a backward step. In the words of one teacher, 'Boys have dreams, but their risk of failure keeps them from going too close until they're mature enough to be able to cope with the possibility of failure. They consider it better not to try than to try and fail.' In the view of this adult man it's only in their thirties that men become willing, and able, to cope with the possibility of failure.

> 'The job you want mightn't be there when you've finished studying, so it's best not to think too far ahead.'

Little boys talk openly about what they want to be when they grow up, but during the project very few boys declared their dreams and those who did, did so very quietly. The majority of adolescent girls I've met seem to talk freely about their dreams for the future or, at the very least, can be easily persuaded to discuss possible future directions. They may, as the boys pointed out, change their minds a number of times, but they generally have some idea of where they're going and how they're going to get there.

Do boys really have no idea where they're heading? Are they quite happy to deal with this issue when the moment arrives, or do a significant number keep silent about their hopes and dreams through a fear of failure? Is living in the moment the safest place for an adolescent boy?

As a result of the classroom discussions I came to believe that adolescent boys are considerably less resilient than girls of the same age. There were moments during the project when their vulnerability washed over me and I found myself wondering how we actually manage to get so many of them safely through to manhood. They often left me with the impression they were accidents waiting to happen. Their childlike naivety (which many of them seem to hold on to longer than girls), their dependence on their peers to define their behaviour, their desire to live in the moment and their associated unwillingness to plan all combine at a time when male hormones are raging through their bodies and the blood appears to be flowing down rather than up. It's a potent mix and one that leaves adolescent boys extremely vulnerable, despite their outwardly strong physical appearance.

A regular topic of discussion was the management and processing of emotion. As we talked it became apparent that the only really acceptable emotion adolescent boys feel able to display is anger. Any other potentially negative emotion, such as grief, hurt or sadness, is transmuted into anger and dealt with accordingly, and when I asked the boys how they dealt with anger, the answer was invariably 'hit something . . . or someone'.

As we'll see later when I talk about Sixth Form boys, the senior students were able to provide a variety of images in relation to anger and grief. They were very clear that only time reduces such emotions and that nothing can be done to hasten the process. They explained that moving away from whatever emotion they are feeling allows them to detach themselves from it and eventually let it go: in that moment it loses its power. They were adamant that talking doesn't generally help and couldn't be persuaded otherwise. As one student put it, 'We do feel emotions deeply, but we actually don't need to always be talking about it.' They seemed to believe that, given time, the hard knocks of life become manageable and life can move on, but that this process can't be hurried.

In time I came to understand that the idea of not needing to talk about some difficult or stressful situation wasn't part of a male conspiracy to keep information away from women – at least not always. Sometimes it really is true that males, both adolescent boys and adult men, don't want or need to talk. They just want time to let the conflicting emotions settle until they can make some sense of them and get a grip on what they're feeling. Unlike me, they don't work out what they're feeling by talking about it. They work it out and then – sometimes – talk about it.

When the students were asked if and when it was OK to cry, they gave a variety of answers, many of them extremely humorous: 'When your eyes are full of mace' or 'Crying is OK for stuff that matters – like when your son crashes your Ferrari.' Generally, though, the standard answer was, 'when someone dies'. Some boys talked of having seen adult men, including their

'We do feel emotions deeply, but we actually don't need to always be talking about it.'

fathers, cry (usually at funerals or immediately after the death of a family member or close friend), but most hadn't and didn't regard it as natural male behaviour.

When I asked what message they might have been given about crying as children, the majority agreed that the 'boys don't cry' concept had been there, though not always as an overt statement. Sometimes it was the sense of disapproval they picked up when they did cry that persuaded them it was time to stop. Most of them had experienced such sayings as 'Don't be a girl'. When I asked when they first began receiving negative messages about crying, some said as young as six or seven, but the more common answer was around ten years of age.

The boys themselves offered some interesting insights into men crying and whether they'd stopped because they'd been told to and so were denying a natural impulse, or because they no longer felt the need to cry. Before undertaking the project, I tended to believe it was the former, that men

'Crying is OK for stuff that matters – like when your son crashes your Ferrari.'

have as natural an instinct to cry as women and that they learn not to cry as adult males in order to meet society's expectations. Now I'm not quite so sure.

The boys talked of not crying in movies not because it wasn't sad, but because it wasn't 'real'. (One particularly articulate boy added at this point that comforting girls crying in movies provided a 'good way to move in'. He moved his arm up into a semi-circle as if wrapping it around a girl's shoulders to show me what he meant.) They talked of not crying when they hurt themselves because, as one student clearly put it when speaking of a broken arm, 'The pain was there', pointing to his arm, 'while crying is here', pointing to his heart, and 'they're not connected' – making it clear that for him crying isn't an instinctive reaction. When asked how they did react when they hurt themselves, they inevitably replied 'swearing'.

They also talked of having stopped crying when it was no longer a way of ensuring they got attention and/or their own way. When we discussed their crying as little boys if they fell over and scraped their knees or tumbled out of trees, they identified crying in those circumstances as largely a reaction to the shock of what had happened and/or a means of getting attention: their crying started for the first reason and was carried on for the second. They explained that the effectiveness of this kind of crying eventually wore off so they stopped and found other ways to get attention. And, as one student put it, 'Crying doesn't change anything, it just leaves you breathless.'

> 'Crying doesn't change anything, it just leaves you breathless.'

Loyalty was a characteristic the students often associated with the concept of a good man; it seemed to be an important facet of their world. When I asked what loyalty looked like, I was told this: 'when a big bastard is coming towards you and you know you're going to get a hiding, but your mate stays with you and gets a hiding too'. My response to this idea was to suggest that it sounded a lot like stupidity to me, but I was assured it was in fact loyalty and that every man and adolescent boy would recognise it as such. I found myself wondering at that point whether loyalty was also the boy who puts his foot down on the

> 'We get over stuff. We keep our friends.'

accelerator and runs an amber light when encouraged to do so by his mates in the back seat and loses his life, and possibly theirs, as a result.

Loyalty to their mates appeared to be the basis for many of the actions taken by the students and seemed to add considerable weight to the potential influence of their peer group. Whenever they were asked who they took guidance from, who knew the most about the fabric of their lives and who mattered to them the most, the answer was always 'my mates'.

I often wondered how much that might change once they became involved with girls, but was repeatedly assured that it was 'mates before dates' or, in some schools, 'bros before hoes'. Only among some Sixth Form students was there any recognition that a relationship with a girl might take precedence over one with a mate, and even then it was dubious.

> 'Loyalty is when a big bastard is coming towards you and you know you're going to get a hiding, but your mate stays with you and gets a hiding too.'

As one senior student said, 'You can always get a girl, but you can't always get a good friend.'

According to another older boy, 'Girls don't really feature. There's too much planning involved in keeping them happy and meeting the responsibilities of the relationship.'

Interestingly, despite their stated view that mates came first, the boys also conceded that they didn't discuss the real stuff of life with their friends because they didn't trust that what they said wouldn't get out and be spread around the school. They would talk to their mates about acceptable emotions such as anger, but they would hold in the other softer emotions such as being in love or being scared unless or until they could talk them over with a girl. They said they did this because 'she won't tell anyone', whereas anything they told even their best mate would eventually find its way into the wider school community.

I struggled with this apparent contradiction. They put their mates before girls, they declared that one of the differences between them and girls was that they, the boys, kept their friends and they talked constantly about loyalty, yet they entrusted their deepest secrets about their emotions only to the girls in their lives, assuming that anything they told their mates would eventually become public knowledge. I'm still not sure how these two realities can exist side by side and can only assume that, in the minds of the boys, loyalty isn't about keeping secrets, but rather about having someone standing at your side as you meet the challenges you're constantly seeking as an adolescent boy.

'Girls think too much during conversations.'

'Girls are always analysing things. Guys – if it's not broke, don't fix it.'

'They talk about stuff we don't want to hear – what moisturiser works, what colour their bedroom's painted.'

'Guys, they tell you what they're thinking. Girls, you've got to read their minds because there's no way in hell they're going to tell you what they're thinking.'

This apparent emphasis on loyalty among the boys led me to think about the impact of peer pressure or what I now prefer to call horizontal learning. Throughout these adolescent years it appeared to be almost entirely through observing their peers, with the assistance of their intuition, that the students were learning what was and wasn't OK. This was particularly true of Year 10 students, who were right out on their own in terms of their ability to dismiss everyone other than their peer group as wankers, losers or geeks, but even the older students, who appeared more willing and able to accept advice and input from other adults, still filtered that advice and input through the attitude of their peers.

The students watched what happened as 'he' did this or said that and if it got a positive response from the rest of the peer group, they stored it away as a word or action they would use at some later date when there was a need to appear cool. If another student made a fool of himself in some way, they made a mental note never to do what he had done. If a member of their peer group noted that a certain teacher was 'OK' or a 'dickhead', there was usually a general murmur of agreement.

Rather than seeing peer pressure as a negative force, I began to see it as having considerable potential for good if we can learn to use the channels it provides to bring adolescent boys the right sort of information. Perhaps we just need to learn to use the filter of their peers' attitude more effectively than we currently do. It seems to me we, the adults in the lives of adolescent boys, expend a great deal of energy pushing against peer pressure rather than seeking to use it for our own ends: to keep the young men we love safe; to challenge them in positive ways as they make their way across the bridge of adolescence; and to help them grow into the good men they have the potential to be.

The inner workings of the minds of adolescent boys continue to be a source of amazement (and amusement) to me, as I'm sure they are to many of those struggling with a son who has suddenly become a monosyllabic grunter. It may appear nothing much is happening inside his head, but the project taught me the opposite: a great deal is going on. Our peace of mind lies in our ability to trust the process, to know he won't be this way forever and to learn to recognise what we're seeing and why he's behaving the way he is. Getting ourselves to this place will allow us to enjoy him and to laugh with him – and there's a lot of laughter waiting.

✦ Recognise their desire to live in the moment, their inability and/or unwillingness to plan their lives.

✦ Have we made education a series of relatively small steps because we think that's what works, when what boys actually want and need are fewer, much bigger steps?

✦ The fatalism evident in boys seems to be an adolescent trait, a sign that they don't yet feel any real control over their lives.

✦ Fear of failure keeps boys living in the moment longer than those of us who love them might wish.

✦ There's a fine line between the perception that girls learn differently from boys and the perception that they learn better.

✦ Boys are considerably less resilient than girls of the same age.

✦ The only really acceptable emotion adolescent boys feel able to display is anger.

✦ Boys often associate loyalty with the concept of a good man; it's an important facet of their world.

✦ They'll talk to their mates about acceptable emotions such as anger, but hold in the other softer emotions until they can talk them over with a girl.

✦ Never underestimate the power of peer pressure or horizontal learning for adolescent boys.

Chapter 4
The Bridge of Adolescence: Years 9 to 13

I've already referred a number of times to the bridge of adolescence. Perhaps it's time to explain the idea in more detail.

This concept had often occurred to me during the raising of my daughter and son. As I approached the bridge with my daughter, the elder of my two children, I was aware that we were entering a new stage in her life but had a sense it was alright to walk onto the bridge with her. She was a girl and her journey across the bridge would make her a woman. I'm a woman and whatever our differing views of the world, whatever path in life she was going to choose, we were destined always to have a great deal in common. Being able to stand on the bridge of adolescence together didn't make the journey all sweetness and light. At times she was running ahead of me with enthusiasm; at others she was walking behind me, sulking spectacularly as only adolescent girls can (and usually for no other reason than you'd held your face the wrong way that morning, or perhaps because this was the day when she'd wondered just why God had made you her mother). But for a significant part of the journey we walked side by side and occasionally we even managed to hold hands.

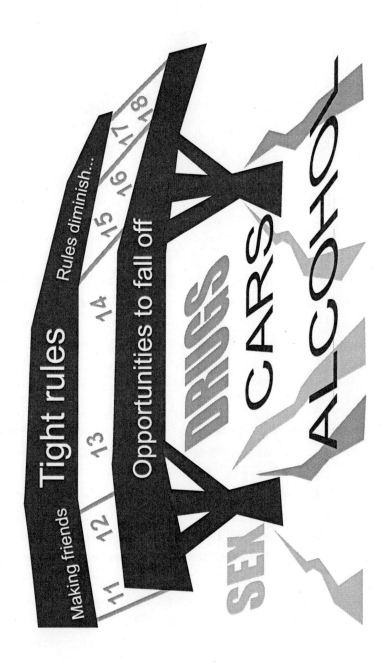

That wasn't the case with my son. As the bridge of adolescence loomed, I felt I shouldn't be going onto it with him. He was on his way to manhood, a concept I barely understood, and I knew I wouldn't and couldn't understand parts of the journey he was about to undertake. I was proud of the special mother-son relationship I felt we enjoyed, but I knew that if he was to become a man, a good man, we would need to separate for a time. But I wrestled with a problem as we drew close to the bridge: if I couldn't go onto it with him, who was going to? His father wasn't a major feature in his life at that time and although there were some good men in my life, the challenge was to find ways of having these and/or other good men more directly involved in my son's life. I'll talk more later of the challenges faced by mothers raising sons without fathers, but suffice to say that as my son was running towards the bridge of adolescence, far too early in my view and at breakneck speed, I felt obliged to walk up onto the bridge even while recognising at some deep intuitive level that I shouldn't be there.

As we'll see, this is the central issue in the lives of adolescent boys: how to get mothers off the bridge and fathers onto it. Mothers do need to step back; there does come a moment when the level of direct involvement in the lives of our sons needs to ease a little in order to assist their passage into manhood. One thing is clear, however: if there isn't a man clearly visible at the edge of the bridge into whose care they can entrust their sons, mothers will walk onto the bridge. They won't abandon their boys. The challenge for fathers is to make themselves clearly visible at the edge of the bridge so they can be seen by both their sons and their wives or partners and so there is plenty of time for all involved to adjust to the impending change. And this is surprisingly easy if we just pause and listen to what the boys themselves are saying.

The challenge to mothers is to willingly usher their sons onto the bridge knowing that, for a time, he'll be on a journey they can watch only from a distance. It's not about mothers abandoning their sons; it's about them accepting that for a time they will walk beside the bridge of adolescence rather than on it, or if they can't quite manage to stay off the bridge, that they at least commit to walking on one side rather than marching down the centre line directing traffic, as I spent much of my time doing. This, too, is surprisingly easy if we just pause and listen to what the boys themselves are saying, although in my experience the boys end up having to say it a little more emphatically because of their mothers' perception that they know best what their beloved sons need.

For now let's return to the issue of what boys might need (as opposed to want) as they move through the various stages of adolescence.

It's apparent to all who work with them that boys like clear boundaries: they like to know what's being required of them and by whom and what will happen to them if they don't do what's being asked. They like things to be kept simple and they're extremely pragmatic when assessing whether they'll do something. Given this, and the fact that in their early adolescent years they'll be swamped with testosterone, it seems entirely appropriate that in the early stages of their secondary school career, boys don't have a lot of discretion about school rules and the way the school does things.

During my time in the classrooms of the various schools, I began to develop a mental picture of boys' education and what boys need to assist their learning and to keep them safe as they move forward on their journey.

These were the questions I initially posed for myself as I sought some sort of visual image that explained what I was seeing: if we were bringing a group of boys into a room in which they were going to spend the next five years of their life, what would the room need to have in it in order to facilitate their learning? How is the room different because boys rather than girls are being educated in it? What changes would need to occur in the room over the five years to accommodate the growth process the boys will go through? My observations of the boys I met in the classrooms left me with these answers.

As he enters secondary school, a boy requires, in a metaphorical sense, to be brought into a large uncluttered room. Anything that might have been on the floor needs to be lifted up and taken away. There must be a vast amount of space in the room because for the next five years he's going to be on the move, physically, mentally and emotionally. This doesn't mean that he can't be asked to sit at a desk and learn, but his head and quite often his body won't be still unless he's asleep and even then stillness can't be guaranteed. Our ability to educate him and take him towards his unrealised potential will depend on our ability to connect with him while he's on the move. He'll spend almost all his time in the room playing, he'll make physical contact, some of it rough, with almost every boy he meets as he plays and it will be through play rather than by being forced to sit still that he'll learn. His learning will happen while he's mobile.

It's interesting to note that, in line with this idea of unceasing movement, a classroom chair has recently been designed that takes into account a boy's need to move. The word from some teachers of boys is that this piece of ingenuity is working magic in classrooms; a number of female teachers who have to cope with the physicality of boys in their daily lives have been queuing up to kiss the designers.

How is the room different because boys rather than girls are being educated in it? In my view, if a girl were going to occupy the room for the next five years, there would need to be a series of pathways laid out in the room. She may not always be able to tell you immediately, but somewhere in the head of an adolescent girl there's always a plan. Today she's going to be a flight attendant, tomorrow an astrophysicist, the next day a vet . . . then it's back to the flight attendant idea. She'll spend much of her adolescence jumping on and off pathways and her motivation to learn will be based on which particular pathway she's on at any one time.

He doesn't want to be on a pathway. Put him on one and he'll immediately jump off. He wants to be able to run and play, to live in the moment and to enjoy the fact that, for now, he's exactly where he needs to be and there's nowhere else he needs to go.

What changes will need to occur in the room over the next five years if we're to accommodate the growth processes the boy will go through? Let's define the changes in line with the year groups he'll make his way through while at secondary school, but as we do so, it's important to bear in mind that, to a significant degree, the changes that will be discussed here are stereotypical. There will always be boys who will move more quickly or more slowly through the various stages and there will be boys who skip some stages completely. What joy it would be to be the mother of a boy who skips the Year 10 stage! Although there will be these differences, I'm confident that the stages of development I'm about to describe are the norm for the majority of adolescent boys, or at least for the boys I was lucky enough to meet and talk to during the project.

Year 9

You can still see the boy in a Year 9 student – he's fresh-faced and bushy-tailed, still a boy, still cute. As he arrives at the age of 13, he's aware that he's starting a new phase of life. His head's up and he's looking towards the Sixth Form boys. When he enters an all-boys' school it's as if he can see a banner hanging above the door that says, 'Welcome to the world of men'. We need to focus his attention in this moment and hold it there, just for a brief time, holding him steady while we plant the idea in his head that one day he'll be there, one day he'll be a Sixth Form student. We need to make the most of this moment because soon his eyes are going to lower and he won't look up again for quite some time. If we can get this idea into his head during his first weeks at secondary school that the day will come when he'll be a senior student at the school, we'll do a great deal towards making that a reality and do society in general a major favour.

In the course of my time in the boys' schools I became a big fan of the idea of keeping boys at secondary school for seven years. It isn't that there won't always be boys who'll leave earlier because of personal circumstances or because of the future pathways they've chosen and I wouldn't want to see a world where boys *have* to stay for the full seven years. What I'd like to see is the glass turned up the other way so that the expectation isn't that a boy will do five years at secondary school and might stay for the extra two, but that the majority will do seven years and only some boys will leave early.

The reasons I now hold this view are linked to my prison experience and the realisation that the main thing a boy needs as he makes his way to adulthood is time: time to come to terms with who he is and who he wants to be; time to find his place in the world that awaits him. Regardless of what he might want to do once he leaves school, staying for the full seven years gives him the time he needs and holds him steadier than might otherwise be the case while he copes with the turbulence of adolescence. And, if we can hold him steady in that way, we lessen the chances of his turning up at a prison gate because, like so many young men, he made a stupid decision.

As he enters his teenage years as a Year 9 student, life is extraordinarily simple for a boy. He's focused on only four things: what do I have to do; when by; who's in charge; and what happens if I don't do it. He doesn't want long, detailed explanations about anything; he doesn't want to know why you've imposed the penalty you have or even why you think he should do what you've asked of him.

There is, however, one small adjunct to the 'what happens if I don't'. He needs to know that in administering any penalty for wrong done or expectations not met, the world will be fair. If he does something and the penalty is this, then if Jimmy does it too, the penalty should be the same. He doesn't want an explanation about how Jimmy comes from a difficult family and we really need to go more gently with him: he couldn't give a damn about Jimmy's background and/or whatever reason you might have on hand to justify treating him differently. His version of fairness goes like this: if this is what happens to me when I do or don't do something, that's what should happen to us all.

The Year 9 boy is interested only in having fun and learning, preferably both at the same time. Given that fact, what else do we need to do to more adequately prepare the space we've created for his education? We've lifted everything off the floor in the room to give him the space he needs, but what else does he require? In terms of the things he's most concerned about – what do I have to do and by when – we need to create a clearly visible boundary that runs without a break around the edges of the room.

He needs to know where those edges are, to be able to see them wherever he stands, so the boundary has to be brightly coloured. It also needs to be firm, because he's going to hurl himself into it on a regular basis over the next couple of years and he must be able to bounce off without hurting himself. Think of the vibrant bouncy castle that kids play on in fairgrounds, or maybe a series of large rubber tyres painted in primary colours. Paradoxically, it's only the boundary – the what, for whom, when and what happens – that gives him the freedom to relax into learning. If he can't see the boundary from wherever he's standing in the room, he'll go looking for it and if he doesn't find it, he'll just keep walking and then we, and he, are in trouble. The first part of his journey in Year 9 is walking the boundary, so it's best we get it in place quickly.

As well as being firm and brightly coloured, the boundary needs one more thing: we have to run a small electric current through it. This is just an extra safety precaution. As he walks the boundary for the first time, he'll touch it to check out how it feels, how real it is, and as part of his learning he needs to feel the light tingle in his fingers. It's this that tells him the boundary is real, that the people in his life are watching, that they do care and are genuine in their desire to keep him safe.

In real terms the electric current is the effort that needs to be put into reinforcing again and again that a certain standard of behaviour is expected and that if it isn't delivered, there are very definite consequences. Year 9 is all about sussing out how serious adults are about the rules and expectations of behaviour they're always (in his mind) going on about. As one Year 9 boy put it, 'Yeah, I know it's a rule but I'm going to have a go at breaking it anyway.' A quick zap from the mild electric current running through the boundary focuses his attention and brings him back into the middle of the room where he will begin the learning that awaits him.

Year 10

And so the real journey begins. As he approaches the end of Year 9 and crosses into Year 10, he starts to demonstrate to all around him, not least his shell-shocked mother, that he now has a very good grip of his world and is keen for the real fun to begin. Suddenly his parents know nothing and anything he's told by an adult is a plot to ruin his fun; his eyes lower and it seems he'll never look up again; testosterone starts to make its presence felt and his interests are inextricably linked to bodily functions; the blood coursing through his body starts to flow downwards and very little makes its way back up again. Suddenly, and with almost no warning, the cute boy has been transformed into a monosyllabic grunter.

'How was school?'

'Good.'

'Anything interesting happen?'

'Nah.'

'Did you learn anything?'

'Nah, just boring stuff.'

'Anything happen I need to know about?'

'Nah.'

The polite, cherubic boy full of hope and promise who entered the school a year ago has mutated into a barely recognisable being. It's best to assume that common sense has vacated the building and isn't going to be back for a while. He's now ten feet tall and bulletproof, and every adult he knows (and every senior boy at school) is either a control freak, a loser, a wanker or a geek – or maybe all four. There's nothing you can tell him that has any relevance to his life; the only information he now willingly takes in comes from his peers. He has the most amazing brain starting to develop, but at the same time he's also developing an extraordinary ability to filter everything that comes down from the adults above him. If, as an adult, you give him one piece of information that he knows or can prove to be wrong, for this next period of his life every piece of information that drops out of your mouth is rubbish and you're not to be trusted.

So when an alcohol and drug educator stands in front of him and says, 'If you drink six cans of beer in an hour you're going to do yourself serious damage', and he's sitting there thinking he drank ten cans in half an hour last Saturday and he's still breathing, the conclusion he draws is that this is just more adult bullshit. As for the educator telling him that when he's 35 there'll be consequences for having given his body a hard time when he was 15, forget it. He's working with extreme diligence to stay in the moment and it's all he can do to think about next weekend. The idea of considering what his life will be like when he's 35, or even when he's 20, is just too big to contemplate. And there's no good reason to do so. It's the present he's concerned with, the present that's occupying his attention, and his prime aim is to turn it into a time of fun.

He's become like a six-year-old boy who wants to take the back off a clock and find out how it works – only now he's not playing with clocks. This is his most dangerous year; this is the time when he's most at risk, both to the rest of the world and to himself. He tips a bottle of whisky down his throat with enthusiasm, his main aim being to see how far he can projectile vomit and whether he can vomit further than his mate, who's just done the same thing. For him it's a science project, nothing to do with reality, and he's fascinated. 'I can drink a bottle of whisky in this amount of time and then projectile vomit that far. My mate can only get it to there. That's interesting. Let's try that again.'

At this time in his life the best thing we can do for him is to provide him with real information, to meet him head-on in his belligerent belief that he knows everything and to take every opportunity that comes our way to remind him as gently as possible that in fact he doesn't. We don't need to work to destroy him; we just need to hold on to our sense that we do actually know a thing or two as a result of our life experiences.

The greatest gift you can give a boy at this stage of his development is not to attempt to provide him with information he hasn't asked for, but when he does come to you with information he has gleaned and is convinced is right because it suits whatever argument he's running, to step right into the discussion with him. Tell him what you know to be the truth for you and hold on to your adult wisdom, even though the going will inevitably get rough owing to his entrenched belief that your views are based on your ever-present desire to ruin his fun.

It's important to remember, as you enter debates with Year 10 boys, that there's a strong chance you're going to lose. He's a very skilled debater when the aim is to validate his position – why he should be allowed to go to the party, why school sucks and the detention was unfair – and in the months since the testosterone began to flow in earnest he's developed a real ability to pick out the facts that support his argument, the pieces that are relevant to him, and discard the rest.

Let me give you an example of a typical debate with a group of Year 10 boys. Whenever I wandered towards the issue of alcohol and drug use, it was common for boys at this level to want to debate the merits of cannabis versus alcohol and why it should be legalised.

'OK, you reckon cannabis is better than alcohol. Tell me why.'

'Oh cannabis is much better for you, Miss.'

'Really, how's that?'

'It mellows you out. Alcohol makes you want to fight and gets you into trouble.'

And from another boy: 'Anyway the cops smoke it, teachers smoke it – they're all hypocrites. How come everyone else is allowed to smoke it except us?'

Having been drawn into the argument, I decided to do

the adult thing and begin to explain the facts as I understand them – THC, fatty tissue around the brain, alcohol clears your system in 24 hours but cannabis is still there six weeks later, it dissolves your dreams, it makes kids too lazy to get out of their own way . . . At that point I stopped and looked around the room. It was obvious there wasn't the slightest bit of interest in what I was saying. I could see my words rolling out of my mouth, sliding across the top of their heads and dropping out the back window. They weren't even registering with the boys in front of me.

I paused, thought about whether I could be sued and decided to take a risk.

'OK guys, there's actually just one reason why you shouldn't smoke dope.'

'Yeah, what's that?'

'Because it fucks your head. It won't fuck it as badly when you're 23, but it's fucking it now because of everything else that's going on in your body at this stage of your development, so I suggest you cut it out.'

In that moment they came right into the conversation. They weren't there long – it was a fleeting moment of connection – but they were there. I don't imagine for a minute I had put them all off smoking marijuana, but at least I appeared to have got them thinking.

In the true style of Year 10 boys, the conversation on this particular topic didn't stop at that point. One boy down the back of the classroom looked up, grinned at his mate sitting next to him and said, 'Hey Miss, you've forgotten one thing.'

'Really, what's that?'

'Dope makes you really good in bed.'

The noise in the classroom escalated as the boys enjoyed

the idea that I might have been caught out. But experience as a prison officer does prepare you for most things, so I just smiled at him as I held his gaze and said, 'Actually, I've got some news for you.'

'Yeah, what's that?'

'Take some advice from an older woman. Dope makes you *think* you're really good in bed.'

The look on his face was a treat and I wondered just for a moment what thought might wander across his mind the next time he picked up a joint.

My advice with regard to Year 10 boys: don't go looking for debate with them, but if it appears in front of you, have the conversation. If you're a teacher, you may have to moderate your language slightly – you won't have the freedom I had in the project – but go as far with them as you can, watching all the time to check that they can cope. Year 10 boys want us to come into their territory and explain the world as we see it, but only when we're invited – and they invite us with their confrontational comments. They're testing us and we need to show courage – moral courage – in meeting them where they've asked to meet us.

So, going back to our metaphorical room, how will it be different now that it has to accommodate a Year 10 boy? It will look exactly the same as it did for Year 9, but now, instead of a small electric current, we need to run the national grid through the boundary. He can feel his strength growing, he thinks he has the world sorted, he considers he is the master of his own destiny and, left to his own devices, he will go over the boundary and out into the world that waits beyond, a world he's actually not ready for. The important thing the adults in his life need to stay focused on is that although he's beginning to look like an adult, he's still just a boy and any impression he gives that he has and is using common sense is an illusion. It will return, but trust me when I say there's not an ounce of common sense operating in his brain at this point and in an attempt to keep him safe and on track parents and teachers must hold hands and work together. He needs to be kept in the middle of the room well away from the boundaries. And this is actually exactly what he wants you to do.

He might be as belligerent as hell and spend a great deal of time at this stage pushing fiercely against the boundary (or launching himself headlong at it), but he does know his limitations and he wants to be kept safe. He won't articulate that fact, he can't, and when I talk later about intuition, I'll explain just why, in my view, he has become mono-syllabic, but he does want the national grid running through the boundary. He wants to know, at some level, that it's what will keep him safe and that it's proof of the love people have for him.

In real terms the increased level of electric current is overt reinforcement of boundaries, swift implementation of consequences and making sure there's a limit to the amount of debate about breaking the rules. He'll expend considerable energy trying to work out new reasons why he shouldn't be held accountable for his behaviour: don't give him too much ground in this regard.

After I'd been involved in the project for a while, one teacher looked at me and said, 'I spend a lot of time trying to work out how to get a better relationship with my Year 10 students.' I laughed and said, 'I wouldn't bother. If you get a relationship it's a bonus, but don't spend any energy trying to get one – just teach them. Imagine that you start the year with a Year 10 class with 3500 seeds in your hand for each boy in the class, and throughout the year you're going to throw the seeds at them. If you get to the end of the year and one of those 3500 seeds has lodged in his brain tissue, you've been very successful.'

A Year 10 boy doesn't want to be caught up in life's complications. He wants things to be simple. Looking back, I realise now that when my son was at this stage in his development, I thought he was going to be there forever and I wondered how on earth I was going to find the energy to cope. I decided that rather than risk him staying there, it was my job to pull him out and I spent a great deal of time with my hands clasping the top of his arms trying to pull him forward, explaining to him in incredible detail the possible consequences of the behaviour he was or wasn't exhibiting. Now I know that he isn't going to be in this phase forever. Coping with him at this point is about waiting, about letting him go through the stage at his own pace, and above all else about keeping him corralled while he does.

In one discussion with parents about the management of Year 10 boys, one mother looked at me and said, 'I can tell him he's not going to the party, but in reality I can't stop him. If I send him to his room, the chances are he'll climb out the window and go anyway.' My response was to confirm that she was probably right but just to make sure he did it only once. 'Every boy I know,' I told her, 'even the worst of them, has at least one thing in his life he loves. You're his mother; you're the person who knows him best at this point in his life. If you don't already know what the thing he loves most is, and I suspect you do, find out what it is and take it off him. And join forces. When he says, "How come I got the mother from hell? Everyone else's mothers are letting them go to the party", make sure you can say, "No they're not, I've just rung them all and no one's going." Or "We've all agreed you can all go until 11.30 and then we're all coming to pick you up."'

This is about guerrilla warfare; this is about parents joining forces with one another and about parents joining forces with teachers. We need to learn to hold him steady and we need to encourage one another in our attempts to do so. In today's world in many ways we're letting him go, thinking he's a grown up, but he's not, and he's dangerous, to others but more especially to himself. He's gorgeous and he's highly intuitive and the time will soon come when we can let him go and watch him grow, but at this stage in his development we must understand how much he needs the boundary, how much he needs us to turn on the national grid.

One Year 10 boy described arguing with his mother about a party, with some of his mates standing around.

'I want to go.'

'Well, you're not going.'

'Oh, you're not fair, everyone else is allowed to go.'

'You're not going.'

'How come I've got the mother from hell? Why won't you let me go?'

She just held the line, and in the end he turned away angry.

When I asked him, 'What did you do next?' he said, 'As I turned away and once my mates couldn't see my face, I smiled. I didn't want to go to the party, but I needed Mum to hold the line for me in front of my mates, so I could say it was her – it was her fault.'

Year 11

And so Year 10 comes to an end eventually and with some relief for all concerned (except perhaps the teachers who will have another class next year – in my opinion, staff working with Year 10 boys deserve special medals). But for those of us able to focus on the next stage of development, we can now see the man beginning to emerge. They are brief glimpses, but very welcome nonetheless. Occasionally, completely unprompted, you'll get a sentence from him that has as many as five words in it and you can enjoy a quiet moment of celebration. As a word of warning to mothers, when the five-word sentence comes, don't turn and face him with a look of excitement. If you do that it will be quite some time before you get another one.

Now that he's a Year 11 student, life has become a little more serious, but there's still plenty of time to play. He will work for short periods on the idea of being a man, but at regular intervals will invariably and with considerable enthusiasm go back to being a boy. In terms of our image, the metaphorical room, nothing changes at this point. Although he doesn't wander across to the boundary as much any more and generally makes no attempt to get over it, the national grid should be kept running and at the same wattage. Its role at this point is not to keep him in; it's to reassure him. If you were to turn it off at this point he would get frightened: he's grown used to the hum now and silence would scare him, telling him that he's now stuck on the pathway to manhood and can't get off. He knows time is passing and he'll soon have to think about leaving school and making some choices for himself, but at this stage his plea is 'not yet, there are more games to be played, more fun to be had'. The hum reassures him that there *is* in fact time for more games, more fun. And some boys may still make the occasional dash for the boundary in moments of madness so for them the national grid has not yet outlived its usefulness or applicability.

Year 12/Lower Sixth

In Year 12, as he enters the Sixth Form the electric current can safely be switched off as the maturation process is now fully under way. He's still a pretty relaxed sort of dude, he still lives very much in the moment and takes advantage of any opportunity to play, but he's also starting to show definite signs that common sense is on its way back. He'll spend significant parts of this year walking over to sit up on the boundary, looking out over the side, considering his options. After deliberating a while, he'll then get down, return to the middle of the room and set about playing another game. He moves constantly between the gateway from boyhood and the gateway into manhood, and as he moves back and forth he looks for every opportunity to hold on to the idea that he's still just a boy, not yet committed to taking life too seriously. He knows the moment is approaching when the world will come to meet him and he wants to defer it as long as possible.

Year 13/Upper Sixth

When a boy walks into school as an Upper Sixth student, it's as if he immediately looks up and, seeing no one above him, says to himself, 'Oh OK, now it might be time to do something.' As I interacted with the various classrooms of boys I struggled to find some sort of explanation for the very real difference I observed between Year 12 and Year 13 students. It was as if all the synapses of their brains had finally knitted together as they entered Year 13 and suddenly, sitting in front of me were these gorgeous and extremely wise young men with much to teach us.

In an attempt to clarify this, I asked one group of Upper Sixth students to tell me what might have happened over the Christmas break. 'How is it you're so different from how you were last year? Did someone inject you with something over the break?' At that point one boy looked up and said somewhat nonchalantly, 'No Miss, it's just that up until now the position has always been recoverable.' A perfect example of the inherent pragmatism of boys.

This is the point at which the boundary needs to be removed altogether and replaced by a white picket fence. There must be a number of large, clearly marked exit gates visible from wherever the boy stands in the room. This will give him plenty of time and opportunity to decide which gate he's going to use to leave the school. He'll spend the Upper Sixth sauntering up to a gateway, looking out and pondering how it would feel to exit through this one, then wandering back to play another game. In the course of the year, he'll check out each of the gates, not hurrying in his decision about which one to use. This is the area that appears to present the greatest challenge to the boys' schools. It's a relatively new experience to consider the complete removal of the boundary which has been in place so long, and which teachers have grown used to. I could detect some trepidation at the suggestion that Upper Sixth boys need to be given a strong sense of the control they have over their own destiny.

During this year everything can come together as far as the school is concerned. The teachers have survived the journey and the students at this level are truly delightful young men with much to offer both the school and the wider community. The boys' schools I visited seemed to have the initial setting up of the metaphorical room and the installation of boundaries about right, but I picked up varying levels of resistance among staff to the idea that the current needed to be switched off in the Lower Sixth and the boundary completely removed in the Upper Sixth. The teachers had managed the students quite tightly during their early years at the school, and they found it hard to consider loosening school rules and procedures to allow for the senior students' need for increased independence. As I contemplated the difficulties some schools were experiencing with this challenge, I felt it was worth remembering that many of these young men were working outside school hours and functioning as responsible adults.

As I said at the beginning of this chapter, there are boys who will sit well outside the stereotypical characteristics I've used to describe the various stages of development adolescent boys go through. That may be the case, but it remains my experience, as a result of the project, that whatever differences there might be, an adolescent boy is an adolescent boy is an adolescent boy, and there are clearly discernible benchmarks in terms of his journey towards manhood. I believe there's much to be gained from recognising the common aspects of the journey, not least the ability to live in the moment with the boys and enjoy them, knowing that it will come to an end all too soon.

+ The central issue in the lives of adolescent boys is getting mothers off the bridge of adolescence, and fathers onto it.

+ It's apparent to all who work with them that boys like clear boundaries.

+ Let's turn the glass up the other way so that it's expected that most boys will stay at secondary school for five years and only some will leave early.

+ The Year 9 boy is interested only in having fun and learning.

+ The Year 10 boy is ten feet tall and bulletproof and everyone else is a loser, a wanker or a geek.

+ Don't go looking for debate with a Year 10 boy but have the conversation if he brings the debate to you.

+ In Year 11 life becomes a little more serious but there's still time to play.

+ In Year 12 there are definite signs that common sense is on its way back.

+ Year 13 boys are gorgeous, wise young men.

Chapter 5
External Forces: Alcohol, Drugs, Sport – and Girls

Having considered what may be inside the heads of adolescent boys, and given some thought as to how they make their way through their secondary school years, we should perhaps now take time to reflect on the external forces impinging on them as they move across the bridge of adolescence towards manhood. One thing I learned as a result of my discussions with both men and boys during the Good Man Project was that an integral part of being a man seems to be the need to belong to something bigger than themselves, to be connected to a common good. And this means they tend to see themselves as part of a whole rather than as an individual. As one teacher put it, 'Girls are more egocentric, that is, what does this have to do with me, while boys are more about what does this have to do with us.' Given this male view of the world, adolescent boys could be vulnerable because, in the absence of an obvious common good, they go looking for one and may choose unwisely in deciding where to place their allegiance. This view may also go some way towards explaining the enormous influence that can be exerted by their peers.

As anyone lucky enough to have a teenage boy in the house knows, peer pressure (or horizontal learning as I prefer to describe it) is an extremely influential part of male adolescence. They move in packs; they graze the fridge and pantry with incredible ease and blow the household budget several times over as they do so, whole loaves of bread disappearing within a matter of seconds; and they seem unable or unwilling to do anything that will in any way distinguish them as being different from their mates. There are, it would seem, quite compelling reasons for them to behave this way and I'll go into those in more detail when I talk about the development of boys' sense of intuition in Chapter 7.

A major external force that came to the fore very early in the project was the boys' use of alcohol. If their stories were to be believed, they were drinking from a reasonably young age and in a number of settings. In the assessment of one group of Year 11 students, their drinking began when they were anywhere from nine to 11 years old and able to sneak small quantities of alcohol unnoticed at family functions. By 13 or 14 they were getting drunk on a reasonably regular basis, in some cases on alcohol bought by the parents of other boys for their son to take to a party. But at this age the most common way of getting access to alcohol was via an older sibling or the friend of an older sibling who would buy it for them.

'Girls are more egocentric, that is, what does this have to do with me, while boys are more about what does this have to do with us.'

In a slight variation on this practice, some more enterprising lads would wait outside the off-licence until a sympathetic-looking adult came along who might be persuaded to buy booze for them. They said it never took long to find someone willing to help and it was usually a person only a few years older than them, rather than someone of their parents' generation. One particularly entrepreneurial group of students talked of paying a homeless person to buy alcohol for them, the price of such a transaction usually being around £2.

There seemed to be definite stages in the students' drinking careers as they moved through secondary school. In their own words, it was in Year 10 that the vast majority of them went through the 'drink till you vomit' phase to determine just what their limit was and to show their peers (and their older brothers) how grown up they were becoming. Once they were through that phase, usually Year 11 or, for some late bloomers, Year 12, it seemed to become a question of drinking to have fun, to be at one with their peers and to find the confidence to talk to girls.

These older students agreed that they did go out to get drunk, believing it was in this process that the fun would begin, but they claimed they no longer actively sought to drink until they could drink no more. If they happened to reach that point, it was almost entirely by accident, a by-product of seeking to have fun and going with the flow. They were articulate in their assessment of why they drank and it was interesting to note how clear they were that, once out of the 'till you vomit' stage, alcohol had no real connection to manhood. Whenever I asked directly whether the ability to drink alcohol had anything to do with being a man, the answer was almost always a resounding 'no'.

The exception was the boy who told me that drinking was about being a man 'when I'm sitting on the couch with Dad, a can in my hand, watching a game'.

As I came to grips with the students' relationship to alcohol, I found one of my fundamental preconceptions about young men being swept aside. I'd always believed the determination of my son and many adolescent boys like him to drink to excess as often as possible was about entry to manhood, some sort of agreed male rite of passage, which, as a woman, I knew nothing about. On the basis of what the students told me, I now believe that to be wrong. It seems to me that alcohol is much more about easing the pressures they're feeling as they leave boyhood and move towards manhood; it's about finding common ground with their peers and with girls; and above all else it's simply about having some fun.

In the words of one wonderfully articulate Upper Sixth student: 'I'll tell you what alcohol is, Miss. For me it's the pit stop of life. When I'm feeling the pressure, I can pull into the pit stop and rest for a time while the race of life goes on around me. Then when I've rested a while and I'm ready, I can rejoin the race.'

> 'For me alcohol's the pit stop of life. When I'm feeling the pressure, I can pull into the pit stop and rest for a time while the race of life goes on around me. Then when I've rested a while and I'm ready, I can rejoin the race.'

As adults, we may be tempted to believe the lives of adolescent boys are without pressure, that a world filled with opportunities lies at their feet. As I listened to that young man and marvelled at his ability to give me such a clear image, I realised the degree to which these boys were feeling the pressure to perform in the different areas of their lives and I began to see why many of them use alcohol as they do. We think they're cruising through life with no worries beyond where the nearest food supply is and what they might have planned for the weekend. In fact they're worrying about whether that girl really likes them, whether they've got what it takes to pass the exams that are looming. They're highly intuitive: they can see the state the world is in and they wonder about their future place in it. Owing to their overwhelming desire and inclination to live in the moment, they're unable to sort the thoughts running around in their head into any logical order and so, when it all becomes too much, which it does frequently at this stage of their lives, they turn the voices off by pouring alcohol down their throats. And given all that's happening for them, this behaviour is completely understandable.

When I asked what alcohol was about, if it wasn't to do with being a man, I got a variety of answers:

'It's about letting off steam, knowing you can get drunk and not be responsible for what you're doing.'

'It's about connecting with girls, getting the courage to talk to the really hot ones.'

'It's about letting the problems of life go for a while.'

'It's about filling in time.'

'It's about telling the truth, getting the confidence to say what you've been thinking.'

'It's about being able to live in the moment and being able to be careless.'

'Drinking makes you social and social is cool.'

These replies, and the many others I was given, all echoed the same sentiment: alcohol is the primary means by which adolescents find the courage to move out into the world waiting for them, and once they've made their way out there, it's the means by which they then take time out from that world.

One recurring theme that begs for further investigation is

the degree to which the boys linked alcohol use with having fun. It was a common occurrence to hear the words 'getting shitfaced' and 'having fun' in the same sentence, combined in a way that suggested the two can't be separated, that it is necessary to get 'shitfaced' in order to have fun. Given the culture of heavy alcohol use in many parts of our community, I'm not convinced this is a phenomenon linked only to the behaviour of adolescent boys, but I do think there's room for a great deal more open and honest discussion on this topic with young people.

In the wider social context, I believe 18 may be too low an age at which to allow drinking. At the age when adolescents are most in need of clear and explicit boundaries (the national grid) – 13-, 14-, 15-year-olds – they can and do easily rationalise that, because 18 is looming, there can't be any real harm in starting to drink now. We love to debate the issue of personal freedom, including the freedom to think and to make our own decisions, and we've told ourselves that this age limit has no real effect because the kids are getting hold of alcohol anyway and it's better to teach them how to use it 'properly', that is, in moderation, rather than letting them run wild with it. But they are running wild with it and in trying to convince ourselves that it's all about personal freedom and encouraging mature behaviour, I think we may have missed the point completely.

My discussions with the students reinforced the reality that 13-, 14- and 15-year-olds aren't generally able to hold themselves steady in the face of external pressures and that when they're looking for things to hold on to, they gravitate towards very practical realities. Is it legal/is it illegal? Who's telling me that I shouldn't do it? Do they know what they're talking about? Are they walking the walk or simply talking the talk?

By having 18 as the drinking age rather than 21, we lessen the ability of students to hold themselves steady during the roller-coaster ride of adolescence and put them at significantly higher levels of risk. And the stories the students themselves told support that view. Even as they claimed the freedom to get drunk if they wanted to, they could clearly articulate the difference between a drinking age of 18 and 21, including the far greater ease with which they can acquire alcohol. Setting the legal age of drinking at 18 just makes it much easier for 14-year-olds to get the same access.

Although the Good Man Project was focused on the world of adolescent boys, it was occasionally possible, through discussion with the students, to get very clear glimpses into the world of adolescent girls. One of the most interesting aspects of our talks was the boys' view of the drinking habits of the girls in their peer group. I was left with the impression that adolescent girls are matching or in some cases even surpassing adolescent boys in their tendency to get extremely drunk on regular occasions. The boys talked of how quickly the girls got drunk and how they often kept drinking to a point of complete oblivion despite the risks involved in not knowing where they were or what might be happening to their bodies. Behind the ever-present bravado of these young men was a concern about the situations some of their female peers get themselves into and an awareness that a young woman who has drunk herself to the point of unconsciousness is in real danger. The idea that girls can do everything boys can do – including drinking the same amount of alcohol – seems to have taken hold in ways we could not have foreseen.

There's an increasing need for upfront discussions with young women about the physical reality of their high alcohol consumption.

The boys and I also talked about their access to and use of illicit drugs. For a number of reasons, not least that I didn't want them to confess anything which might leave them vulnerable at school, I made it clear that I wasn't interested in knowing what drugs individual students might be using and always geared my questions to extract general rather than specific information, for example 'Could you, if you wanted to, gain access to cannabis or ecstasy?' I concentrated on trying to establish how available drugs were in their world rather than on who in the classroom might be using what.

As a result of these discussions, I believe we adults need to be aware that almost every illicit drug is available in any secondary school in the country. The students indicated quite clearly that they don't have to go too far out of their way to gain access to cannabis and so-called party drugs and that the social settings in which they'd been moving since late childhood had exposed them to people who were regularly using recreational drugs. I reached the conclusion that most adolescent boys will decide whether or not to use cannabis for the first time at around age 13. (Unfortunately any community or social worker will tell us that for some the decision comes a lot earlier than that.)

It's worth noting at this point that the hypocrisy of some adults didn't go unnoticed by the students: in terms of using illicit drugs, adults often tell them to do as they say, not as they do. The boys spoke of this double standard several times, making the point that many of the adults they were supposed to be looking up to, because of their position in the community, were known to be regular users of cannabis and heavy users of alcohol. Because of this the boys regarded what these adults said as nonsense, which should be ignored.

I was pleasantly surprised by what the students told me about the scale of their drug use. On the basis of the information they gave me, and they were reasonably candid, it would appear the use of illicit drugs by students attending boys' schools is significantly less than that of their peers in society at large. The majority of the boys, particularly senior students, seemed to consider drug use 'not cool' or 'stupid' and often cited examples of former peers who had fallen by the wayside through drug use as the primary reason they weren't interested.

This wasn't a scientific study and the information I was given was entirely anecdotal, but the picture of a low percentage of drug users within almost every school I visited did continue to build, and gave me considerable food for thought. When I talked with the heads about this, we identified three possible contributing factors.

The first was the fact that most boys' schools have a zero tolerance approach to drug use. Any student recently caught with or under the influence of drugs had been moved out of the school and so wasn't among the boys I spoke to.

The second was the role sport plays in the lives of the boys. To quote one student, who demonstrated yet again the pragmatism of boys, 'Why would I use drugs? I can go out on Saturday night after the game, get totally off my face on alcohol and have a great time. I'll be sick on Sunday, seedy on Monday, but by Tuesday I'm ready for practice. If I go out on Saturday night and get off my face on drugs, I'll have a great time, but I'll feel crap all week and I'll probably have to miss practice.' A number of students echoed this view, all making the point that drugs have a much worse effect on sporting performance than alcohol.

The third possible contributing factor was summed up in the words of one head: 'They cherish their place in the school and know there are other boys waiting to take it, they know the school has a zero tolerance approach to drugs and they know they'll eventually get caught.' Again we see adolescent male pragmatism at work: I like being here, if I use drugs I'll eventually get caught – others have, so it's best not to use drugs. It's not high-level thinking, just high-level pragmatism.

> 'If I go out on Saturday night and choose drugs rather than alcohol to get off my face, I'll have a great time, but I'll feel crap all week and I'll probably have to miss practice.'

It often seemed to me as I talked to both staff and students that if the schools can work at keeping the boys busy when they're most at risk of starting to experiment with drugs, in Years 9, 10 and 11, then by the time they're senior students, the message has had time to sink in. By then they've developed considerable self-esteem and a sense of purpose in terms of sport and other interests and so have mechanisms at hand to help them decide not to become involved. At this stage in their school career it was obvious that they regarded using drugs as uncool and the culture of the school and among the boys themselves constantly reinforced this message. Whatever boys' schools are doing in the battle against drugs, they appear to be getting it right most of the time and are to be congratulated for that.

That said, it needs to be remembered that easy access to illicit drugs is a constant external force in the lives of adolescent boys. They like having fun, they like a challenge and they're constantly seeking the approval of their peer group. These factors, coupled with their fear of failure and the ever-present sense that they're moving towards the gateway to manhood whether they want to or not, mean they'll continually be tempted by the temporary disconnection from reality drugs can offer.

Because of this, my focus is now primarily on the need to give young people a reason to say no when they're offered illicit drugs rather than on shutting down the supply. It's important that every effort is made to curb the sale of drugs to children and adolescents, but I believe we'll only make real progress when we've managed to perfect the art of linking young people to their dreams and linking those dreams to their need to refrain from exposing themselves to undue risk. Some will dismiss this as an idealistic approach, but it's one I've seen work again and again in the recovery of people from serious drug and alcohol addiction.

Now that we've looked at two potentially negative external forces affecting the lives of adolescent boys, it's perhaps time to talk about a potentially positive external force about which I learned a great deal – and completely changed my mind – during the project. I had entered boys' schools more than a little cynical about the ubiquitous culture of sport embraced by both the teachers and the students. I didn't believe that sport sat at the core, or anywhere near it, of what boys need as they mature; I assumed it was a side issue in terms of their journey to manhood. Once again, I was proved quite wrong.

After talking with the students and watching them in their daily school lives, I now regard sport as an integral part of the journey to manhood for the vast majority of boys. The reason? Its competitive nature coupled with the sense it can give them of being a part of something bigger than themselves. The wide range of sporting opportunities to which the students had access allowed them to experience success and to develop a sense of pride. Through sport they could continue to build a positive relationship with their body and to use their high energy levels. For some boys I met during the project, sport seemed to be the only thing keeping them at school, the only thing giving their world a sense of structure and balance when nothing much else was making sense.

As I've already mentioned, I consider boys to be a lot less resilient than girls and when life hits a difficult moment, they seem much less able to cope. If, in the midst of the chaos, the student remains part of a sports team and has responsibilities and a goal to reach for, he seems able to hold himself steadier than might otherwise be the case. Sport focuses him outwards, in the first instance giving him an excuse to ignore what's happening until he can begin to make some sense of it, and then giving him the time he so desperately needs to think through the issues impinging on his life.

Two other inextricably linked external forces affecting the lives of adolescent boys, which gave rise to a great deal of laughter during our discussions, are adolescent girls and adult women. One facet of the project I haven't yet discussed was the boys' seemingly ever-present fear that they might be accused by their mates and other males of being gay. And this fear meant that they were constantly seeking ways to overtly prove their masculinity. One obvious way to prove their mates wrong, even before the accusations start flying, as they seem inevitably to do, is by the endless pursuit of adolescent girls, something to which many of them seemed to devote a great deal of time and energy.

I was fascinated by the degree to which the boys believed women were in charge, both within their world and in the wider community. This attitude was clear in comments such as these: 'I pick an answer and hope it's the one she wants to hear', 'They can have sex any time they want while we have to work out whether they're up for it', 'Part of being a man is putting up with women.'

This isn't to say the students considered all their relationships with women to be negative, but many of them were clearly putting a great deal of their energy into placating the women, and girls, in their lives, in order to keep their world manageable.

Almost all boys I spoke to had close female friends within their immediate peer group, often referred to as 'girl-mates'. The discussion about how a girl became a girl-mate, given that the students had previously agreed they viewed all girls of their age as potential sexual conquests, was always entertaining, the most common explanation being 'she said no'. Again, boys saw girls as the ones who called the shots: he asked,

'Who's in charge in your relationships with girls?'

'They are – the girls.'

'In all the relationships you have with girls?'

'Yes.'

'So how do you manage your relationships with them?'

'Tell them what you think they want to hear and hope it's the right answer.'

she said no and thus the parameters of their friendship were defined.

Students at all levels in the schools I visited talked of the freedom not having girls on the campus gave them. In fact they saw not having to concern themselves with appearance as the major benefit of being at a boys' school: in their words, it 'lessened the pressure'.

They often spoke of not wanting to appear a fool in front of girls, which meant they tended not to speak in their presence. And, as we've seen, alcohol came in here: many boys said they drank to gain the necessary confidence to talk to girls. Almost all the Year 9, 10 and 11 students I spoke to felt that having girls in their classes would make them much less willing to take part in discussions and that their behaviour would 'tone down' and become less boisterous. There it is again: the girls calling the shots.

'Is it true that you look at every girl as a potential sexual partner?'

'Pretty much.'

'How is it then that you have girl-mates?'

'They said no.'

This belief that women were in charge extended to the adult women in the boys' lives. They regularly told me that female teachers needed to be placated about things their male teachers didn't consider important and referred to all women 'sweating the small stuff' and requiring negotiation. They gave clear examples of how they managed the flow of information to their mothers in order to make their own lives less stressful (I'll discuss this in more detail later) and often evaluated the value of a relationship with a girl in the context of just how much effort was required to keep her happy. I was often intrigued by the degree to which even the junior students had developed this view of women, wondering how it had happened so early in their lives. However they learn it, as I listened to boys (of all ages) describe their relationships with women and how they manage them, I often felt as if I was watching an extremely skilled public relations firm in action.

+ Adolescent boys are drinking alcohol from a reasonably young age and in a number of settings.

+ Alcohol is about easing the pressure of moving towards manhood, about finding common ground with their peers and girls and simply about having fun.

+ Adolescent girls are matching or even surpassing adolescent boys in the tendency to sometimes get extremely drunk.

+ Adults need to be aware that almost every illicit drug is available in any secondary school in the country.

+ With regard to drugs, the hypocrisy of adults doesn't go unnoticed.

+ Keeping boys busy in Years 9, 10 and 11 allows time for the anti-drug message to sink in.

+ Sport is an integral part of the journey to manhood for the vast majority of boys.

+ Most boys believe that women are in charge.

DIARIES

Girl

Saturday 17 November

Saw John in the evening and he was acting really strangely. I went shopping in the afternoon with the girls and I did turn up a bit late so I thought it might be that.

The bar was really crowded and loud so I suggested we go somewhere quieter to talk. He was still very subdued and distracted so I suggested we go somewhere nice to eat. All through dinner he just didn't seem himself; he hardly laughed and didn't seem to be paying attention to me or to what I was saying.

I just knew that something was wrong.

He dropped me back home. I wondered if he was going to come in; he hesitated, but followed. I asked him again if there was something the matter but he just half shook his head and turned the television on.

After about 10 minutes of silence, I said I was going to bed. I put my arms around him and told him that I loved him deeply. He just gave a sigh, and a sad sort of smile.

He didn't follow me up, but later he did, and I was surprised when we made love. He still seemed distant and a bit cold, and I started to think that he was going to leave me, and that he had found someone else.

I cried myself to sleep . . .

Boy

Saturday 17 November

Liverpool lost to Chelsea. Had sex though.

Chapter 6
Adolescent Pragmatism: Why They Do What They Do

We've taken a detailed look at what can make raising and coping with adolescent boys a challenging and sometimes very frustrating process. Now it's time to look at the surprises the Good Man Project delivered, the gifts and talents contained within these young men that I hadn't known were there and that I came to delight in: their pragmatism, their intuition and, in the case of Upper Sixth students, their extraordinary wisdom.

Had I known when I was on the bridge of adolescence with my son what I know now about these special qualities of adolescent boys, I strongly suspect the journey we were on together would have been significantly smoother and more enjoyable for both of us. Having this knowledge won't take away all the concerns adolescent boys generate or totally remove the difficult moments as a Year 10 boy pushes against the boundaries with absolute determination. For me, though, as my awareness grew during the project, this knowledge gave a shape to what was happening in the lives of the boys, a shape I now strongly believe can help us to make clear decisions about getting them safely over the bridge and onto the other side, while retaining our own sanity.

Let's talk first about their pragmatism. I had no sense of this before undertaking the project, but once I got an inkling of the pragmatic way in which boys decide what to do and when to do it, I began to see it everywhere, in the lives of both boys and adult men.

How did I first stumble on the pragmatism? I was interested in the reasons the boys were at single-sex schools and wanted to know whether they'd made a conscious choice to be there rather than at a co-ed school, so early on in the project I began to ask, as an opening question, 'So, why are you here at a boys' school?'

'Cos my mum said.' (It was almost always Mum, not Dad.)

'How many of you would like to be at a co-ed school?'

Almost all the hands in the room went up.

'What would be good about a co-ed school?'

'Duh, girls!'

'Yes, I realise it's about girls, but what about girls? What would be good about being at a school with girls?' (I was hoping, pushing even, for a discussion about the challenge in the classroom or something equally deep and meaningful.)

'Something good to look at . . . I'm sick of looking at him.' This was said looking sideways at his mate.

'So it's just about having something good to look at?'

'Yeah.'

'OK, you're going to go home tonight and your parents are going to say you can now go to a co-ed school. Who's going?'

Three hands went up.

'Come on guys, I'm offering you a chance to go to a co-ed school where there are girls to look at. Why aren't you going?'

'Nah, I'm here now . . . too hard.'

As I looked around the room, I swear I could see them thinking that moving would mean they'd have to pack their lockers, and it would all just be too hard. It was as if they were balancing a set of scales in their head, effort versus pay-off, and the scales weren't tipped far enough towards possible pay-off to justify the effort.

'OK, I'll make it easy for you. We'll bring the girls here. You don't have to do anything except vote. Tomorrow morning you'll come to school and the school will hold a vote about whether this school goes co-ed. Who's voting yes?'

Three hands went up, a different three.

'Come on guys, I'm making it easy for you. You don't have to actually do anything and it would mean there would be girls here in the school to look at. Why aren't you voting yes?'

'Where would they come from?'

Detail, they wanted detail.

'Oh I don't know, how about the girls' school just down the road?'

'Nah, they're dogs!'

'Oh, so they have to be good-looking girls?'

'Yeah.'

'So who would pick them?'

'We would.'

They were now fully involved in this discussion.

'So there'd be a selection panel and only those girls who scored seven or above out of ten would get in?'

'Yeah, works for me.'

'So some poor girl turns up and she's only a six, so you tell her to bugger off, she's ugly.'

'Yeah.'

I was wanting to discuss the philosophical issue of whether there were definite advantages to being at a single-sex versus co-educational school; they were focused on making sure that if their school environment was to change in the way I was suggesting, they could get the best-looking girls onto the campus. Pragmatism, or at least adolescent male pragmatism – what's in it for me, what's the pay-off, why should I do this?

> 'I have one beer and then I can't drive home. There's no point in calling a taxi when you've only had one beer, so I might as well keep drinking until I get completely shitfaced.'

Once I became aware of this aspect of their thought processes, I began to see examples of it everywhere. I've mentioned some already: being at a boys' school meant ten minutes extra in bed because without 'girls to impress' there was no need to apply hair gel; having platonic girlfriends, girl-mates, because 'she said no'; choosing alcohol over drugs as the way to have fun on a Saturday night in order to make training on Tuesday. These are all extremely pragmatic decisions.

'I have one beer and then I can't drive home. There's no point in calling a taxi when you've only had one beer, so I might as well keep drinking until I get completely shitfaced.' (Getting a taxi home after having had only one beer would be a complete waste of money; there's less financial waste involved if there's a greater degree of intoxication.)

So the challenge then becomes how to use the pragmatism of adolescent boys in a way that supports their development and helps mothers in particular to stop expending energy on trying to make their sons into something they're not.

The young man who talked of choosing to use alcohol instead of drugs to 'get off my face' on a Saturday night was making a clear, pragmatic decision. We adults often talk to adolescent boys about what they need to be doing in order to be happy, healthy members of society when they are 30 or 40. He's thinking about having fun on Saturday night and making training on Tuesday, a three-day time span, and would have extreme difficulty trying to envisage what life will be like when he leaves school, let alone when he's 30. In order to connect with him and encourage and assist him to make good decisions, we need to step into his timeframe, his way of being in the world rather than trying to get him to step into ours. This young man wants to have fun *and* be at training. His sport is obviously important, and he's showing us plainly what matters to him and what we can work with to keep him safe while he's on the bridge of adolescence.

I spoke in an earlier chapter about boys always working to a last-minute deadline when getting their homework done. How many parents use up a great deal of energy trying to cajole and/or force their son into at least starting the assignment that's due next week? And they do this even though they know from past experience that, despite their best efforts, there'll be a flurry of activity the night before and the atmosphere in the house will take a decided turn for the worst as tempers fray and the adults ask why the work wasn't started earlier.

Most adolescent boys will do the work when the moment arrives and not before, and no amount of cajoling is likely to have any effect. Send him to his room to do it by all means, but don't expect him to be working on it. Unless he senses the time is here, or he can't find anything else to do and he's not willing to risk the consequences of leaving his room either through the door or the window, no degree of coercion will make any difference.

When he knows it's up to him and only him whether something does or doesn't get done, when he's able to link action with consequence, then he'll begin to make good decisions for himself. A classic example of this is the students who were made aware that this was the last chance in terms of their art portfolios and so galvanised themselves into action. Their pragmatism means adolescent boys have to be able to see and/or feel the consequences of doing or not doing something before it becomes real enough to matter and to motivate them. If they sense that something will 'happen anyway', if they sense that in the end their efforts won't make any real difference, they'll simply choose not to act because, in their minds, there's no reason to do so.

I believe it's worth investigating ways in which we can effectively use the pragmatism of boys. As an example, when I was talking to one group of students about homework deadlines, they mentioned in an almost offhand way that if they had an assignment due on a Monday, they usually started work on it early on Sunday afternoon. I was immediately curious as to why they would spend available leisure time on a Sunday afternoon doing schoolwork (as opposed to cramming it in on a week night) and asked them to explain.

'You might as well.'

'What does "might as well" mean?'

'Well, you've done everything else you wanted to do: played the game on Saturday, been out and had a good time on Saturday night, slept in on Sunday morning. Nothing much else to do, so you might as well do some schoolwork.'

So only because he has nothing much else to do, he turns his attention to the assignment that's due to be handed in the following morning. He possibly gets up to four hours' work done on it before something else grabs his attention (dinner?), as opposed to the two hours he would have achieved if it had been due on any day other than a Monday.

It might not work every time and it might be a somewhat simplistic solution from an educational perspective, but it did occur to me as I listened to the boys explain their reasoning that there may be considerable merit in having every assignment due on a Monday. Who knows what quality of work might result.

Do I believe it would be possible to get a boy to work on a Sunday afternoon on an assignment not due until the following Thursday or even the following Tuesday? No. The time span is too great and his desire and commitment to live in the moment will ensure that there will always be something better to do if the assignment isn't due on Monday. His gaze will be firmly fixed on the fact that Monday night is still available to do the required work.

There will, of course, be adolescent boys who sit outside the stereotype I'm describing, boys who do work consistently on assignments throughout the week, who are able to motivate themselves so they're not always working at the last minute. If you're the parent of one of these boys, all I can say is, 'Enjoy it.' I wasn't such a parent and during the project I couldn't help but notice that no matter what age group I was talking to, up to and including Lower Sixth, no matter what the level of academic ability of the students in front of me, there was general and almost universal agreement that homework is done the night before it's due.

It was true that I detected more evidence of planning and consistent work effort when talking to Upper Sixth boys, but this, too, was linked to their pragmatism. They realised that the time to move had arrived, that the position was no longer 'recoverable'. They were able to talk about being aware that the passing of each day brought them closer to the moment when they would be leaving school and entering the next phase of their lives. Why did they have this level of awareness? What had prompted this development in their thinking? Their pragmatism. They could look up and see there was no one above them. They were made aware every day in a very physical way that they were the senior students, that their time at the school now had a use-by date and that the time for decision-making was fast approaching. It was in the midst of this reality that their work patterns changed and they began to commit themselves to the work in front of them. Because it was now up to them and they weren't simply satisfying the demands of a nagging parent or teacher, they moved.

This is the other reason for my belief in the value of keeping boys at school for five years. It's true that a number of boys have done well and will continue to do well in life having left school at an earlier stage. This isn't about insisting that they stay no matter what. It's about recognising that something happens when a boy becomes an Upper Sixth student and realises that his destiny is now in his own hands. It's about him motivating himself rather than being motivated by others. There has always been someone else in charge; at this point, if the school mechanisms to support this next level of his growth are in place, he begins to take charge and miracles can happen which have a positive flow-on effect on the society this boy is about to move into.

As I draw this discussion on the pragmatism of adolescent boys to a conclusion, it's perhaps a good time to share what became the question of the project – the ultimate pragmatic response from an adolescent boy.

'Who do you talk to about sex?'

'My mates.'

Great, I thought, no doubt there's an abundance of good information out there!

'Would you ever talk to your dad about it?'

The first time I asked this question the noise in the room was amazing. The boys were laughing so hard that they were rocking on their chairs and holding their sides, and the word 'embarrassing' was ricocheting off the walls.

'Come on guys, why wouldn't you talk to your dad about it? It seems entirely logical to me – you're a bloke, he's a bloke . . .'

Pause.

'What would I ask him, Miss?' (There's the pragmatism again: he was into the detail, trying to work out exactly how the suggested conversation might work.)

'I don't know! What happens when? Is this normal?'

Another pause.

'Nah.'

A student at the back of the room looked up. 'You're not getting it, are you, Miss? It would be embarrassing to talk to my dad about sex.'

'No, I'm not getting it, so you're going to have to explain it to me.'

'Well, think about it, he's having sex with *my* mother.'

As his father tells him that women like this, respond to that, all the boy is capable of thinking is 'He's done that to my mother!' The student who was sharing his thoughts with me put his hand over his face at this point, saying 'Too much visual!'

'Have any of you had advice about sex from your father?'

'Yep, my dad told me to always say please.'

We adults, particularly women, think it entirely logical that a man should discuss with his adolescent son whatever he needs to know about sex. Not so. From the boy's perspective, a perspective driven by his pragmatism, it's far better to get the information he needs from someone who isn't in a sexual relationship with his mother.

And finally, let me make a comment on the pragmatism of adult men. Make no mistake – they don't lose their pragmatism once they come off the bridge of adolescence or at any point thereafter; they retain it all their lives. But if they've successfully completed the maturation process, it seems to me that the pragmatism has taken on a slightly different shape from that of adolescent boys. The challenge remains for we women to accept who the men in our lives are and to stop wasting our energy trying to make them into something they're not.

So what *is* the difference between the pragmatism of adolescent boys and that of mature adult men? The pragmatic lens through which an adolescent boy looks is very narrow and has room only for himself. The pragmatic lens through which a mature adult man looks has widened and can incorporate the idea of doing things for others, those he cares about and those for whom he feels a social responsibility. But, and it's a significant but, if he can see no reason for doing something within that framework, he won't do it, no matter what coercion comes his way.

There's no better way to illustrate this than by describing the task of putting out the household rubbish, which needs to be out for collection by 7.30 each Wednesday morning. It's his job. We women think the best idea is to sort the rubbish and put it out the night before, allowing for such possibilities as the truck coming five minutes early or the entire household sleeping in and missing the deadline. He, on the other hand, considers that getting it out there at 7.28 on the Wednesday morning is time enough and that's what he intends to do. We get increasingly agitated on the Tuesday evening when he shows no sign of doing what we'd like him to do – put it out now. Eventually we somewhat huffily gather up the rubbish and put it out ourselves, muttering as we do so about how hopeless he is and why can't he do the one thing that's actually his responsibility. We then sulk for the rest of the night.

What we need to understand is that as we gathered up the rubbish and took it out, in his brain there was a tick: 'She's just done what I expected her to do. Now I don't need to do it.' He's watched our increasing levels of agitation as the evening has worn on, knowing that eventually we'll be annoyed enough to act and he'll be saved a job.

Some women will see it as entirely appropriate that men do things according to our schedule rather than theirs, usually because they consider we 'know better', 'are better organised' or 'can multi-task and anticipate possible problems'. Men, on the other hand, are fully aware of the possibility of the household sleeping in or the bin men coming early, but, like their adolescent counterparts, they would deal with the problem if either of those things were to happen. And anyway, there could be an earthquake or a flood overnight and then it would have been a complete waste of time expending effort to put the rubbish out.

What are we women to do in the face of this male pragmatism? It's simple really, and not unlike learning to walk inside the pragmatic minds of adolescent boys to get them to do what needs to be done or to keep them safe. We need to accept the reality of men rather than forever wanting to change it and them. There are two possible approaches. We can decide to leave it entirely up to him when the rubbish goes out, having agreed in adult negotiations that it will be his job, and that any consequences from not getting it out in time are his to deal with. Or we can decide that it's such a potentially stressful issue for us, given the way we view the world and what we need to feel adequately organised in our lives, that we'll put it out ourselves. Simple really.

Why should we accept men's pragmatism and not try to change them into creatures who do things our way? Because there's so much fun to be had when we let them be who they are. Because their strength and male beauty lie in their pragmatism. Because if we look beyond the frustration we feel (and we do feel it) as we try to understand the pragmatism driving their lives and their decisions, we begin to see their intuition and their wisdom and we increase the chances of our sons and our grandsons growing into good men.

+ The challenge is how to use the pragmatism of adolescent boys in a way that supports their development and helps mothers in particular to stop expending energy on trying to make their sons into something they're not.

+ To connect with him and encourage him in making good decisions, we need to step into his timeframe.

+ Adolescent boys have to be able to see and/or feel the consequences of doing or not doing something before it becomes real enough to matter and to motivate them.

+ The pragmatic lens through which an adolescent boy looks is very narrow and has room only for himself. The pragmatic lens through which a mature adult man looks can incorporate the idea of doing things for others.

+ Women need to accept the reality of men rather than forever wanting to change it and them.

Chapter 7
Intuition and Wisdom: The Hidden Gifts

I started the Good Man Project believing that men have intuition but that they very rarely, if ever, use it. I ended the project having learnt that I was half-right. Men have intuition? Yes. They very rarely use it? No. In fact they use it all the time, and very effectively, in their everyday lives. Why didn't I see this before? Because I and other women don't immediately recognise it as intuitive behaviour. It may look different, and men may use it differently, but intuition it is – a highly developed skill that most males use with almost no conscious awareness of exactly what they're doing. It's simply part of their way of being and they seldom pause to question or analyse it.

I first became aware of these male intuitive skills in my discussions with Year 10 boys, those delightfully obnoxious know-it-alls who, in a matter of months, have been transformed from fresh-faced boys into a species of alien that has a concentration span of 30 seconds *if* the subject fits their definition of interesting, and who are unable to do any more than grunt when asked a question. Obnoxious they may be, know-it-all they may be, but it's not all bad news. There are some fairly amazing things going on below the surface (and no, I don't mean below the waist), things that have huge potential in allowing the adults in his world to believe he really will be OK.

Very early on in the project I became aware of the language of insult used by the boys. Words such as 'gay', 'queer', 'faggot' and 'homo' were clearly audible in the boys' conversations with one another and seemed to be used almost as terms of endearment. Having observed this phenomenon in a number of settings, I decided to investigate further and asked a group of Year 10 students about it. They liked my description of it being a language of insult, laughing among themselves at the idea, and confirmed that, despite using such derogatory comments, the boys they were addressing were their mates. When I asked why they always used words that make reference to homosexuality, they replied, 'Cos it's the worst thing you could be, Miss.'

I didn't want to pause at that moment to talk in any more depth about why they considered it such a negative thing to be homosexual, but opportunities to discuss this did arise at various points in the project and have left me with some thoughts which I'll share in Chapter 11.

Moving the discussion on, I asked the boys why they never said anything nice to their mates and, in true pragmatic style, one lad looked up at me and said, 'Like what, Miss?'

'Oh, I don't know . . . "You're looking good today"?'

'Oh nah, Miss, that'd be gay.'

Having failed to convince them there was merit in speaking less rudely to one another, I turned back to their use of insulting language.

'So, how do you know when you've gone too far?'

'There's usually blood involved.'

'Nah there's not, Miss,' said another while hitting the boy who'd just spoken. 'It's not like that; you just know.'

'Tell me about "just know".'

Long pause.

'Well, he goes kinda quiet . . . you expect an insult to come back and it doesn't.'

'Or he moves away . . . goes quiet.'

'Or the skin colour around his neck changes.'

At this point I re-entered the discussion, which had been meandering around the classroom. Surprised by the insight in this boy's comment, I asked him to repeat it.

'Oh you know, Miss. If someone's upset, the skin colour around their neck goes a different colour.'

These boys have entered a phase in their lives that some adults have classified as monosyllabic neo-autism and yet here was one of them talking to me about body language! From then on I began to observe their behaviour a little more closely and so came to understand, at least to some degree, the framework of men's intuition.

When a boy moves from Year 9 into Year 10 he seriously begins the journey across the bridge of adolescence and into manhood that has only been hinted at until now. He now has a reasonable grip on his environment both at school and at home and the physical changes in his body are telling him in a very obvious way that he's on his way to a new and exciting place. But he's nervous, despite all external signs to the contrary, uncertain of what's expected of him, and so he begins

'If someone's upset, the skin colour around their neck goes a different colour.'

to seek out information. And this is when the development of the intuition he's always had begins in earnest. He's stopped automatically accepting the information being passed down from the adults in his life, considering most of it simply a plot to ruin his fun, and has started to run his own radar through which he filters the information he gathers from his peers. His aim? To find out what it means to be a man.

His mate Dave uses that word and everyone thinks he's cool, so he stores the word in his brain to use too; Jack does something and everyone thinks he's a complete and utter geek, so he stores that away as something not to do. But the challenge for all boys at this stage in their development is that things can and do change really quickly, sometimes hour by hour rather than day by day. The cool word becomes a geeky word, and the geeky thing becomes cool. So now he's got a non-stop flow of information coming in and out, in and out. Not much of it's landing yet. Running down through the centre of his being is a beam – imagine it as a thin strip of wood – which in time will expand to incorporate the qualities he'll have as a man; just now, though, it's very narrow. As his maturation process continues, pieces of the information he's gleaning from those around him about what makes a man, and a good man at that, will attach themselves to the beam, causing it to expand. At the moment the information is just rolling relentlessly in and out and nothing is sticking. This is why he can't talk beyond the occasional monosyllabic grunt: there's so much happening on the inside that his ability to even begin formulating a question or comment beyond 'What's for tea?' is virtually non-existent.

Having gained some sense of the way in which the boys were using their intuition to manage their environment, I watched more closely and was able to see numerous examples of male intuition at work.

Boys' schools seem to create an environment in which it's safe, in an emotional sense, for the boys, regardless of age, to play. Wherever I looked out at the school grounds during morning breaks and lunch breaks, I was able to observe boys playing and it seemed as if the games had been set up with almost no verbal communication; there was no declaring of rules, no drawing up of boundaries, no overt picking of teams. I'm sure that these things had happened as the games got under way, but they weren't done obviously as would probably have happened if girls had been involved.

Let me give you one example of male intuition at work.

It was lunchtime and four boys, Year 9 students, were playing a game on the concrete area in front of the main school building. The head came down the stairs on his way to do something and noticed the boys. He paused and watched the game for a minute or two, working out exactly what it was the boys were doing. Having sussed it, he joined in and played with them for about five minutes before moving on. No words had been exchanged between the various parties at this point.

Three days later the head came down the same stairs and saw what appeared to be the same group of boys playing the same game. He didn't hesitate this time because he considered he knew the game, so he stepped in and began to play. He told me later that he thought he'd been in the game about 30 seconds when he realised something different was going on: the game had evolved in some way. At the very moment that he, an adult man, realised there was something different happening, a Year 9 boy looked straight at him and said, 'Keep up, Mr B, or bugger off.'

It isn't just about boys' intuition and how boys communicate, it's also about male intuition, male communication styles. I'm now convinced that, in general, about 80 per cent of men's communication is silent and if men are communicating with other men, that ratio rises to about 90 per cent. They communicate with hand gestures, with their eyes and eyebrows, with their head, and then and only then do they speak. In complete contrast to women, they don't talk unless there's something to say.

At a conference I attended recently as a guest speaker I was sitting waiting to address a group of around 300 women. As I watched them come into the hall, I began to take note of the noise they were making. It seemed they were all talking at once. I decided to see if I could focus on just what had them so energised: perhaps they were discussing the world situation in the context of the Iraq war or maybe the political situation here at home. But no, they were talking about which chair they were going to sit in – 'Hey Mary, let's go up the front', 'Sally, I think we should go over here', 'Has anyone seen Jude? She might want to sit with us', 'Where do you reckon you'll hear her better, up the back, or over here?', 'Are the seats allocated, do you think? Will it be alright to sit here?' The discussion continued for several minutes then gradually came to a halt as the women settled into their chairs, checking as they did so that everyone around them was happy with the seating arrangements.

There's nothing wrong with the scene I've just described and I'm not in any way condemning or judging the women for behaving as they did. No doubt I would have behaved in exactly the same way had I been a member of the audience. In highlighting this incident, I'm focusing on the comparison between how men and women act in such situations.

I'm reasonably sure I can guarantee that if 300 men were

coming into a hall in similar circumstances, there wouldn't be one conversation about which chair to sit in. If there was any conversation at all, it would be low level, short bursts of speech and equally short responses. 'Good game last night.' 'Yeah.' 'Michael Owen seems to have hit his stride.' 'Yeah.' But if you actually watched what was going on, you'd see a lot of communication occurring. If one guy wanted another to sit next to him, he'd just nod towards a chair and raise an eyebrow and the other man would know exactly what he meant. He wouldn't speak; he wouldn't need to. He'd just sit down.

As part of the project I was lucky enough to spend some time in workshops with the heads of the various schools. It was in these that I came to understand how much silent conversation is always going on between men. We women know nothing about it; it happens around us and a great deal of the time we have no idea that it exists. Then, when we don't hear anything being said, we try to articulate what's happening. So, when a father raises his eyebrow towards his son as a result of what he's just said or done, Mum catches the tail end of the look and says, 'Did you have to be that hard on him?' Then she turns to the boy and says, 'What your dad was really trying to say was . . . ' There was actually no need for the translation. There may be disagreement between the two parties, but the message has been received and understood. If there's more to be said, the two males will find their own way to the next part of the conversation – and the chances are high we women would miss that too.

Men are highly intuitive, and they appear to use their intuition as a communication tool with considerable success. The challenge for women is to recognise the communication that is occurring in the silence and trust it, let it be, rather than insisting that everything be openly discussed.

I've often reflected on what I might have done differently with my son during his adolescence had I known then what I now know about the power of male intuition and the way it develops. I think the answer is that I would have talked to his intuition rather than to his belligerence. Instead of going at him repeatedly using the word 'should', as I can recall doing on more than one occasion, I would have reached around behind the visual image of a sullen adolescent boy and spoken to his intuition. I could, for example, have said, 'But we both know that's not OK, don't we?' He wouldn't have hugged me and said 'Yes, Mum, we do', but I now know he would have heard me. And by doing it that way I would have been encouraging the development of his intuition and assisting him on his journey towards manhood.

The pragmatism and intuition of the boys were two big surprises of the project. The third was the discovery of the extraordinary wisdom contained within the Upper Sixth boys I met. When in discussions with students at this level, I was often taken aback by their ability to talk in depth and with amazing insight about some of the hard issues. I didn't have to raise the topic of youth suicide, they did, often displaying a high level of awareness of the various aspects involved, and they were more than capable of finding the words they needed to explain how the world looked to them in this regard and many others.

I'm not suggesting they had totally become mature adult men as they crossed the boundary from the Lower into the Upper Sixth. This was definitely not the case: they were still boys at heart, taking advantage of any opportunity that arose to join in a game, play a trick on a fellow classmate or inject fun into whatever was happening. What I did see was young men who were on their way out of adolescence, who had a strong sense of the world around them and what their place in it might be, and who were willing and able to articulate their views about the subjects I was raising.

Before I go on to share some of the insights I gained from these wise creatures, I feel the need to add a word of warning. While it's true that the Upper Sixth student is a gorgeous and apparently mature young man moving confidently towards the end of his school career, there is a strong chance he'll take what will seem to be a backward step during his first year away from school. He may well become a moron who is focused on getting drunk and/or laid and little else. (I'm drawing here on my experience of first-year university students.) That he becomes such a creature does not make a nonsense of my description of Upper Sixth boys as wise and insightful young men. It's simply that in the Upper Sixth he reaches a plateau and pauses. As he leaves school, he moves off that plateau and begins to make his way towards the next one. In the first little while, unaccustomed to the sudden and complete freedom involved, he takes a few backward steps. In time he'll become steady again – it may take a while, but it will happen. What happens as he swings away from the structure of school is all just part of the process.

When I raised the subject of emotions with students at all levels it was interesting to note how anger was the most acceptable emotion and how every other emotion seemed to be transformed into anger. It seems that fear became anger, grief became anger and sadness became anger. How,

I often wondered, does this happen? Are boys receiving a message that says anger is the only valid emotion for men, or do they transform whatever emotion they're feeling into anger in order to make it more manageable? I'm not sure I yet know the answer to that question and I'm reluctant to put a female spin on any possibilities, knowing as I now do how much my view of the world differs from that of a male.

It was very common in the course of my visits to find myself at a school that was mourning the loss of a student or a recent graduate, either through suicide or death on the road. As I watched the schools grapple with this situation time and again, I became aware that the reality of death sits very close to the lives of the boys, possibly a lot closer than it did for people of my generation. A significant number of young men are taking the option of suicide or are driving themselves and their mates to death or injury on the roads and as a result adolescent boys are feeling deep and painful emotions as part of their everyday lives, even if they don't appear to be affected. It was during my discussions with Upper Sixth students about suicide, death and grief that the window was opened on their natural wisdom.

'Who has had someone close to them die?'

Several of them put up their hands.

'Can someone give me a visual image of the grief?'

There was no pause at all before one student looked up saying, as he cupped his hands, 'Mine's a small hard ball.'

'And you're holding it now?'

'Yeah.'

'So it fits in your hand?'

'Yep.'

'OK, now you've got it in your hand, what do you do with it?'

'I put it down here and go over there and play a game.'

'Does the game involve physical contact?'

'Yep, the harder the better.'

'So you've played the game. Now you look back towards the grief; has it changed shape?'

'No.'

'Has it got any smaller?'

'No.'

'Will anything make it smaller?'

'No.'

'Talking?'

'No!'

'So it just stays that size?'

'Yeah.'

'Permanently?'

'Time might make a difference.'

'But it will be a part of who you are forever?'

'Yep.'

The boy next to him picked up the image.

'Miss, mine's not a ball,' he said. 'I know it's a cliché but mine's a bottle – I put the grief in the bottle and screw the top down.'

'Does the bottle ever get full?'

'Yep.'

'What do you do with it?'

At this point he made as if to throw something over his shoulder.

'Does it hit someone?'

'Yeah, usually.'

Both of them, you'll notice, talked about physical contact (in one case, the harder the better) as a way of coping with grief.

Another boy then joined in. 'Mine's a bottle too, Miss, but I don't ever have to throw mine away. I've got a hole drilled in the bottom and it drips away at a pace I can cope with.'

His neighbour added, 'I've got a bottle too, Miss, and it's got one of those cords' – he was miming an intensive care drip – 'and I can move the clip as necessary to increase or lessen the flow.'

I'd been in a conversation about grief with this group of Upper Sixth students for only about five minutes and already we'd developed some very clear imagery for what's involved in the management of heavy emotions. The conversation continued for another ten minutes or so along these lines and the imagery just got stronger.

I've already referred to the student who, when I talked about young men committing suicide because they couldn't see their way out of the darkness in which they'd become stuck, replied that the answer to this dilemma was simple really: we just had to keep reminding boys that there will be more moments. This is where the real learning can occur for those of us involved in the lives of adolescent boys; this is the place where we can connect with the boys' natural wisdom and find the answers to the questions that worry us above all others. How do I keep him safe? How do I keep him from overdosing on drugs, from killing himself in a car, from making a stupid decision that will lead him directly to the gates of a prison? We don't have to look far: the answers to these questions sit within the heads of Upper Sixth boys. We simply have to find the time to ask the questions and develop our ability to hear, really hear, the answers.

But at the very time we could and should be pausing to gather this information, both for our own education and to improve our teaching and management of younger boys, including those challenging Year 10 students, the school curriculum allows almost no room for such an activity. It doesn't have to be a teaching module; in fact it shouldn't be – to turn the idea into a teaching module would be to kill it. What I'm talking about is developing our ability to have a conversation with Upper Sixth students whenever the opportunity presents itself. I'm suggesting 15 minutes here, 20 minutes there, posing a question about life as it looks to them, asking about such topics as sex, drugs, alcohol, manhood and relationships in the same way I did; daring to ask, listening carefully and without judgement to the answers and continually gathering a stronger sense of what the world looks like through their eyes.

+ Male intuition is a highly developed skill that most men use with almost no conscious awareness of exactly what they're doing.

+ There's so much happening on the inside for a Year 10 boy that he can't talk beyond the occasional monosyllabic grunt.

+ About 80 per cent of men's communication is silent and if men are communicating with other men, that ratio rises to about 90 per cent.

+ The challenge for women is to recognise the communication that's occurring in the silence and trust it, rather than insisting that everything be openly discussed.

+ When in discussions with Upper Sixth students, I was often taken aback by their ability to talk in depth and with amazing insight about the hard issues.

+ In his first year away from school he may well become a moron who is focused on getting drunk and/or laid and little else.

+ Anger is the most acceptable emotion for adolescent boys. Every other emotion seems to be transformed into anger.

+ The reality of death sits very close to the lives of the boys, possibly a lot closer than it did for people of my generation.

+ We need to have conversations with Upper Sixth students whenever we can – 15 or 20 minutes here and there, asking them about such topics as sex, drugs, alcohol, manhood and relationships.

Chapter 8
Stop Making His Lunch: What Mothers Should Do

At a fathers and sons breakfast held recently at one of the schools that had participated in the Good Man Project, I gave the boys sitting alongside their dads a piece of advice. When your mother asks you what happened this morning, what was talked about, tell her that all she needs to know is that you and your dad were here together, you had breakfast and you listened to me talk for a while. OK? That's all she needs to know: I was there, Dad was there, end of story. It was men's business, your stuff. If she goes on about it a bit, trying to get you to tell her what I said, whether you said anything or your dad said anything, who else said something, just tell her she doesn't need to know. Say it again: it was men's business.

As I said that to the group in front of me, I could see the looks going between the boys and their fathers and between the men in the room, looks that if translated into words would probably have said something like, 'You've got to be kidding. The minute I get home she'll be lined up wanting to know what went on and she won't stop going on about it until I've told her what she wants to know . . . or until I've made up something that satisfies her curiosity.'

That may sound like a very harsh translation, one that makes women the bad guys. But that was exactly what the men were thinking, and not without good cause. I've talked about the good surprises of the project; well, this was another surprise, but one that wasn't quite so good – the degree to which mothers, particularly white middle-class mothers, are overly involved in the lives of their adolescent sons. I hadn't gone looking for this as part of the project. I began to have meetings with parents at the schools where I was working because the heads thought it would be a good idea to inform the mothers and fathers about the project and why the school had decided to become involved. The meetings were called to inform the parents, but they ended up informing me. And when the decision was made, at one school, to talk to men and women about their sons in separate forums, that became a regular feature of the project. At these meetings, what I've come to consider the 'real' information about parents and their roles began to flow.

I mentioned in an earlier chapter, when discussing the concept of a bridge of adolescence, that the project has left me believing that the central issue in the lives of adolescent boys seems to be how to get mothers off the bridge and fathers onto it. While the challenge for fathers is to make themselves clearly visible at the edge of the bridge, the challenge for mothers is to let go the hands of their beloved sons and to allow them to walk onto the bridge at their own pace and in the company of other males. When I explained this concept to the mothers of the students in various schools, there were definite 'aha' moments, as the women recognised their own behaviour and understood the vulnerability they'd been feeling as their sons moved, often at breakneck speed, towards the bridge. It wasn't uncommon for a mother to look at me after a presentation about the project and say with a laugh, 'I'm camped on the bridge, now tell me how to get off.'

When I talk about mothers walking onto the bridge of adolescence and spending their time up there directing traffic, I'm not talking only about other women, I'm talking about myself. I was one of those mothers and with the benefit of hindsight there are a number of things I wish I'd done differently.

Before I begin to discuss what I observed about mothers during the project, perhaps it would be a good idea to share some of my own experience as the mother of an adolescent boy.

I'm the mother of two and my son is my second child. I married young, divorced young and, as a result, raised my children as a single parent from the time they were six and four years of age. Their father lived overseas for a long period during their formative years, but I had the support of my family, his family and a wide group of friends as I brought them to adulthood.

Until he was 12, my son was gorgeous, a good-looking boy with long eyelashes and a great smile who grinned at the world and encouraged it to grin back. He had no difficulty getting the world, me included, to give him whatever he wanted, and he spent a lot of time sitting behind the protection of his sister – she worried and worked hard to be responsible; he had fun. And then he started his journey across the bridge of adolescence, an alien invaded his body and I spent the next few years wondering where my boy had gone. I had a strong sense he was going to be a good man if he did make it to adulthood, but was he going to live long enough? There seemed to be a very real possibility that he would accidentally kill himself as a result of the risk-taking behaviour he regularly indulged in, despite my best efforts to control him or, perhaps more likely, that I would kill him out of sheer frustration.

I had sent him to a boys' school in order to immerse him in a male world, thinking that this would help in teaching him how to become a good man. While I'm sure there were some calm and relatively uneventful days over the next few years, they're not the ones I remember. Looking back, it seems as if he developed a close relationship with the discipline master at the school from day two, and that he maintained that relationship for the next three and a half years, at which point I gave us both a break and finally let him leave.

What I didn't know then, but know now with absolute clarity, is that from the school's perspective I was very likely the mother from hell. I'd sent him to the school in the hope they would wrap him in positive male values and show him the pathway to manhood. Having made that decision, I then spent the next three and a half years telling them what they weren't doing for 'my boy'. What I really meant, now I'm prepared to be honest with myself, was that they weren't doing what I wanted in the way I wanted. They were doing exactly what I'd sent him to the school for – attempting to hold him steady and guide him towards manhood while educating him – and I kept interrupting the process. The discipline master is now the headteacher at the school and when I met him again recently, I acknowledged how hard I must have been to manage and how much I must have interfered. He looked at me in that noncommittal way men have and said, 'No, you weren't

that bad really. There were others who were much worse.'
This reply didn't do a lot to reassure me that I hadn't been
a complete pain in the neck.

As I negotiated the journey through adolescence with
my son, I spent a great deal of time thinking, What am I
supposed to be doing with him? How am I supposed to show
him how to be a good man, and what is that anyway? What
are the rites of passage that take a boy from boyhood into
manhood? I wondered and worried about him, knowing
that the essence of the boy was good, but that things were
stepping in his way. He was a risk taker: he was constantly
out there, doing things that I sensed he needed to do, and
while he was doing them, I was wondering whether I would
have to find the strength to bury my son. He bought a car
and owned it for only 24 hours before he wrapped it around
a telegraph pole. Luckily it was a big car and neither he nor
his friends, nor anyone else, was hurt in the accident, but I
was frightened by his behaviour. I didn't want to turn him
into a weak-willed individual dominated by his mother and
always having to consider my feelings and insecurities when
making decisions about his life, but I did want to keep him
alive and see my gorgeous boy grow into a good man. The
question was how.

Another strong influence on my thinking and my concern
for my son emanated from my work experience. At the time
my son was drawing close to the bridge of adolescence and I
had begun to think about the task ahead and my role as the
single parent of an adolescent boy, I was a prison officer in
male prisons. As I walked the wings of the prison I noticed
how many of the inmates were just like my son. They were
boys, boys in men's bodies, boys who weren't inherently
bad, who'd been born full of magic as every child is, but who

had made stupid 30-second decisions, and they, and their families, were living out the consequences. Like the young man who'd 'borrowed' his father's car, gone for a drive with his best mate in the passenger seat, decided to outrun the cops when they attempted to pull him over for exceeding the speed limit and crashed. His closest friend was dead and he was in prison for seven years for manslaughter. He was a good boy; he'd just made a dumb choice.

To my woman's eye, it seemed that many young men were entering prison as part of some kind of quest for manhood. Unfortunately, many of the symbols of manhood in our culture involve alcohol, violence and fast cars, and boys go after those things, thinking they're acting like men. They think it's manly to get into a car, put your foot on the accelerator and take the car up to 100 miles an hour. They hit a lamppost and they die, or their best mate in the passenger seat dies and they go to prison and live forever with the knowledge that their friend is dead because of them.

It's not that they wake up and think, 'Gee, I think I'll go to prison today', but they do wake up and think, 'I'm a man now, I can do this.' So they drink that alcohol, accept those drugs when they're offered, having no idea what their brain's going to get them to do when they're drunk or high and can't remember where they are. There must be another way, I thought; there must be some other rites of passage I just don't know about that can and do assist boys to come to manhood in a less dangerous way.

I can still vividly recall the sense of powerlessness I felt as I watched my son move across the bridge of adolescence. I wasn't sure what I was supposed to be doing, I wasn't sure how to draw men into his life, I wasn't sure what role I was supposed to be playing in trying to open or reopen his relationship with his father. In the end, I decided that the only thing I could do was to go up onto the bridge with him, knowing even as I did so that I shouldn't have been there.

Why shouldn't I have been there? Quite simply because he was on a journey to manhood and I wasn't a man. There are strong differences between the genders, enjoyable differences, and there are a number of moments in life when those differences need to be acknowledged and allowed for. One of those moments for women is as our sons begin the journey into adulthood.

One of the lessons I learned in this regard came on a number of occasions when I watched male teachers discipline students. I often found myself thinking that I would handle the situation better: I would explain the issues more clearly to the boy concerned, I would be gentler, I would have a stronger sense of fairness and so on. I've stopped thinking that way now; I stopped not long after observing the incident I'm about to describe.

I had walked into a head's office not realising as I pushed the door open that a Lower Sixth boy was in the room. I quickly realised something had been going on that I was interrupting. There was a black cloud visible over the boy's head: he was an obviously angry young man. Sitting behind the desk was the head, doing some work. Not quite knowing what to do next and to ease the situation I said to the boy, 'So, in a spot of bother, are we?' He grunted at me and then resumed staring at the floor. As he did so, the head stood up, came around from behind his desk and started to move towards the boy. This kid was very angry.

The head was moving towards the boy with his hand out, and appeared to be aiming for the boy's collar, which wasn't straight. I'd been a prison officer; I'd watched what happens when you touch angry people – you usually get a smack in the mouth. So there I was, in my supreme knowledge as a woman thinking, this will be interesting. Touching this boy could produce quite a reaction. Why is he worrying about the boy's collar at a time like this? What does it matter that it's crooked?

As the head moved towards the boy with his arm extended, and while I was congratulating myself inwardly for knowing better, he said, 'Yeah, he is in a spot of bother. He nicked a mobile – he knows he nicked it, he knows that I know he nicked it, and some time soon he's going to tell me about it.' Just as he finished speaking, his hand reached the boy's collar and he proceeded to straighten it. The head then dropped his hand onto the boy's shoulder, saying as he did so, 'But we're going to get through this.' The boy didn't hit him. He waited about ten seconds, taking in the feeling of the older man's hand on his shoulder; then, to recover his mana (composure), he shrugged the hand away. But for those few seconds, a younger man was told by an older man that though what he'd done wasn't OK, *he* was OK, and that there would be a way through this situation that would leave him intact. It was a stunningly skilful interaction between a man and a boy and I don't believe there's a woman on earth who could have delivered that message as effectively. This is what happens when we let men attend to men's business.

Boys are extraordinary creatures. Their intuition and their pragmatism make them incredibly humorous, incredibly frustrating and gorgeous. Men's business at this point in the lives of boys is to guide them through adolescence. Our job is to step back, to let the men do what they do so well and to enjoy watching from the sidelines, participating occasionally, knowing that it's their time and their turn.

I have a message for mothers, a message from your sons. When I asked the boys what I could tell their mothers on their behalf, their answer was simple and clear: 'Chill out.'

The first time I asked this question I was a little taken aback by the speed with which they answered, and responded by saying, 'OK. I'll tell them to chill out, as long as you can tell me, one, that you know they're there, and two, that you'll make sure they know the big stuff.' They looked straight back at me and said, 'Of course we know she's there, we don't need you to remind us. We know she's there and we will go to her for the big stuff, but she needs to let go of the small stuff.'

So what is the small stuff? Listen to the following conversation.

'So, what's the main difference between men and women?'

'Women sweat the small stuff.'

'Really? Like what?'

'Like what colour the room's painted, what colour nail polish you're wearing, what so and so said about so and so.'

'Who are you talking about? Your mothers, your girl-friends, your sisters . . . ?'

'Nah, all women.'

It's important to note that, as he said 'all women', he, a boy of about 15, had a look of complete resignation on his face. Is this stuff somehow absorbed through their skin when they're in the company of older men? Are there secret communication channels out there running between men and boys that we women know absolutely nothing about? How is it that a 15-year-old boy can be so resigned so early that all women sweat the small stuff? The discussion continued and I got more examples from the boys of the subjects they considered too trivial to talk about, but that women love discussing.

A student sitting down the back of the classroom had been only partially engaged in the conversation. His main preoccupation had been doodling on the pad in front of him. At this point in the conversation, he caught my eye, put down the pen he was holding and said very nonchalantly, 'Yeah, you lose a sock – she goes out and buys you five new pairs . . . and it's only a sock!'

And then there was the other young man: 'My mother wakes me up ten minutes earlier than I need to be out of bed every morning.' (Note the pragmatism – 'ten minutes earlier than I need to be out of bed'. He'd calculated exactly how much time he required to get out of bed, do what's necessary and get to school on time – there wouldn't have been any spare moments in there.)

'Really? What for?'

'She wants me to get up and fold the clothes that are thrown on the spare bed in my room.'

'Do you ever get up?'

'Nah.'

'Are you ever going to get up?'

'Nah.'

This boy's mother gave herself ten minutes of angst every morning trying to turn her son into a clothes-folding adolescent – she was sweating the small stuff. In the context of what else was happening in this boy's life, what did it really matter that there were clothes thrown on the spare bed in his room? He wasn't being disrespectful to his mother or deliberately disobedient. He just couldn't see the point in wasting good sleeping time folding clothes that at some point in the next six months he was going to put on, or recycle through the laundry.

I wasn't very far into the project when I began having discussions with the various heads about the role of parents in helping the school educate their sons. It was a topic they raised. They had the impression that whereas it used to be common for parents to back the school in any decisions made in the management of their son, especially when discipline issues were involved, the reverse was now the case. Now it's the norm for parents to assume that the school has got it wrong and has treated their son unfairly by taking whatever action they've decided on. My discussions with parents themselves have led me to go one step further. I believe there are a significant number of mothers – mothers, not fathers – who think that the school rules should apply to everyone except their son; mothers who are all too ready to step in and defend their boys no matter how obnoxious or unacceptable their behaviour. I was told a number of anecdotes that support this view and I'll share some with you. But first, let's talk about where the fathers are in all of this.

The heads told me again and again that when two parents come in for a chat because their boy's in trouble, it's the norm for the mother to do all the talking. The head looks towards the father and it's obvious he has something to say, an opinion to offer, but she won't shut up long enough for him to actually say it. Initially I wasn't sure I totally believed the heads on this one. I thought it might be an overly prejudiced view, so decided to investigate a little further. The opportunity to do so arose when I found myself in front of a group of fathers.

'Listen guys, I just want to check something out with you. Apparently when you and your wife are in the head's office because your son's in a spot of bother and you've been called to the school, you're really quiet, you just don't talk.'

'No,' came the reply from one man.

'Why not?'

'Because I'll get it wrong.'

Somewhat naïvely, I replied, 'No, you can't get it wrong, he's your boy.'

'Oh no,' he said, looking straight at me, a now-familiar look of resignation on his face, 'I'll get it wrong . . . and I'll get a bollocking when I get home.'

As he said this, several heads in the room nodded, the men seeming to relish the fact that someone had identified a situation with which they were all very familiar.

After a bit more discussion on this topic with the men, I headed back to talk to their wives and partners and, as I did so, I found myself thinking that the views expressed by the men were probably a little unfair and would offend the women I was about to talk to. I couldn't have been more wrong.

'The guys have just told me that when they're in the head's office with you, they don't talk because they'll get it wrong.'

One woman didn't even hesitate; she looked straight at me and without the slightest hint of the embarrassment I was expecting, she said, 'He will.'

'And he reckons he'll get a bollocking when he gets home?'

'I won't wait that long – I'll get him in the car.'

There seemed to be universal agreement with her comments and the conversation continued with one woman saying, 'I take him to parent-teacher evenings, but he just won't talk.' By this time I was thinking, Yes, and I think I'm beginning to see why, so I said, 'Well, there's one possible solution.'

'What's that?'

'You could send him by himself, then he's going to have to talk.'

At that moment the entire group of intelligent, articulate middle-class women looked as if I'd just asked them to eat snake. (No power and control issues here, I thought to myself!)

One woman bravely put up her hand at that point and said, 'I could do that, I could send him by himself.'

'Great,' I said, 'great.'

'As long as I got a detailed list of what he talked about.'

'The guys have just told me that when they're in the head's office with you, they don't talk because they'll get it wrong.'

'He will.'

'And he reckons he'll get a bollocking when he gets home?'

'I won't wait that long,' was the reply. 'I'll get him in the car.'

The point here is: actually you don't need to know. This is men's business and it's time for us to back off. The men I talked to in the course of the project were good men, intelligent, articulate men who, having accepted the responsibility of going to the parent-teacher meeting, will willingly tell you the important stuff. You just have to accept that what he tells you is what meets his criteria of important, not yours. I'm not sure how or why we've reached the situation where many women seem to believe they need to know it all, but we appear to be there and for the sake of our boys it's time to realise that we need to change. When your son starts his journey towards manhood in earnest, it's time to lighten up and let go. Perhaps above all else it is time to trust the boy's father to find his way through the challenges now presenting themselves, helping him where you can, rather than pushing him aside on the pretext that somehow you'll be better at this.

I'm not saying this on behalf of the men I spoke to in the project. I'm not a self-appointed advocate of men. I'm saying it on behalf of the boys, because they echoed what the men told me in this regard and they're the ones the project was about: 'Mum wants to know everything. You tell her anything at all, she has a hundred more questions. It's easier to keep quiet.'

'If you tell your mum something voluntarily, she'll just ask a whole lot of questions. It's rude to say "Enough", so it's best just not to talk at all.'

'I came home,' one boy said, 'and told Mum I'd met a girl I liked. "Really? What colour's her hair? What does her dad do? What school does she go to?" Mum, I just met her, I'm not marrying her.'

Another boy: 'I stopped telling my mum stuff when I was about 11.'

'Really, that's pretty young. What made you do that?'

'I told her I'd had my first kiss. At the next family gathering it was obvious she'd told everyone – they were all looking at me funny. So I just stopped telling her things.'

Notice the intuition working here. You think it's OK to talk about him and what he might be up to when he's not around, but his intuition is working really well, working overtime in fact at this point, and he knows when those conversations have occurred. When you go into your boy's room and go through his wastepaper basket, looking for hints about what's going on in his life, and you read a note from a girl, you think he won't know but the minute he walks into the kitchen after school it's written on your forehead in glaring lights: 'Is it serious? Is she a nice girl? Have they had sex? Should I be getting his father to talk to him?' Don't believe he can't see it: it's in your face. He doesn't need to see the obvious clues mothers sometimes leave, such as a neatly made bed and folded clothes. The intuition of boys is amazing.

> A 15-year-old boy was attacked by a shark but didn't tell his mother.
>
> 'She wouldn't have been interested?'
>
> 'No, she would have been too interested.'

A number of women have talked to me with some sadness about how their sons don't talk to them as they used to, how they miss the closeness they used to share. As part of his adolescent journey, a boy will need to pull away both from his mother and from women in general while he gets his head around the changes occurring in his body and his life. It's inevitable, therefore, that there'll be some distance, some change in how he relates to you, but what the project taught me is that he withdraws further than he might otherwise do because of our behaviour – because of our overzealous interrogation, because we keep walking towards him and asking questions long after we should have stopped.

I think one of the very important roles mothers have is to continually remind their adolescent sons that they have intuition. Think of it like a muscle that you're making him exercise. Use 'I' statements: 'I don't like it when you . . . ', 'I feel scared when you . . . ' Let his intuition pick up the reality of what you're saying. Don't spell it out for him. Remember, he doesn't need lecturing, he needs reminding.

'If your mum stopped asking, would you go to her for the important stuff?'

'Yes. Trust that I'm okay and I'll come for help if I need it. Silence doesn't mean trouble.'

It will be his intuition that keeps him safe, keeps him from making dumb decisions, and you can help him to develop it. This is something I believe you'll do better than his father. He's testing his intuition all the time at a subconscious level, asking himself whether what he's seeing or feeling is real, whether he's right to be worried. Your role isn't to go in and drag those feelings out and name them; your role is to name your own feelings so he can find his place alongside them. You're tremendously important to him and he builds his world on the idea you're there. He just needs you to trust that he knows you're there and to pull back a little to give him the room he needs to think and breathe.

And as you pull back remember this, for it can be something to hold on to in the hard moments that will come, the moments when you show real courage and let men tend to men's business: every bit of information you push into his head before he turns 13 and the testosterone starts to move, every bit of it stays in there and will eventually re-emerge. Trust me, none of the values and principles you work to instil in him will be lost; it will appear to be lost and you'll doubt your effectiveness as a parent, but the time will come when a good man stands before you and you can take a bow.

My son is 28 now and working as a diesel fitter in a mine in Western Australia. He's turned into a good man – sometimes I think it's in spite of me rather than because of me – and he's gorgeous. In the conversations I've had with him recently I've listened to the threads of the information coming out of his mouth and realised that none of the hard work was wasted: he got it and he's kept it. He's the sort of man I hoped he would be, the sort of man he always had the potential to be. Yes, your boy's going away for a time, but he's coming back; he knows you're his mother, and he knows you're there. Trust that process, trust your intuition and trust his.

> Police dog Blade is being hailed a hero again after tracking three youths for 10 miles through farmland
>
> . . . One of the youths was found 20 feet up a tree and only came down after being assured Blade would not bite him. It is understood he was on a mobile to his mother.

Without question some mothers are overly involved in the lives of their adolescent sons. Some examples:

A Year 9 student tells the deputy head that he doesn't have any lunch.

'Why not?'

'Because my mother didn't put it in my bag.'

'I beg your pardon?'

'Well it's her job.'

Students standing within the hearing of the school office staff using the phone to make a call home to get their mother to pick them up.

'What do you mean you can't come now?'

Mothers who, according to their sons, continue to make their 18-year-old sons' beds and lunches every day.

Many mothers I talked to readily acknowledged their behaviour in this regard and often showed a clear desire to act differently, but had no idea where or how to begin. Wondering just where their little boy had gone and if he would ever reappear, they were comforting themselves with the idea that as long as they prepared good wholesome food for him to take to school and kept making his bed and doing his washing, all would be well.

Given their concern about their beloved son turning into a barely recognisable adolescent and their sense of powerlessness about the changes occurring in his body and his mind, it's little wonder that many mothers end up in heads' offices defending their sons against perceived injustices. I've known that feeling of 'I can't change that, but I can change this.'

It's difficult to consider letting him feel the consequences of his actions because we often realise just how big those consequences can be. As a first step, could I ask that, if your son is now a secondary school student and you're still making his lunch, you seriously consider stopping? There's a reason for my asking this: it's a tangible, practical thing you can do to begin allowing him to learn the link between action and consequence, something he needs to learn as part of the journey to manhood. Some of you will immediately be thinking, 'But if I don't make his lunch he won't eat healthily, and he won't learn in the afternoon.' This is where adolescent male pragmatism comes in, particularly since food is involved.

You need to give him some warning: tell him the week before that there'll be no lunch on Monday and that from this point he's to make his own. He doesn't really believe you, thinks you're kidding. You're his mother, after all, and you've always made it your mission to ensure he has enough to eat. On Monday morning he gets out of bed on that carefully calculated journey he makes each day from his room to the school gate, and he's surprised to see that the lunch isn't on the bench where he expected it to be. So, there he is, kind of angry because the lunch isn't there, and now he'll be late for school if he stops to make it. He's brassed off, but he's going to need food, so guess what he does: at lunchtime he goes to the school canteen and spends his own money feeding himself. It takes him about two days, in my reckoning, before he realises, one, that it's his money he's spending, money he could be spending on the weekend, and two, that he's not as full as he was when the food came from home. And so, on day three, he calculates ten extra minutes into his morning, gets out of bed and makes his lunch. As long as you've got the food in the pantry, he'll be fine.

I'm keen on this idea because it's actually quite serious. We women aren't letting our boys learn about action and consequence because we keep interfering in the process. Some significant stories came out of the Good Man Project in this regard.

The students weren't allowed mobiles in the classroom,

but one boy had one, which the teacher saw and confiscated. The boy sauntered up at the end of the period and said, 'When can I have my phone back?' The teacher replied, 'This is Tuesday, you can have it on Friday, that's the rule.' The boy said, very calmly, 'The last time you took it my mother rang up, and you had to give it back the same day.' The teacher said, 'Oh, so you've done this before. Now you've lost it until Monday.' Guess who rang up that night demanding that the phone be returned immediately? School rules apparently applied to every other boy but hers: her implied question was, 'Why should he have to actually follow the rules?'

As a teacher drove out of the school at 3.30 p.m. he saw a boy in uniform standing outside the school property. The boy turned towards the teacher and with a belligerent look on his face raised the middle finger of his right hand. The teacher wound down the window and said, 'The headteacher's office, 9 o'clock tomorrow morning.' The next day the boy arrived at school carrying a letter from his mother: 'Dear Mr . . . , I don't believe you have the right to correct my son's behaviour when he's not on school property. I've instructed him not to be at the headteacher's office at 9 o'clock. If you want to discuss this any further, you can talk to me.' What had she just taught her son? That he's her little darling, and that with her blessing he can disrespect any adult he chooses and she'll back him.

We're not doing boys any favours when we act in this way: if they're to have any chance of a successful and enjoyable life, we have to let them feel action and consequence. Let him work out that when he's hungry he has to do something about it (you'll also be doing a favour for the woman he's going to live with sometime in the future). But more than that, let him feel the results of his decision. When we wrap our sons in cotton wool, when we step between them and the school, between them and the rest of the world, all we're really doing is excusing their appalling behaviour and ensuring they remain self-centred individuals who will forever find it difficult to accept responsibility for themselves and the decisions they're making.

I want the first decision he makes to be nothing more significant than deciding to get out of bed to make his own lunch so that he doesn't spend the day hungry. I don't want the first decision he makes to be to put his foot on an accelerator, run a red light and die. If we don't give our boys the opportunity to practise making decisions, the first ones they make will be dangerous and potentially fatal: 'Do I drink this extra bottle of scotch? Do I try the party drug I've just been offered? Do I get in that stolen car? Do I try and outrun the cops?'

Remember, he's pragmatic: as long as you keep doing it – making his lunch, making his bed, running interference for him with the school – he'll let you. But if you let him start when he's quite young, he'll get used to decision-making and will come to understand that he has to choose to get up ten minutes earlier to make his lunch so he won't go hungry, to choose not to risk losing his mobile by taking it to school, to choose not to try the party drug because he wants to be at practice on Tuesday. I'm serious in this plea, and I make it on behalf of your son. Step back. He loves you and you love him, and he knows that. You don't have to make his lunch to prove that you're a good mother.

I talked at the beginning of this chapter about the need for mothers to get off the bridge of adolescence and for fathers to get onto it. I made that comment as a mother who spent a lot of time up there. When I started the discussions with men and women about their different roles in the lives of their sons, I said women should stay off the bridge altogether. As the project progressed and I talked to more parents, my view modified slightly, helped to some extent by the group of mothers who, having been challenged about being up on the bridge, were adamant that they had no intention of getting off. I'd discussed the idea of the bridge with them before leaving them to talk among themselves while I went to speak to their husbands and partners. When I came back into the room, I was quickly informed that while I was gone they'd voted and the majority view was that they were staying put on the bridge. 'OK,' I replied, 'you can stay – I'll build you a clip-on lane. But please, for the sake of your boys, stop sitting in the middle. You're holding up traffic.'

In the discussions we've continued to have about the role of mothers, Salvi Gargiulo and I have agreed that if you feel you can't get right off the bridge, you must do some good things up there and make a positive contribution. The plea that comes to you from Salvi is: 'Just let go of his hand . . . please.'

Instruction manual for mums

1. Don't worry for us.

2. Let us make mistakes,
   be hungry, be late.

3. Chill out.

+ Mothers, particularly white middle-class mothers, are overly involved in the lives of their adolescent sons.

+ There seemed to be a very real possibility that my son would accidentally kill himself or, perhaps more likely, that I would kill him out of sheer frustration.

+ Men's business at this point in the lives of boys is to guide them through adolescence. Women's job is to step back.

+ In the context of what else is happening in the life of an adolescent boy, does it really matter that there were clothes thrown on the spare bed in his room?

+ As part of his adolescent journey, a boy will need to pull away both from his mother and from women in general while he gets his head around the changes occurring in his body and his life.

+ It will be his intuition that keeps him safe, keeps him from making dumb decisions, and you can help him to develop it.

+ Every bit of information you push into his head before he turns 13 and the testosterone starts to move stays in there and will eventually re-emerge.

+ If your son is now a secondary school student and you're still making his lunch, please seriously consider stopping.

✦ We women aren't letting our boys learn about action and consequence because we keep interfering in the process. We must do so if they're to have any chance of a successful and enjoyable life.

✦ The first decision he makes should be nothing more significant than deciding to get out of bed to make his own lunch so that he doesn't spend the day hungry. It shouldn't and doesn't need to be deciding to put his foot on the accelerator, running a red light and dying.

Chapter 9
When His Father Isn't There: The Single Mother's Journey

For a number of women reading this book, those who are raising their sons without direct input from the boy's father, the previous chapter won't have been much help. You'll be thinking it's all very well talking about women taking a step back from the bridge of adolescence and creating the space for men to step forward and become more involved, but what if his dad isn't there? What then?

There are significant numbers of women who are raising their sons without the direct and ongoing support of fathers and there are probably similar numbers raising their sons with the help of another man, who willingly or unwillingly takes the role of the boy's stepfather. In the latter case there's endless potential for conflict and I'll talk about some of those issues in the next chapter. For now I want to focus on what steps women raising their sons alone might take to make the journey across the bridge of adolescence a little easier – for their boys, and themselves.

The simple reality for an adolescent boy, which many women find hard to accept, is that he needs to know who his dad is, what sort of man he is – or was, if he's dead. I've watched many women grapple with the fact that the man they once loved enough to have this child with, they now consider a less than desirable creature, an emotional cripple or an idiot (or a combination of all three); and the last thing they want is for their son to have ongoing contact with him and risk becoming the same sort of man. There are also the women who were never in love with the boy's father, who regret they ever had the physical contact with him, but who don't regret the result. And then there are the women who wonder how to explain to their son that his father is in jail for murder, for drug dealing or for molesting children.

This is another instance where the decisions about how to proceed need to be based on our knowledge of the pragmatism and intuition of adolescent boys rather than on our female perspective.

He's pragmatic: he wants to know the facts, he wants to know whose blood flows through his veins. One way to think about it is that, having reached the point where he's attempting to take some measure of control over his life, if he's lived much or all of his existence away from his father, his first steps will be to try to put the pieces together. How did I get to be here? Did my parents once love each other? Who is my dad really? Do I matter to him? Am I like him now? Will I be like him in the future? Do I want to be like him? These are the questions that will be beginning to find their way into his head even if he can't articulate them. You, his mother, don't need to keep checking with him about whether the questions are there yet; he'll let you know, often in quite indirect ways, when they're starting to form. Your job is to be ready when they do and to show courage in responding to his need to know.

I don't believe there's a set time when this will happen. My son was 11 when he came back quite distressed from a holiday with his father in Western Australia. The cause of the distress was the conflict he was feeling because he'd reached the point of wanting to know his father better, but didn't want to hurt me. After further discussion, I offered him the opportunity to live with his dad in Australia for a year. It was without doubt one of the hardest decisions I've ever had to make, but I knew then and know even more now, that it was the right one. He went into the Australian desert for his last primary school year and it wasn't easy for either him or me. I suspect there were more than a few nights when he cried himself to sleep and I had a permanent tear in my heart while he was gone, but it was a choice he made, and one he was fully capable of making, even at 11 years of age.

He lived with the consequences of his choice and, I'm sure, had many moments of fun and laughter as well as moments that were highly challenging. He came back with a much clearer sense of both himself and his father, something I believe has made a significant difference to who he is now. I didn't then, and still don't, know much of what went on that year, and I don't need to. It was men's business. I knew he was safe, I had enough trust in his father to know that, and that was all I needed to know. I realise not all single mothers can be sure of that and that others know their son certainly wouldn't be safe in similar circumstances. There's one thing I'd ask on behalf of the boys being raised by their mothers: Is it really concern for his safety that's stopping you from letting him spend time with his father or is it a cloak you're hiding behind for other reasons? Whatever our problems with the fathers of our sons, whatever level of justification we feel there is for our hurt, anger or grief, we have to remember that they're our issues, our feelings, not our sons. They have to be allowed to form their own view and we have to trust them to do so.

As I keep saying, your son's pragmatic. We worry what will happen when he learns that his father didn't stick around much beyond conception point, that he's in prison for rape or murder or that he died in a car accident while driving drunk, killing another person in the process. We think he'll be traumatised by the knowledge and that it will do immense damage to his psyche, so we work to keep the knowledge away from him, telling ourselves we're doing it for his sake. I believe a better way to think about it, in light of his extreme pragmatism as he begins the journey into adolescence, is to think of it as the equivalent of a science experiment. At this stage he's not seeking to examine the deeper issues; he'll come to that in due course and when he has the maturity and wisdom to think through the wider implications of the knowledge he now has about his father. He'll pursue the truth until he's sure it's the truth rather than just your version of the truth and then he'll go back to playing a game.

I don't believe he'll ask any questions until he's ready to handle the answers and I think that, because of his high level of intuition, he already knows the answers to most of the questions he may be about to ask. In asking them, he's not so much seeking answers as confirming where the world he's been in to date, your world, and the world of his father, intersect. He's beginning to explore the practical implications of the fact he's been raised by his mother away from his father and he just wants answers, straight answers. I'm not for a moment suggesting this is easy; it isn't. But I am suggesting that it doesn't have to be as hard as some women seem to want to make it, often for their own ends and often with serious consequences for their sons.

If he doesn't get the information he needs to begin putting the pieces of his life together, he'll just go on looking, and he'll be 55, with a string of broken relationships behind him, before he has any sense that the real issue is whether his father did or didn't love him. We women need to understand that the answer to that question isn't the primary issue – it's the not knowing that matters. It's the not knowing that will make him into an angry man who uses people for his own ends, never sure of just what has left him feeling so empty inside and rendered him unable to sustain intimate relationships. In time his natural and deeply embedded pragmatism will allow him to work through the issues stirred up by either answer, but until he knows, he can't move forward.

The other thing to remember is your son's intuition. This can provide some comfort for those of you who are worried that he won't see what a hopeless case his father is – should this in fact be true. Time with his father will allow him to work it out for himself; he doesn't need your help with this. He may well come to conclusions about his father that match your opinion entirely, but whether or not you end up holding the same view, you must leave him to find out for himself. This is his journey, not yours. You knew his father as a sexual partner; he knows him as his dad.

If his father is dead, what he needs are conversations in which he hears his father's name mentioned, conversations with you and with others that allow him to get a sense of who his father was, good or bad. If his father did die in a car accident while driving drunk and did kill someone else, he needs to have those facts told to him as non-judgementally as possible . . . when he asks. Again he won't seek this information until he's ready to manage the possible answers, which he actually already knows at some level. When he's got an answer to one question, you may be inclined to keep talking to try to take advantage of the moment, but he may well react by going back to his computer game or heading outside to kick a ball around. Remember, he needs time to think so let him have it. Let him dictate the pace at which he moves through this process.

Whether you want it or not, you, his mother, are responsible for informing him about his father, the man with whom you conceived him. And it's incredibly important that you do it when he's ready to receive the information; that you let him dictate the pace at which he absorbs your answers; that you give him straight responses where possible, and where that's not possible because of your experiences with his father, that you're honest in identifying the bias you can't rid yourself of; and, that unless you can be sure he wouldn't be safe in his father's company, you remain open to the idea that time in his father's company is one of the key factors in getting him across the bridge of adolescence safely so that he'll grow from a gorgeous boy into a good man.

Many boys being raised by their mothers live in a female-dominated environment. Their home contains no men; their teachers are predominantly women; and their social scene is bereft of male influence. In the course of the project I was often asked by women raising boys alone what I thought they should do in the absence of good male role models to ensure their sons were exposed to what it means to be a man and encouraged in their quest to do well in whatever interested them. After giving the matter some thought, I came up with the following idea. You might like to include your son in the activity I'm about to suggest, or you might like to do it by yourself to give you a sense of just how many men there actually are, or are not, in his life.

Sit down with a piece of paper. In the middle of the paper put an X; this is your son. Around the X draw three concentric circles. In the first circle, write the names of the men your son meets on a regular basis, that is, at least once a week. In the next circle puts the names of the men he meets less often, once a month or so. In the third circle write the names of the men he meets only occasionally. Now draw a line between the various men and the X. If the relationship is a strong one, make it a dark and solid line; if it's an OK connection, use a lighter line; and if it's a tenuous relationship, go for a broken line. Now work out where his father's name belongs. If his father's dead, still include his name in whatever circle feels appropriate, but instead of drawing a line from his father's name to the X, draw the line to the name of the man most able to give your son a sense of his father. For the reasons I explained earlier, it's vital that his father's name is there.

Your task as a single mother now becomes to work out which relationships are likely to be helpful in getting your son across the bridge of adolescence and then to figure out how those relationships can be strengthened or maintained at their current level. This doesn't require you to be involved in the relationship, just to be as aware and supportive of it as you can. For example, it might be that he has a good relationship with one of your brothers, with your father and/or with his paternal grandfather. If so, it might just be a case of asking your father to take his grandson out once a fortnight on his own for a couple of hours and do something with him, perhaps fishing. You might want to think about asking your brother or your son's paternal grandfather to be the one who goes to watch him play football each weekend in the winter.

It might be that your son has formed a bit of a friendship with the young guy just down the road and always stops to talk to him whenever he's outside working on his car. You could make a point of saying hello to the young man next time you go past, identifying yourself as your son's mother and thus giving the contact some legitimacy rather than leaving the older boy to think this is something your son does without your knowledge or blessing.

I'm not talking about formalising the contacts your son has with older males in a major way; it isn't the formal relationships that will make the real difference. It's the informal contacts that happen in the course of an ordinary day that will count: the ten-minute conversations that happen between the other stuff of life.

This is why I'm keen on single mothers of boys approaching adolescence doing an exercise like this: there are actually more men in our sons' lives than we realise and this allows us an opportunity to check that reality out. It's important that we increase the number of male teachers in nursery, infant and primary schools. Another piece of the puzzle, however, is to be as aware as possible of the resources you have at your disposal in terms of the men already in your son's life.

Had I turned my head sideways as I approached the bridge of adolescence with my son, I would have noticed some very good men, platonic friends of mine, standing just over to the side. I've no doubt that, had I asked them, they would have been more than willing to spend some time up on the bridge with my boy. Why didn't I ask? Because I didn't realise it was OK; I assumed that to ask for help would be to admit failure in the raising of my son. I'd chosen to have him, I'd chosen to leave the marriage; it was now my job to get him safely over the bridge. These were the thoughts that ran through my mind. I realise now, with the benefit of hindsight and with a new level of awareness after being involved in the Good Man Project, that to have asked for the help of these good men would have made the trip across the bridge easier for both my son and me. Perhaps most importantly, it would have allowed me to have more fun while on the bridge with him.

+ Many women find it hard to accept, but an adolescent boy needs to know who his dad is and what sort of man he is – or was.

+ For now he just wants to know the facts and, when given them, will handle them as objective information.

+ If he doesn't get the information he needs to begin putting the pieces of his life together, he'll just go on looking, and he'll be 55, with a string of broken relationships behind him, before he has any sense that the real issue is whether his father did or didn't love him.

+ This is his journey, not yours. You knew his father as a sexual partner; he knows him as his dad.

+ Your task as a single mother is to work out which male

relationships are likely to help get your son across the bridge of adolescence and then see how those relationships can be strengthened or maintained at their current level.

+ I assumed that to ask for help would be to admit failure in the raising of my son. Asking for help from good men would have made the journey easier.

Chapter 10
Men's Business: Letting It Happen

Given that the title of the chapter written for mothers of adolescent boys includes the words 'what mothers should do', it wouldn't be unreasonable to expect that the title of this chapter, written with fathers in mind, should include the phrase 'what fathers should do'. There's a very simple reason why it doesn't: I have absolutely no intention of telling men what to do. I think enough of that has gone on already and from where I'm standing, there doesn't appear to be any sign of a let-up in the current tendency for women to tell men not only what to do but how to do it. I'm a woman. My life experience, which includes raising a son on my own and being involved in the Good Man Project, gives a certain legitimacy to suggestions I might make to other women struggling, as I did, with the raising of their adolescent sons. That's the reason, the only reason, I agreed to write this book in the first place.

All I really needed in the worst moments of the journey across the bridge of adolescence with my son, the moments when I felt there was a real possibility I would lose him, was another woman to look at me and say, 'He'll be OK.' I've written this book so other women now in that position will hear those words loudly and clearly and will then be able to relax and enjoy the journey.

So if I'm not going to tell men what to do, what am I going to do in this chapter? A number of things. I'm going to revisit the reasons for my involvement in a project looking at the definition of a good man in the 21st century when I'm a woman and I believe this is largely men's business; I'm going to tell you a few more stories about how the world looks to men, in particular the world of women, and I'm going to share what I was told by the boys I met whenever the subject of their fathers or stepfathers was raised. Some of the boys' comments in this regard were extremely acute and I think they deserve to be heard. My main intention, in straying into the world of fathers when this book is being written primarily for mothers, is to honour men – their humour, their intuition, their strength and, above all else, their maleness.

I believe men are greatly undervalued in our society today. I'm sad that men's voices aren't heard as clearly as they should or could be, and that it seems acceptable to poke fun at men. As I've mentioned, I consider myself a feminist, I was the first woman in New Zealand to work as a prison officer in a male prison, and I can give as good as I get. There's also definite fun to be had in exchanges with men about which gender does things better. But if I change my perspective slightly, from having an intellectual debate or a hard-case session with one of my male contemporaries towards the world my yet-to-be conceived grandson might enter, I feel some concern about how men are perceived.

Recently a shop was selling merchandise aimed at the young female market. Bags bore the words 'Made in the stupid factory where boys are made' while the slippers said 'Boys are stupid, throw rocks at them'. As I thought about the inappropriateness of this and how I would feel if I had a grandson old enough to read such things, I was also aware of the silence on the issue, knowing that had the reverse been the case – bags that called girls stupid, slippers that urged boys to throw rocks at girls – a media furore could practically have been guaranteed. It's highly likely that, in such circumstances, the Prime Minister would have been asked to comment and would have done so willingly and spokespeople from Women's Refuges around the country would have drawn parallels and connections with our rate of domestic abuse incidents.

When concerned men drew the issue to the attention of the media, it initially got limited traction, but eventually, and thankfully, the product line was withdrawn. As the debate continued I did some radio interviews and was struck by the female interviewer who stated that, in her view, it was all just a bit of fun and that I appeared to have lost my sense of humour. Perhaps I have, on this topic at least. When I think about the young men who end their lives because they're unsure of their place in the world or because they feel unable to cope with rejection by a young woman; when articulate, intelligent, gorgeous young men tell me with absolute sincerity that they believe they came out of the womb dumber than girls or that they think there's no point in competing against a girl because she'll win anyway; when I watch the resignation on the faces of young men who are tired of seeing themselves being portrayed negatively in the media and weary of being watched by shop assistants who assume they're trouble just because they are adolescent boys – then I find it hard to discover the humour in a pair of slippers that say boys are stupid and deserve to have rocks thrown at them.

It was my time in male prisons, my experience as the single mother of an adolescent boy and my perception of the increasing social dislocation of men that sat behind my initial conversations with Salvi Gargiulo about the world of boys' schools, and it was these factors that pushed me to consider being involved in the Good Man Project. I've spoken already about the potential conflict inherent in a woman spending time in boys' schools discussing the concept of a good man and what might constitute legitimate and effective male rites of passage. But I decided that my experience could prove a distinct advantage. The heads agreed that the lens I'd be looking through would allow me to see things they don't see, not because they aren't there, but because they're things that men take for granted.

I don't think you men necessarily know how intuitive you are or how that intuition manifests itself in your daily lives, or that you could explain easily how you communicate with one another so effectively, yet so silently. It's just what you do. You've always done it and you'll continue to do it and to a large extent there's no need for explanation. It's women who need the explanation, who need to know that this male communication is happening even though they can't see it. In many ways, this, in a nutshell, is what the project was about and why I became involved.

And then there's the other, somewhat regrettable, reason why the heads and I decided it made good sense to have a woman involved in the project – the matter of what today's world considers acceptable and unacceptable for men to say. The media came to me, a woman, to get a view on whether those slippers were OK, suggesting that the legitimacy of their concerns depended on a female analysis. Before I was challenged for lacking a sense of humour, the discussions I had on the topic suggested a widely held view that men should simply get over themselves and not be so sensitive.

It seems to me there's a tendency in society at the moment to assume that views expressed by women are right until proven wrong and that those expressed by men are wrong until proven right. I don't want it to be so and I was keen to take part in the Good Man Project partly to prove this idea wrong. Unfortunately the project didn't do that; rather it added considerable weight to my impression that this is exactly how things stand. As a result, the project, and this book, became focused on getting women to step back as they approach the bridge of adolescence with their son and allow room for his father to come forward; to be quiet at times and note the conversations that are actually occurring between men and boys; to see the inherent beauty and strength in men when they're allowed to be themselves rather than the sort of men we think we want them to be.

This is why it was considered a good idea that a woman was involved in the Good Man Project. Can you for a minute imagine it being acceptable for a man to say what I'm saying? Any man doing so would undoubtedly be told to stop being so sensitive, to develop a sense of humour and to realise that he's not yet off the hook for the sins of the past committed by males.

As I write this, I'm recalling a comment made by one man at a fathers and sons evening held at a secondary school recently. I'd been discussing the enjoyment to be had when men become more involved in the lives of their boys and when women step back and let men interact with their sons in whatever way they consider best, including on discipline matters. I was clear that this process involved women being told firmly to back off, something I've been doing, and I was encouraging the men present to try it for their sons' sakes, as well as their own. At this point in the discussion one father looked up at me and said in a delightfully laconic way, 'Great idea. Have you got any suggestions for how, after telling her to back off, I cope with the three months of cold shoulder that will follow?'

The noise in the room at that point indicated that almost every man present was wondering the same thing. As it happens, I couldn't offer him any advice about dealing with the aftermath, but I did promise that I would continue to do my best to get women to see the merits of backing off. My hope was that if they heard the message from me, a woman, first, there would be less cold-shoulder treatment to cope with.

In terms of the problems men have to grapple with when trying to take more of a role in the lives of their sons, I'm reminded of comments made by one group of men when we were discussing the concept of a bridge of adolescence. (As the imagery associated with the bridge grew during the project, there were many humorous moments.) One man said to me, 'I like that idea of me being on the bridge of adolescence with my boy, but could I just ask where she would be?' The concept of the bridge was still relatively new to me at that stage so I said, 'Well, I think I'd like her to be walking alongside the bridge, with the idea of meeting you and your son at the other end.' 'Nah,' he said, 'that won't work. She'll be yelling instructions from the side.' At that point the guy sitting next to him said, 'Yeah, mine'd be the bloody troll under the bridge!'

I'm not suggesting there are no problems with men and

> 'Have you got any suggestions for how, after telling her to back off, I cope with the three months of cold shoulder that will follow?'

their behaviour; there are and some of them are serious. Men need to stop beating their wives and killing their kids and their stepkids; men need to confront other men about selling drugs to children, about taking money that should be used to feed their children to feed their own alcohol, drug or gambling addiction; men need to stand up and be more accountable as fathers. But despite this it's also true that only some men are doing these things, only some men are being less than they could be. There are many more good men out there, and I met a number of them during the project, striving to do the best for their families, and it's them I'm thinking of as I urge a rethink of just where our push for girls to be able to 'do anything' has taken us. Girls and women should be able to do anything, not *everything*: several times during the project, I was left believing that we women are often confusing the two. I think of a quote from one man I met – 'What most men want to do is to offer something of value and meaning to the women around them.' I think he's absolutely right.

'Well, I think I'd like her to be walking alongside the bridge, with the idea of meeting you and your son at the other end.'

'Nah, that won't work. She'll be yelling instructions from the side.'

It's important to remember that I was never going to be the one who would decide the definition of a good man in the twenty-first century; my definition isn't important. I was seeking the views of men and boys about what makes a good man and it's those views I'm putting up for further discussion. It doesn't matter to anyone but me what I think constitutes a good man and it doesn't matter, either, what women in general think. What's important is what men think a good man is – their ability to define it; their ability to live it; and their ability to communicate it to boys moving towards manhood.

I want to pause at this point and explain something to women, something I think they'll find useful in their day-to-day interactions with men. It's something men know about and take for granted, but which we women have very little idea about at all. It's the concept of the 'uh-oh' question.

My awareness of this started when I asked a group of Year 10 boys, 'So, what about when a girl asks you how you feel?' The boy immediately in front of me screwed up his face and said, 'I don't understand that question.' The boy sitting just behind him, 15 going on 23, said, 'Oh, I understand it, I'm just sure as hell not going to answer it.'

'Why not? If you're angry, why wouldn't you just tell her you're angry?'

'Hell no. She's going to want to know why I'm angry and she'll keep asking questions and eventually I'll get one wrong and then I'm booked!'

'An "uh-oh" question is one of those that when your partner asks it, your whole body goes "uh-oh". In that moment your entire relationship's under threat. . . I know it's not logical, I'm just telling you how it is. When I get asked a question like that by my wife, I have to step back, think about the fact that she only wants to know how I feel and rejoin the conversation.'

I couldn't quite believe my ears. Where were they getting this stuff from? These boys were only 15 years old and yet they already had this deeply entrenched view of women wanting too much information, and then 'booking' them.

Thinking I might have somehow got a rogue class of boys, I decided to do a little further research. I went into the school staffroom and spoke to a male teacher, describing what I'd just been through. He looked back at me, showing no surprise at all, nodded and said, 'Yeah he's right, that's an "uh-oh" question.' When I asked exactly what that was I got this reply: 'It's one of those questions that when your partner asks it, your whole body goes "uh-oh". In that moment your entire relationship's under threat.'

This man appeared intelligent, articulate, emotionally literate even, so I asked, 'Are you married?'

'Yeah.'

'How long have you been married?'

'Twenty years.'

'Would you consider it a good marriage?'

'Yeah.'

'OK,' I said, 'just so I've got this right: you've been married 20 years, it's a good marriage, she asks you how you feel and your entire relationship is under threat?'

'Yeah.'

He held my gaze for a minute, then smiled and said, 'I know it's not logical, I'm just telling you how it is. When I get asked a question like that by my wife, I have to step back, think about the fact that she only wants to know how I feel and rejoin the conversation.' (And obviously be careful about his answer!)

'We've given girls permission to be who they are, whoever they want to be. Boys need to be given the same permission.'

I had other conversations with a range of men about this

and it would seem to be a universally agreed reality. There's apparently a whole realm of 'uh-oh' questions that sit in the communication channels between men and women, particularly in their intimate relationships. These include: 'Does my bum look big in these jeans?', 'Should my mother come and live with us?', 'Whose place will we have Christmas at this year?' and, on a Saturday, 'What do you want to do today?'

'Men have tunnel vision and when something's in our vision, it gets done and done properly.'

We women need to understand that generally, when we ask a man an 'uh-oh' question, he doesn't go inside himself to find the answer. It's not about what he thinks. He looks up and there are about 300 words circling his head; his job in that moment is to pick the one that will get him in the least trouble.

I've talked about the situation when two parents are called in to discuss their son with the head and the mother does all the talking. The father obviously has something to say, but can't get it out because the mother won't stop talking long enough for him to get his thoughts organised. When I put this to a group of men, they explained that they don't speak because they're afraid of getting it wrong.

'Uh-oh' questions

'Does my bum look big in this?'

'Should my mother come and live with us?'

It's not OK that women are interfering in this way, wanting to know what's happening, running every aspect of their sons' existence. It's time to let fathers into the lives of their boys, and fathers have to decide whether they're willing to step up to this role.

That's a decision only you, the father, can make, but what I can do is to tell you on behalf of your sons, one, that they want you to step up, to (metaphorically) elbow their mothers aside if you have to in order to step up, and two, that they don't want you to be anyone else, any closer to Superman than you already are; they just want you to be their dad.

Whenever I asked groups of boys, 'How many of you want to be like your dad when you grow up?' initially not many hands went up. Eventually I realised it was their pragmatism getting in the way; when I asked them why not, they replied 'Because he's bald' or 'Because he's a plumber.' 'No,' I'd explain, 'I don't mean what he does, or what he looks like, I mean the sort of man he is. Now how many of you want to be like your dad?' A few more hands would go up, but still not a lot.

> 'What's the one thing about your dad you would change if you could?'
>
> 'He'd get his sense of humour back.'

I decided to phrase the question another way: 'What's the one thing about your dad you would change if you could?' Time and again the answer came: 'He'd get his sense of humour back.' Not 'He'd get a sense of humour' but 'He'd get his sense of humour *back*.' It seems to me – from a woman's perspective, looking in on the world of men – that you're great with your little fellows: you roll around on the floor, you fight, you have a lot of fun. And then the moment comes when you're not getting up off the floor unless he lets you, and in that instant a tiny switch goes down in the back of the male brain, and you say to yourselves, 'OK, I need to be a proper father now.'

So you stand up ready and willing to be a proper father and meanwhile he's looking around thinking, 'I wonder where my dad went, because this grumpy old bastard sure isn't him.' One boy said it in a very insightful if incredibly sad way: 'I used to think my dad was my hero. Now he's just a bloody idiot. He keeps telling me stories about how it was in his day, and every weekend he lectures me about drink driving . . . he just doesn't know I'd never do it.'

If the boys were to be believed, it would seem many fathers are absent in the lives of their sons, if not physically then emotionally. A common theme of the conversations I had with many of the students was their lack of what they considered a real father-son relationship. Many had either no or only intermittent contact with their dads. A significant number of students had stepfathers. In some cases these appeared to be positive relationships; in others they clearly weren't.

I was surprised by the number of students living with their fathers in single-parent households and found myself wondering whether parents no longer living together are coming to recognise the merits of building a stronger father-son relationship as their boy enters adolescence. Or are mothers simply finding themselves unable to cope and placing their sons in their fathers' custody in the hope they'll be able to manage them more effectively? Whatever the reason, it's vital that, whatever the circumstances, raising a boy should, where at all possible, remain a partnership between his mother and father if he's to have a real chance of becoming a good man.

Those students whose fathers were physically present in their lives weren't always there emotionally. Often during the project I wished the fathers of the boys I was talking to could have been listening in an adjoining room in order to understand just how much their sons yearn for their attention.

Stepping onto the bridge of adolescence doesn't mean you have to learn any new skills; it simply means being in your son's life. If there's one message I'd like to get out to all fathers, it's this: no matter what he's saying or how he's behaving on the surface, your son's hanging on your every word. He's looking to you to see how a man should act and he's desperate to know that you really see him. It

> 'Dad spends time with me. I like it when he does things with me and doesn't send me to ask my brother.'

doesn't matter what you actually do together: all he wants is your time, even it's just five minutes a day. He wants you to notice him. One boy described with absolute joy and pride how his father comes in at the end of each day, sits on the edge of his bed just before he's ready to turn the light off and asks, 'How was your day?' Just a five-minute conversation each night allows that boy to know his father cares.

One boy described how his father had started the practice of asking him each night, 'So what question did you ask a teacher today?' The boy said that to start with, he had to ask a teacher what he or she had had for lunch, just so he had something to tell his dad. But eventually he managed to ask a question in class, and he was really excited that he

> Men looking at their children: in their eyes concern, fierce pride, awkward tenderness.
>
> *Sara Donati,*
> *Lake in the Clouds*

would have something to impress his dad with that night.

Your boy would walk across broken glass for you; you'll

be doing him a great favour if you can remember that. He wants to know that, when you're talking to him, you're fully present. He doesn't want you to give up work, to look after him 24 hours a day or to completely invade his world – if you were to do so, I think it would be fair to suggest you'd scare him half to death. What he does want is for you to know what his favourite food is, what music he likes, who his best friend is, what scares him and what his dreams are. He knows implicitly his mother has that information because that's what mothers do – one way or another we find out everything – but he yearns for his father to know it too.

One boy described how excited he was about a car that his mate had just bought, but when he asked his dad to come outside and have a look, the reply was, 'What for? I'm not into cars.' The boy wasn't asking his father to get excited about cars; he wanted to draw him into the world that excited him. It's not about your world; it's about his. You might wonder why he likes what he does, why he's not into the same things as you. My advice would be, just be patient. In the majority of cases he'll find his way back to the things that matter to and interest you, but much of the journey at this point is about trying to establish his own identity, and one of the tests he's setting you as he does so is whether you care enough to cross into his world.

He wants you to connect with him as he is now, not as you might want him to be. Think about stepping into the moment with your boy whenever the opportunity presents itself, and it will. Be aware that the very fact you're his father makes you the right person to be there. You don't have to add any skills, you don't have to become any different from the guy you've always been. You just need to look towards your boy on a regular basis, and to think about organising your life in a way that allows you to spend some time with him.

The other thing you don't have to do is to lecture him. That 'proper father' thing seems to leave you feeling that by continuing to fool around with him, you're in some way being a negligent dad. It's as if there's now a list you consider you have to work through, giving him a lecture on each of the main topics of life – alcohol, sex, cars, and so on. Actually you don't have to give him any lectures at all. You just have to be prepared to answer any question he asks as honestly as you can when he asks it; if you need time to consider your reply, tell him that. Needing time to think is something he understands extremely well. If you do need time to think and tell him you'll get back to him, make sure you do – keeping your word is one of the main indicators of your awareness of your son.

I noted earlier that a significant number of the boys I spoke to had stepfathers, and most described their relationships with these men as a negative aspect of their lives. It's difficult, being the stepfather of an adolescent boy. Even if you've been in the boy's life for a long time, as he begins his own investigation of manhood, you'll come under immense scrutiny and whenever he feels anger at being controlled in the way he needs to be as an early adolescent, he'll be comparing you with his father, who will inevitably appear the better man. Even those boys who said they had a great relationship with their stepdad, and a number went so far as to state without embarrassment that he was a great guy and they really loved him, would then say, 'but he's not my dad'.

This is perhaps the only real advice I can give those stepfathers wanting to know what they should be doing as their stepson moves towards the bridge of adolescence: whether physically or emotionally, make room for his father. If you can talk about his dad, mention him at least. In that way you're giving your stepson a chance to put the pieces together. It doesn't mean he'll love you any less – there's enough love for you both – and if you're worried about the choices he might make because of his father's influence or the reality of his life, tell him that. But tell him objectively, not in a way that implies the boy is an idiot if he gives any credence at all to his father's view of the world. You may well be the only one who can talk to him about his father in an objective way; his mother may still be immersed in the anger or hurt attached to the breakdown of the relationship. In those circumstances, you have enormous potential as a stabilising influence.

The only other comment I would make in this regard is that if you are newly on the scene in an adolescent boy's life and in a sexual relationship with his mother, go carefully. Don't for a minute assume that because you're with his mother, he has any duty or responsibility at all to respect you any more than he would any other adult. The fact that you're with his mother sets the scene for a highly charged emotional environment. In some situations he'll perceive you as having usurped his role as the man of the house. Challenges will come. You're the adult and you're the newcomer. Go carefully with him, give him some space – a lot of space – and (this is a plea on his behalf) please don't try to become his father. If you earn his respect, he'll give it to you, but it will take time.

I'm very conscious that I started this chapter pledging not to tell fathers what to do, so I'm stepping carefully here. If you were to ask my opinion about your role as a father in the life of your adolescent son, on the basis of what the boys told me I'd answer that you should be on the bridge of adolescence, to show your boy what manhood is. Your role is also to create pathways to other men, so that the stuff that he can't talk to you about, because he's so pragmatic, he can talk about to another male. Accept that he will talk to another man, because there are some things he can't talk to you about (especially if you are in a sexual relationship with his mother!). Being a good father doesn't mean that your son talks to you about absolutely everything; being a good father is simply being there. In his eyes, you're enough exactly as you are now, simply because you're his father; you're special because you're the only one he can call 'Dad'. That's all he's focused on. Continue to be who you are, continue to walk beside him and he'll be the good man he has the potential to become. And you'll both have a great deal of fun along the way.

> **Instruction manual for dads**
>
> 1. Show an interest in what we do.
>
> 2. Ask questions.
>
> 3. Trust me.

+ All I really needed in the worst moments of the journey across the bridge of adolescence with my son was another woman to look at me and say, 'He'll be OK.'

✦ Men's voices aren't heard as clearly as they should or could be and it seems acceptable to poke fun at men.

✦ There's a tendency in society to assume that views expressed by women are right until proven wrong and that those expressed by men are wrong until proven right.

✦ Girls and women should be able to do anything, not *everything*. Women often confuse the two.

✦ Your sons want you to step up, elbowing their mothers aside if you need to.

✦ Your boys don't want you to be anyone else; they just want you to be their dad.

✦ The moment you can't get off the floor until he lets you, you say to yourself, 'OK, I need to be a proper father now.'

✦ Where at all possible raising a boy should be a partnership between his mother and father.

✦ All he wants is your time, even if it's just five minutes a day.

✦ He wants you to connect with him as he is now, not as you might want him to be.

✦ You don't have to give him lectures. Just answer any questions honestly and when he asks them.

+ As your stepson moves towards the bridge of adolescence make room for his father, physically or emotionally.

+ Don't for a minute assume that because you're with his mother he has any duty or responsibility to respect you more than he would any other adult.

+ Fathers must also allow their sons to talk to other men about the stuff they can't discuss with their dads.

Chapter 11
Growing a Good Man: What It Takes

And so it's time to draw together the final strands of information and consider what other steps we might take to help our gorgeous boys to grow into good men.

The Good Man Project was started in order to establish an agreed definition of a good man which could be promulgated and which would form the basis of further work to be done in boys' schools concerning rites of passage and the entry to manhood. With this aim in mind, I took every opportunity to ask the men I met and each class of boys I talked with to tell me what they thought were the top three qualities of a good man. As you can imagine, there was a wide variety of answers and the extensive list of the qualities identified appears at the end of this chapter.

To a certain degree, many of the answers were those I had expected and/or hoped for, but there was one major surprise: the top three qualities of a good man emerged as trust, loyalty and a sense of humour. I easily accepted the first two, but initially whenever a sense of humour was mentioned, I would try to dismiss the idea, considering it a nice quality to have, but not something that was an intrinsic part of being a good man. In the end, however, I was forced to concede the point, especially in light of the boys' assertion that they would, if they could, ensure their fathers got their sense of humour back. Also, as the project progressed, I could see how big a part humour plays in the lives of men. Wherever they are, humour is there too; despite their best efforts, women who want a situation to be taken seriously usually find that they're pushing against the tide. Men will do what needs to be done, they'll deal very well with serious and solemn situations, but if there's any chance at all that humour can be brought into a situation while still achieving the required outcome, they'll make sure this happens.

It wasn't long before the heads and I agreed to abandon the idea of developing a definition of a good man. It very quickly became obvious that what we were looking for was far too fluid to be set down in a few words or phrases and that trying to do so could reinforce male stereotypes that would work against our basic aim of freeing boys up to explore what makes a good man. A definition set in concrete could do more harm than good and stop ongoing examination of the concept of manhood in the twenty-first century.

In assessing those top three qualities of trust, loyalty and a sense of humour, it's possible to offer the argument that they're not qualities unique to men. Women can be loyal, women can be trusted and extend trust and women have a sense of humour – it's perhaps not as extensive as men's in some instances, but we do have one. So are there really differences in the attributes considered ideal qualities for good men versus good women, and if so, where do those differences lie? My thoughts on this issue are still relatively underdeveloped, but my view at the moment is that the differences lie not in the qualities themselves but in how they're manifested.

For instance, what does loyalty look like to me, a woman? Loyalty is when I ring a friend and tell her I need to talk and she makes herself available as soon as she can without stopping to ask whether the situation is really that urgent. Loyalty is about her then listening without judgement, regardless of how much of a fool I might be making of myself in the situation I'm describing. As I've mentioned, when I asked a group of boys what loyalty looked like, they said it was staying with your mates in the face of threat.

And this is where the work can begin in our attempts to keep more of our boys alive. Knowing that in their eyes loyalty is seen as part of being a man and means standing by your mates, we can perhaps understand a little better why they put their foot down on the accelerator when urged to do so by their best friends. They don't think about the risk they're taking; they think about being a man and about being loyal and they and their friends die when they wrap their cars around telegraph poles or trees. We have to get them to understand that loyalty is keeping your mates safe; it's stopping at orange lights and staying within the speed limit.

Although I believe that the majority of the characteristics listed at the end of the chapter can be applied to both men and women, there's one that I think might be unique to men, or at least more applicable to men than women. It's the need and/or desire for men to belong to something bigger than themselves, to see themselves as part of a whole. The words given to me by the men and boys I spoke to included 'committed to', 'belonging to', 'being part of something', 'attending' and 'participating'. Men asked to consider at what point in their lives they'd become a man often talked about when their father died. A man stands linked to the past by his father, to the future by his children, and his place in the world is defined by the line that stretches between the three. So when his father dies and he's forced to a different place in the line, his world shifts and, in his own eyes, he finally becomes a man, even if he's been there for a while as far as others are concerned.

As a society I think we've been hooked for some time on the idea that the lack of highly visible, positive male role models is contributing to our high rates of male suicide, imprisonment and road death. Before the Good Man Project I shared that view, but after my conversations with boys, I'm not quite so sure.

Time and time again I asked the students who their role models were and who influenced their view of what makes a good man, and almost always they replied in a way that separated the men in their immediate circle from the so-called role models in the public arena. They made a very definite distinction between the men they admired and those they actually wanted to be like and were very clear in their assertions that they needed to know a man personally before they could decide whether he merited being described as a good man.

In our discussions they identified three distinct groups of men, each of whom acted as role models for them in different ways. There were the men who had access to what the students might want in later life (wealth, cars, power); the men who had achieved excellence in their particular field of interest; and the men they might actually want to be like.

In the first category they spoke of men in the public eye, usually international figures, including the footballer

David Beckham and a number of celebrities. These men were considered role models because of their wealth, the glamorous life they appeared to be living (cars and women featured heavily in the boys' assessment of the glamour factor) and the fact they were wealthy enough to always be where they wanted to be, doing what they wanted to do.

In the second category they spoke of sportsmen, including racing driver Michael Schumacher and international football or cricket players. It was their achievement of excellence that made the boys look up to these men: they admired their willingness to dedicate themselves to something and to stick with it.

Having identified these two categories and the difference between the two, I then went on to ask whether these men were good men. The boys invariably replied in their pragmatic way, 'Dunno, don't know them', that is, they couldn't answer that question because they had no idea what sort of people these men actually were.

That is what led me on to the third category, which I'm inclined to call heroes. These were the men they knew personally, the men they actually aspired to be like. In this group were their grandfathers, their uncles, their older brothers and their mates' older brothers, their teachers and their coaches and, on rare occasions, their fathers. It's here rather than in the public arena that we should be looking for potential 'positive' male role models.

I understood better how the boys differentiate between men in what we might consider public role model positions and those men who actually influence their day-to-day behaviour when, sometime during the project, a famous cricketer appeared on the front page of a Sunday paper after having been involved in an incident in a nightclub while on tour. Given that I was immersed in the issues associated with adolescent boys, I felt angry on their behalf, considering it was less then helpful that a prominent sportsman should behave in that way. I might just as well have saved my energy. When I raised the matter with a group of students, expressing my view that he had set them a bad example, they stared back at me blank-faced: they had absolutely no idea what I was getting so excited about.

As I continued to expand my thoughts about this man being a poor role model and so on, they proceeded to reject every argument I offered to support my belief that his behaviour had been inappropriate – 'there were nine days until the next game', 'you can't trust what was being reported', 'if he wasn't famous, the media wouldn't be picking on him'. The boys agreed that they wouldn't want, and wouldn't be allowed, to behave in such a way while away with their school sports team because it would let their team-mates down. But this fact did nothing to undermine their belief that, despite this behaviour, this player was a good guy and that whatever had happened in the nightclub was completely irrelevant to the main issue – his ability to play a good game of cricket for his country.

I thought, and many other adults would too, that the boys would assess his behaviour and decide that if he could do it, so could they. For the boys I was talking to, nothing could have been further from the truth. They lived according to different expectations, their behaviour was motivated by loyalty to their mates, and they separated the behaviour of this supposed role model from the issue of whether he played well and thus represented his country honourably. Their sense of fairness was evident too. In their eyes this player was being targeted only because he was well known and what was being reported in the media couldn't be trusted.

It was this conversation that led me to seriously question whether the supposed lack of highly visible positive male role models does contribute much at all to our negative youth statistics. Good role models are important; there can be no argument with that. But I now believe that the real answer to such problems as youth suicide, youth offending and imprisonment and the increasing youth road-toll lies in strengthening boys' links to the good men in their immediate circle, their heroes, and in helping fathers to remain heroes and positive influences in the lives of their sons.

The answer also lies in getting ordinary men's stories into the cultural fabric of our society. During the project I spent an evening with the head teachers involved during which each of them spoke for five to ten minutes, sharing their stories of when they had become men. It will remain one of the most memorable nights of my life. To watch adult men reach back to find that moment and then find the words to share it with their peers was to know the strength, humour and pure delight of men when they're affirmed for being who and what they are. If men can begin to share these stories with their sons, with other men and perhaps even with their wives and partners, and if we can honour those stories within our society as they deserve to be honoured, we'll be taking a significant step forward in guiding our young men successfully across the bridge of adolescence and into manhood.

But in terms of strengthening boys' links to the good men in their immediate circle, another dilemma presents itself. If the challenge is our ability to put heroes – good men – into the lives of boys, we're going to have to address, and soon, the matter of getting more men into teaching, and at all levels. There are a number of reasons for the dearth of male teachers at early childhood and primary level, not least the political correctness that is strangling us as a society. The solutions won't be easily found, but find them we must.

What of actual rites of passage? What is being done or might be done to allow boys to recognise that they're on their way into manhood?

All the boys' schools I visited during the Good Man Project put a considerable amount of time and effort into celebrating excellence, both at school assemblies and on a number of other occasions. The boys heard positive language about manhood as a matter of course; they were regularly exposed to conversations that affirmed the value of being male. And they could see evidence of success through effort every day in the photos and plaques on the walls and in the display cabinets of awards. It was this that made me focus on the need to provide boys with positive rites of passage rather than the potentially fatal ones of alcohol, drugs and fast cars (or a mixture of all three).

I believe the opportunities to create positive rites of passage for boys are there within the structures of both single-sex and co-ed schools. Entering the school in Year 9, moving into the sixth form in Year 12 and the step from Lower to Upper Sixth all appear to be natural gateways that schools can highlight and use – and many boys' schools are already doing so.

The Year 9 boy needs affirmation, overt affirmation, that when he arrives at the gate of secondary school for the first time he's moving onto the bridge of adolescence. As

I've said before, his eyes are up and he's looking towards the senior students, thinking about the journey ahead. In whatever way works best, given the particular school environment, it's important to make him as aware as possible of the significance of this particular moment.

The boys themselves spoke of the impact of becoming a senior student and realising that they were moving towards manhood and greater levels of self-responsibility. To some extent, the move from primary to secondary school is the moment when a student really decides to be part of the wider school. At this point they're in effect choosing to be at school – they no longer have to be there. Most of the Lower Sixth boys I talked to confirmed that this made a difference to their attitude. They agreed that going into the Lower Sixth also meant an increased workload, though they had more choice about when and if they actually did the work required. There was general agreement, however, that the step from the Lower to the Upper Sixth was the big one, the point at which they became noticeably more in control of their own lives.

The various schools I visited marked the entry into secondary school in slightly different ways. There was often a change in uniform and sixth formers often had their own space within the school and/or could leave the school grounds without having to seek permission. Prefect systems took differing forms in each school, some having moved towards the idea of leaders and mentors.

The other rite of passage noticeable within boys' schools was the graduation of students from the Sixth Form, often celebrated in great style. This rite of passage is one every school appeared to honour, with a clear sense of history and tradition that the boys obviously enjoyed.

Emotional literacy, emotional resilience, emotional confidence – these phrases were all part of the conversation when the heads and I discussed the needs of boys before the Good Man Project got under way. Emotional literacy was the phrase we were using at the start of the project, the one everyone seemed most comfortable with, but as time went on, we began to question whether this was in fact the right way to explain what they were reaching for on behalf of their students. It seemed to suggest the need to have a significant number of words on hand to describe whatever feeling a person might be experiencing. After considerable discussion, the heads decided they preferred to work with the phrase emotional confidence. That was what they wanted for their students.

What is emotional confidence? How is it different from emotional literacy? This is the definition agreed by the heads: the ability to ask and answer reflective questions; the ability to think about the world around them and their part in it; and the ability to find the language to describe how they see that world. Focusing on emotional confidence rather than emotional literacy means not only having a number of options on hand when looking for a word to explain a feeling, but also having the freedom to decide whether talking is necessary and, if so, what needs to be said.

In my initial conversations with the students, I was struck by how many of them seemed to lack a satisfactory word bank: it wasn't that they didn't have anything to say, rather that they lacked the words to say it. The pauses, the repetition of certain well-used words, the shrugging of the shoulders if they gave a one-word response and I asked another question – all these appeared to indicate an inability to find the words (not to be mistaken for their need to pause and think before they answered).

The contrast between the sexes in this area was made very obvious when I visited a school that incorporated girls into its senior classes and spent some time with a group of girls, asking them the same sort of questions I'd asked the boys. I only had to ask the girls one or two questions and the entire time available was then filled with conversation and discussion. They required no prompting: they needed to know only the general direction I wanted for the discussion before taking control.

Some of what I was seeing was directly attributable to a basic gender difference – most women I know seem to have no difficulty (at least in men's eyes) in expressing an opinion or describing their emotions – but I came to believe that at least some of the difference I was seeing was a direct result of the boys' lack of an adequate word bank.

Often, when you ask an adolescent boy how he is or how his day has been, he'll respond with one word – 'good'. If it's his mother or perhaps even another woman asking the question, she'll tend to wait for some expansion on the concept of 'good' and if it isn't forthcoming, she'll proceed to ask several more questions until she gets what she considers to be sufficient information. (She'll often ask these follow-up questions while peering into the boy's face, thus ensuring that she'll get very little additional information.) We don't need to expand the word bank of adolescent boys so they can answer their mothers' questions satisfactorily – they don't actually want to answer them for reasons already explained – but we do need to work to ensure they have the necessary range of words on hand when they need them.

There are two reasons, I think, why mothers aren't generally satisfied with the answer 'good'. The first is that they still see their son as the small boy who confided in them on a regular basis. The young man standing in front of them looks like their son, but suddenly he's not acting as he always has. This shutting down of communication is frightening to mothers. They've been aware, through the antics of other family members and via the media, that boys change as teenagers, but have never realised that their sons, too, would disappear behind the wall of adolescence. It's panic that drives them to go on interrogating their boys, panic they believe will be calmed only by acquiring more information.

The second reason mothers don't stop asking questions is because they're used to the flow of language. Women (and I include myself here) won't be satisfied with one word when ten would be better. As a gender we women love talking and when life presents a challenge, we respond by talking our way through it. We discuss problems with our colleagues, our best friend or friends, our doctor – and sometimes with anyone who will listen. In this way we find solutions and because that's our experience, we often assume that talking to our sons will calm the ever-present sense of panic we feel as our boys show they're approaching adolescence. On the basis of my own experience and the many conversations I've had with the mothers of boys, it seems we women convince ourselves that if we keep talking to our boys, all will be well. It makes no difference that the boys don't answer willingly; that just makes us all the more determined to keep asking the questions.

In contrast to mothers' reactions to the 'good' response, when I talked with heads and fathers there was general agreement that there are times when that is all boys need or want to say – and that the same can be said of adult men. Many men I spoke to, both parents and teachers, said they often felt that a single-word answer to a question was enough, though their wives and partners were completely unable to understand why.

'Do you ever talk about your feelings?'

'No, not really.'

'Why not?'

'Because talking about it just brings it all back up again. No point in that.'

In the wings of male prisons, I noticed again and again that, when a man's emotions, predominantly anger, were stirred and he couldn't find the words to articulate what he was feeling, he either shrugged and walked away or, if he was angry enough, used his fists. On a number of occasions I saw the same thing, albeit to a lesser degree, in the classrooms of boys' schools.

It stopped a long way short of fights breaking out, but I often saw students, annoyed by their inability to find a word or series of words to explain the idea in their head, eventually shrug and give up, retreating behind a monosyllabic answer and adding to an ever-present sense of frustration. On some occasions I saw them deflect that frustration by targeting another boy either verbally or physically, often doing substantial damage in the process.

As I watched a boy trying to articulate the idea in his head, and as I considered, increasingly, the vulnerability of boys, I found myself wondering how many young men end their own lives because they can't find the words to say what they want to the important people in their lives.

The gorgeous boys currently attending our secondary schools are going to move out into a complex and constantly changing world. They'll be expected to deal with a wide range of situations and they're going to have to negotiate relationships with, among others, their partners, their children and their employers. If they're to develop the emotional confidence they need to cope well in the world they must have an adequate word bank.

One last issue remains to be discussed: homosexuality and the homophobia that was easily detectable in the schools I visited. I've spoken of the language of insult that appeared to operate within all the schools I visited, and that almost all of it featured words that referred to homosexuality in a derogatory way. Words such as 'gay', 'faggot', 'queer' and 'homo' were regularly used by the students when talking to and about each other and were a common feature of discussions in the school.

Whenever I raised their use of this language with the students, they were quick to point out that they weren't actually accusing the boy they were talking to or about of being homosexual. They were seeking mainly to annoy and occasionally to wound someone, most often one of their own friends. When asked when they'd first begun using insulting language as a way of communicating with other boys, the usual reply was 'at the start of secondary school'. When I asked one group of students why they used language connected to homosexuality to insult, they replied because being gay 'is the worst thing you can be'. This sentiment was echoed on several other occasions.

To a certain degree it was possible to see why this particular language had gained such currency. The students attending all-boys' schools were often singled out for attack by those at neighbouring co-ed schools and their insults all focused on the issue of homosexuality – the assumption seemed to be that only boys who were gay would attend a single-sex school. Some students spoke of being taunted with chants about having flies on both sides of their trousers; others talked of being ribbed about attending school on 'homo hill'. But this language of insult is by no means confined to boys' schools. Rather, it appears to be a characteristic of current youth culture: it's very common to hear young people describe something negative as 'gay'.

I was intrigued that the students I was meeting were demonstrating such a high level of homophobia and spent some time talking with them about it. It was primarily a case of peer learning: he used it and got a laugh and everyone thinks he's cool, so I'll use it too. Most students seemed to have learnt it from their peers, but some had copied older siblings.

Why they were so afraid of homosexuality I'm not sure. Perhaps an erection at an inappropriate moment in a changing room had left them wondering. In any event it was clear the little bit of knowledge they did have was a potentially dangerous thing, likely to send them off down a path of proving they weren't gay. They did this both by the active pursuit of girls and by displaying what they considered to be overtly macho behaviour, such as drinking to get drunk and driving cars too fast.

The host of assumptions behind boys' use of homophobic language needs to be challenged. On one level, such assumptions make the school environment an unsafe place for any student who might be uncertain about his sexual orientation (and I believe a great many are, even if only in a very temporary way). On another level, many of the students attending these schools will go on to work in prominent positions within their communities and, if unchallenged, will take these assumptions into the workplace with them.

There can be no denying that the homophobia being overtly displayed by adolescent boys has been influenced by the views of the adult men around them. Until men are willing to confront their own homophobia, and the reasons for it, we won't see any improvement in the behaviour and attitude of adolescent boys in this regard. I'm not asking men to condone homosexuality if it's something they struggle to understand and/or deal with themselves. I *am* asking that they show courage in identifying whatever personal bias they might have and that they don't expect their sons to take on the same prejudices before they've had a chance to form their own views.

As I draw this book to a close, the horror of yet another news report of one young man being stabbed to death by another still sounds in my ears, along with the words of a journalist that sum up very effectively the reality of adolescent boys – 'Young men by law, boys by nature'. That's indeed what they are. We have the challenge of finding the ideal balance between letting them grow towards their potential and keeping them safe when they're unable or unwilling to do that for themselves. It's a tough challenge and in many instances we'll continue to get it wrong. What we have to remember is that we can only do it, mothers and fathers, parents and step-parents, parents and teachers, if we hold hands. We can't do it alone.

What are these young men? They're gorgeous boys on their way to becoming good men, boys who will contribute much to the world that awaits them if we, the adults in their lives, do our job to the very best of our ability.

+ Men need and/or want to belong to something bigger than themselves, to see themselves as part of a whole.

+ Boys make a very definite distinction between the men they admire and those they actually want to be like. They need to know a man personally before they can decide whether he merits being described as a good man.

+ We should be looking for potential positive male role models, heroes, not in the public arena but among the men in our boys' lives – their grandfathers, uncles, older brothers, teachers and coaches and, most of all, their fathers.

+ Both single-sex and co-ed schools have opportunities within their structures to create positive rites of passage for boys.

+ Emotional confidence is the ability for boys to ask and answer reflective questions; the ability to think about the world and their part in it; and the ability to find the language to describe how they see that world.

+ Many boys lack a satisfactory word bank.

+ Women convince themselves that if they keep talking to their boys, all will be well.

+ How many young men end their own lives because they can't find the words to say what they want to the important people in their lives?

+ Homosexuality is connected to insult because, for boys, being gay is 'the worst thing you can be'.

+ Boys seemed to think that homosexuality is something they're at extreme risk of catching.

+ Until men confront their own homophobia and the reasons for it we won't see any improvement in boys' behaviour and attitude.

Characteristics of a Good Man

Trust
Loyalty
Humour

Laid-back
Motivated
Honest

Has dreams and goals
Hard-working
Generous

Compassionate
Humble
Self-reliant

Respected
Respect for others
Sets a good example

Able to persevere
Able to lead from the front
Acts with forgiveness

Has the strength to express
  his emotions

Principled – sticks up
  for what he believes in
Strong enough to know
  when to ask for help

—

Self-confident (will have a go)
Has the courage to be who
  he is (knows who he is)
Follows through on what
  he promised

—

Committed to belonging
  to something
Being part of something
Attending
Participating

—

Brings sense to a situation
Brings humour to a situation
Challenges convention

—

Confident
Carries his authority
Pursues his uniqueness

—

Humour, humour, humour
Capable of lasting relationships
A risk taker

Straight talker
Honest
Empathetic

Enjoys his own physicality
Controls his anger
Shows love

Listens
Expresses his feelings
Can slow down and
  enjoy his own company

Can laugh at himself

Can have fun without alcohol

Good men don't sulk

Printed by RR Donnelley at Glasgow, UK

HOW IOWA
CONQUERED THE
WORLD

HOW IOWA CONQUERED THE WORLD

The Story of a Small Farm Small State's
Journey to Global Dominance

MICHAEL RANK

Five Minute Books
A Fevkalade Publishing Company · Kansas City

Requests for permission to reproduce material should be sent to Permissions,
Five Minute Books
Published by Five Minute Books, 12604 Barkley St. Kansas City, MO 62209

Http://michaelrank.net

Cover Design: Justin Eccles, *Landscape of Iowa*. Courtesy of The Art Studio,
Istanbul, Turkey.

Rank, Michael M.

How Iowa conquered the world: the story of a small farm state's journey to global
dominance / Michael Rank.

Summary: "Iowa is considered a backward farm state full of bumpkins who wear
Carhartt jackets and do little besides give the world corn. But what if that
understanding is wrong? What if Iowa has done more to influence the modern world
than any other population group? It turns out that it has.
In this new book by #1 best-selling author Michael Rank -- himself a native Iowan -
- find out how this underdog state: saved billions of people from starvation in the
20th century; created Silicon Valley in the 1960s and inspired the startup culture of
egalitarianism and hoodies; decides who will win the presidential election every four
years; was the multicultural center of America and hosted more utopian communes
and transcendental meditation centers than any other place in the United States;
created the General American English accent spoken by all actors and broadcasters.
People the world over are learning to speak like an Iowan, even if they don't know
it. This book tells the story of Iowa's outsized influence on global events, but it is
more importantly about how an underdog can defy the odds and truly make a lasting
impact on the world." – Provided by publisher.

Includes bibliographical references.
ISBN: 1503333574
ISBN-13: 978-1503333574

Printed on acid-free paper.

Printed in the United States of America.

To Melissa, Ellie, and Sophie.
As creative as Dixie Gebhardt,
As memorable as the butter cow.

ACKNLOWLEDGMENTS

Being a native Iowan simplified the writing of this book because it put me in touch with Iowans whose knowledge of the state is staggering. More importantly, I had access to kind people willing to give much of their time and go down any rabbit trail, and I had plenty.

I would like to thank the historians of Iowa that gave me the context to to frame all these issues. To Paul Nienkamp, who gave exceptional insight into the university system of the Midwest and for sharing his doctoral research with me. It would have been nearly impossible to find all this information on my own, as I would not have even known what questions to ask when approaching the subject. Kenneth Wheeler's knowledge on the same topic but from a different angle was no less helpful. His profiles of Iowan students and notable graduates added color to a chapter that might have otherwise been duller. Similar thanks go to Joseph Anderson and his knowledge of the global agricultural revolution in America.

Nobody can approach the summit of Iowan politics without the sherpa guidance of Steffen Schmidt, whose mental feats on the topic are no less impressive than the physical feats of a sherpa guide on Mt. Everest, carrying hundreds of pounds of hikers' luggage at an altitude of 28,000 feet. Dr. Schmidt was my professor at Iowa State and helped me get into grad school with his recommendation. His energy is inexhaustible, as he is willing to talk to any media outlet that calls him up – this included me when I was a student reporter at The Iowa State Daily.

I would also like to thank the other researchers and professors at Iowa State University who made the writing of this book possible. In particular I would like to thank Steve Coon, Tom Emmerson, and Dick Haws. The cadre of the journalism department, circa 2002-2004, taught me the craft of writing and reporting. As most of them started their careers at small papers in rural Iowan markets, they also showed me how to explore the state's social landscape and mine it for the human element, bringing to light the stories of real people that can often get buried in images of a quaint farm life resembling a Norman Rockwell painting.

To Mark and Lori Raymie, who let me test out this material before a live studio audience at Coffee Connection in Knoxville, Iowa. If anything was amiss in my material, then the attendees were certainly going to let me know it. I appreciated their contacting the local media and working to promote this book project before it was anywhere close to being finished.

To early readers Helen Klinepeter, Cathy Peper, Billy McCorkle, Bernd Muckenfuss, Nancy Taylor, Kendra Enders, Andreas Wettstein, Jeremy Brock,and Joanna Gould. I couldn't have caught all the things I missed without you, nor would I have realized which parts to expand and which parts to contract.

I would not have even considered writing this book if not for the influence those who embody the values described in this book. In no particular order I would like to thank Nathaniel and Amber Adkins, Paul and Bonnie Beck, Tim Gartin, Peter Swanson, Greg Karssen, Phil Hays, Josh and Rochelle Beck, the staff at Cornerstone and Salt Company, Greg Stults, Brad Wilson, Grant Nelson, Brian Fenoglio, and John King.

Most of all I would like to thank my family. Although I never grew up on a farm, they did their best to instill the values of hard work and putting in grunt work but never bragging about it. But I also lucked out in that I didn't actually have to follow through on much of those – no 5 a.m. feeding of the livestock or walking corn rows in the summer. Instead my mornings were spent asleep in our suburban house and my summers were spent bagging groceries in an air-conditioned supermarket. To my father, who was a jack of all trades but accomplished more than any jack could ever hope to do, whether campus minister, auto mechanic, small business owner, Kiwanis president, or school board member. To my sister, who was there throughout my odd childhood and has become a great friend as an adult, along with my brother-in-law Chris. Kendall and Jack will be awesome. To my mother, who helped me become a writer. Giving a child a quarter every time he used a large word correctly incentivized me to use ten-dollar words when a dime word would suffice, much to the annoyance of my journalism professors. But it started me on a path of words and ideas, which I am always working to improve.

Lastly I would like to thank my wonderful wife Melissa. She may not be an Iowan, but I consider her to be an honorary Iowan. This is the highest compliment that our people can give to an outsider, short of carving a life-size image of them in butter and displaying it at the Iowa State Fair. Thanks for being a rock of support in these last few years and a source of happiness as I churned out books and whiled away in the PhD program. And for giving us two wonderful daughters, Eleanor and Sophia. I can't wait for them to discover their Iowan roots!

TABLE OF CONTENTS

INTRODUCTION

ONE SMALL STATE'S IMPACT
ON MODERN HISTORY

When Troy Davis stepped off the bus to his new life at Iowa State University in 1993, a world away from the nightclubs and beaches of his home in Miami, he knew that he wouldn't fit in.

The 5'8", 198-pound running back was a football sensation in high school but passed over by the Florida universities, partly because of his poor academic record, but more so because of he was simply too small to play great football. His size made him an oddity on the field. Only kickers were as short as he was, and they didn't have to fend off tackles from behemoths twice their weight. College coaches in Florida saw little potential in Davis.

So Davis's choices were few. Iowa was far away and very foreign to this Floridian, and the team drafting him was abysmal. A year after Davis's arrival the team's year-end performance was a winless 0-10-1. Not the stuff gridiron dreams are made of.

However, the perception of Davis as being undersized and unimportant proved to be terribly wrong.

Davis's moment came in the first game of his sophomore year against the University of Ohio, when by halftime the ISU team had already fallen into a familiar losing pattern and were playing like a poor

1

high school squad. With little to lose, new head coach Dan McCarney sent Davis into the game, even though the young player had spent most of the previous year on the bench.

Within a few minutes of play, Davis astounded his teammates, coaches, and fans. He created openings in the defensive line that didn't exist, smashed through linebacker tackles, and leapt for first downs. Defenders missed him completely. By the end of the game, he had set a team record for single-game rushing for 291 yards and was instrumental in generating the first win for the Cyclones in nearly two years.

Then, three games later, Davis rushed for over 300 yards against UNLV. The pattern was repeated over and over again, with Davis running an average of nearly 200 yards per game. By the end of the season he ran a total of 2,010 yards, the fifth running back in NCAA Division 1-A history to pass the 2,000-yard mark.

Even though his team still did poorly that year, Davis earned All-American honors and finished fifth in Heisman voting. Davis nearly won the Heisman trophy the next year – in which he ran for an astonishing 2,185 yards and 21 touchdowns and finished first in all the Heisman voting regions but one. He ultimately lost to Danny Wuerffel, who was on a winning team and headed to a bowl game.

Davis also was nominated for the College Football Hall of Fame in 2014 but did not receive enough votes to be inducted. Even though he is the only NCAA running back to have back-to-back seasons with more than 2,000 rushing yards, many believe the specter of playing for a losing team diminished the recognition of Davis's legacy.

The snubbing of Davis sadly continued into his professional career. He left for the NFL after his junior year at Iowa State, forgoing his senior season of eligibility and opting for the 1997 draft. He was selected in the 3rd round by the New Orleans Saints and played for three unremarkable years before joining the Canadian Football League. The league had smaller stadiums, meager pay, and games in the bitter cold. He had successes here in the modest league but was mostly forgotten by Americans. Davis finished his CFL career in 2007.

Davis might have been a transplant to Iowa, but his story runs parallel to that of his adoptive state. Both Iowa and Davis accomplished amazing results, even though each was/is perceived as unremarkable.

Instead of being honored, both were usually labeled as insignificant or under-performers. In the case of Davis those unaware of his accomplishments wrongly disparage him as an academically challenged rusher on a losing team in a second-rate conference. In the case of Iowa stereotypes suggest it to be filled with overall-clad farmers that respond to every statement with a simple "Ayup."

But when one takes a closer look at Davis the football player and Iowa the state, anomalies emerge. Davis is statistically one of the best college football players in history. And I have discovered that Iowa has produced more innovations in education, technology, science, and culture than Silicon Valley and Hollywood combined. In fact, it invented or built of both of those.

The goal of this book is to make an extremely difficult argument. I will attempt to convince you why Iowa is the greatest cultural force in the world. Not in the Midwest or the United States, but in the world. Its culture of creativity, hard-work, and lack of class structure has allowed its inhabitants to cultivate their skills and rise to extraordinary heights. The state's egalitarian culture has spread out across the country, influencing everything from the way Americans speak English to utopian communes. Due to all these factors, I will make an argument that few would ever consider and even fewer believe – that Iowa has, with its influence on modern global society, conquered the world.

Iowa has certainty attempted to brand itself as a success story. For instance, Iowa license plates through the years contained such slogans as "Fields of Opportunity," "A State of Minds," and at one time, the straightforward, "The Corn State." But slogans like these have trouble sticking when public perception might more easily suggest: "Iowa, So Easy to Forget."

Most in the U.S. have heard of Iowa, of course, and guess it might be somewhere near the center of the country.But besides a general sense that corn and pork are produced here, and information gets fuzzy.When I told Californians I was from Iowa, most frequent responses were divided almost equally between, "That's the one with the potatoes, right?" and "Isn't Columbus the capitol of Iowa?"

Unfortunately, the knowledge that does get disseminated about the state doesn't put our best food forward. Take, for example, the way an Onion article from 2012 decided to make fun of two notable Iowa institutions: the first-in-the-nation presidential caucuses, and the Iowa State's Fair annual exhibition of a life-sized sculpture of a cow, carved from a giant slab of butter.

The tongue-in-cheek report was titled: "600-Pound Butter Cow Sculpture Wins Iowa Caucus." The text reads that the ever-popular butter cow received 64 percent of all votes, defeating the entire slate of Republican opponents.

"For one thing, I'm more familiar and comfortable with the butter cow," a fictional Iowa voter was "quoted" in the article, and went on to say he'd cast his vote for the creamy sculpture because of its even demeanor, its pro-agriculture agenda, and the fact that it was not Mitt Romney.

However, I can't fault The Onion for its choice of targets, because I've done my share of mocking my home state and home town, as well. I hail from Knoxville, Iowa (population 7,313). Knoxville is a former coal center that is slowly diminishing in population, like many small towns in the state. While it is the global capital of sprint car racing (high-powered race cars that dart around circular dirt tracks), its largest employer – the VA hospital – closed in 2009. Many stores in the town squares have closed and too many for-sale houses have no buyers.

But even before Knoxville's downturn, I never had delusions about its grandeur. When I was in high school my gym teacher, Mr. Cunningham, doubled as the town's mayor, juggling his gym teacher duties along with political ones. For instance, he would duck into his office during our dodge ball games and take calls from the city commissioner.

Mr. Cunningham may not have been our most notable mayor, but he was always able to coast to easy re-election. His only real opponent came in 1998, when a former VA mental patient and unrepentant drug user named Josiah Dillinger ran his own mayoral campaign.

At the time of his campaign, Dillinger was homeless, living in storage sheds until owners discovered and evicted him. Dillinger's bold campaign planks included such gems as adding an adults-only section to the local library. But I found his most interesting proposal to be an offer to solve the town's methamphetamine problem by using his knowledge as a licensed American-Indian medicine man to administer peyote to those suffering addiction.

He lost the election.

I told stories like these because like others, I had bought into the popular perception that Iowa's fumbling backwardness meant it deserved whatever ribbing it took. However, I stumbled over an unavoidable challenge to the practice of demeaning my home state – and I found this challenge in the most surprising of places, in the history of the Middle East.

I am a historian, researching Middle Eastern History at Central European University in Budapest. But as I was studying the intellectual history of the Middle East in the late 19th century, I started to notice something strange; incongruent, actually.

In the final decades of the Ottoman Empire – the Middle Eastern power that controlled southeastern Europe, Turkey, and the entire Arabian Peninsula – Iowans began popping up in the most unexpected places. In the period from the 1860s until World War I, dusty little villages in Anatolia had Iowans visit them and even inhabit them.

What were Iowans doing on the other side of the globe in tiny Middle Eastern provincial towns, at a time when Iowa had only been a state for a few decades America itself was still expanding west? The answer? These transplants from Iowa to the Middle East came spreading agricultural technology and Christianity, with remarkable results.

George E. White was a good example. He was born in the Ottoman city of Marash in 1856, where his Congregationalist missionary parents had arrived some years earlier. Later he returned to the United States to study theology at Iowa College in Grinnell. He came back to the Ottoman Empire in 1890 when the American Board of Commissioners for Foreign Missions appointed him to Merzifon to serve as the dean and treasurer of the Anatolia College in Merzifon. White taught theology, science, agriculture, Hebrew, Biblical Greek, and mathematics to young Armenians, Greeks, and Turks.

White was a scholar, but he brought his Iowan farm knowledge, mechanical skills, and love of tinkering along with him. With these skills, he helped transform the Merzifon missionary compound into the technological and educational center of the region. The eight acres of the missionary station were filled with schools, houses, mechanic shops, a bakery "already famous for its good bread," and about 2,000 books in the library. White and the Americans introduced the first telephone, sewing machine, heating system, and farm implements to the region. Their station even had a small farm that imported new agricultural techniques from America. White and other missionaries taught students and local farmers irrigation and crop rotation – new forms of farming that were decades ahead of anything else in the

Middle East. Also, their schools were of such excellent quality that Sırrî Pasha, the Ottoman governor of the province, noted that the foreigners taught the Turkish language better than in the state's own Turkish schools.

When I saw that Iowans like White with a notable place in Ottoman history, I began to wonder if there were other ways that Iowans had influenced the world in unexpected ways. What other arenas had Iowans exercised influence that I would not have expected?

After digging into more research, I was more than a little surprised by the answer. In amazingly diverse fields of achievement – whether the biological sciences, the development of the digital computer, global politics, or even communist movements – there were Iowans. We were in the background and foreground of countless technological and social developments of the 19th and 20th centuries. Sometimes we quietly supported a project; other times we were out in front directing it. Was it serendipity that put so many Iowans into influential positions in recent history, or was something else going on?

I found that it was the latter. Iowa life had two features not found in most parts of the world, or even in many parts of the United States. First, its young people were exposed to hands-on work, whether on the farm or elsewhere. Second, they were also given an excellent education. Public schools became commonplace in the state by the late 19th century, even if they were the one-room variety. Even the most isolated farm children could become literate, learn mathematics, and develop professional competency. Throughout history most people had one but not the other – either they worked at manual labor but were denied education, or they received fine instruction as a part of an elite class but were never exposed to the hard work that would enable them to transform theories into change-drivers.

Because of this combination, a small-town tinkerer like Robert Noyce could experiment with a transistor at his Grinnell college, then go on to found Intel, a company known for its egalitarian, Midwestern culture. A farm boy like Norman Borlaug could get a Ph.D. in genetics but still spend his career in the fields of Mexico and teach millions of farmers how to avoid crop failure. A beloved Iowa radio personality named Ronald Reagan could go on to acting and political fame but keep an amiable, humble personality throughout his life.

This book will tell the stories of people and groups that made Iowa the cultural force it is today. It will explore larger-than-life figures whose stories have largely been forgotten or never showcased in the first place.

Norman Borlaug is a perfect example. The crop scientist isn't a household name today, but nobody saved as many lives as he did in the 20th century. Borlaug's on-the-ground experiments in wheat cross-pollination made crops drought and disease resistant. This was a godsend to nations at risk for famine such as Mexico, Pakistan, Ethiopia, and India. Western experts wrote off these third-world nations as unrescuable, their people doomed to starvation.

However, when Borlaug finished his work, he left behind the tools to create harvests so large that in Pakistan, for example, public schools and government offices had to be closed and used for temporary grain storage. Countries previously forced to import wheat now have sufficient crops to export the grain. Today Borlaug's story is ignored in favor of more daring protectors of human life like Oscar Schindler, but Borlaug actually saved more lives by a factor of one million.

Also, a state that's assumed to be monolithic and provincial was — and still is — the setting for dozens of experiments in communal living and New Age societies. Many utopian communities sprung up in Iowa in the 19th century; the state had more of these than anywhere else in America. Most notable were the Icarians, who built America's longest-lasting secular communist society in Corning, and the German settlers of the Amanas, where tens of thousands of transplanted religious pietists shared food, housing, furniture, and beer in common.

In the 1980s Fairfield, Iowa became home to thousands of followers of Maharishi Mahesh Yogi and his brand of meditation called Transcendental Meditation. There they set up a university and even built a new community called Vedic City. The town has traditional Vedic architecture and bans all non-organic food, giving it a higher concentration of organic grocers than the most hipster of Brooklyn neighborhoods.

Iowa has broadcast its influence to the farthest corners of the world. Every university around the globe that teaches career-oriented skills owes its origin to the land grant university revolution that took place in 1850s Iowa.

Furthermore, anyone who is learning to speak English with an American accent — and more than a billion are doing so — is unknowingly learning how to speak like an Iowan. Because of the disproportionate number of Midwestern-born broadcasters and actors during Hollywood's golden age, general American English is based on the Iowan accent.

Iowa even leads the selection of the U.S. president. The Iowa caucuses have the power to launch a presidential campaign that will go all the way to the White House, as it did for Barack Obama in 2008, George W. Bush in 2000, and Jimmy Carter in 1976. For this reason Iowan voters are so valuable that politicians spend approximately $200 in campaign expenses for each vote they win during the Iowa caucuses. (In contrast, campaigns spend as little as *a tenth* of this in other early-voting states.)

Not bad for a state thought to have nothing but corn, a cow made of butter, and more pigs than people.

This book will tell the untold history of Iowa. It will examine the state in terms of its own development, but also its influence on national and world affairs. It will explore Iowa's unique attributes and what made its people so influential, hard working, and capable of generating great change on the world.

Let's now take a look at how Iowa conquered the world, and what the world got out of it in return.

CHAPTER ONE

HOW IOWA CREATED THE GLOBAL UNIVERSIY SYSTEM – AND SILICON VALLEY AS A BY-PRODUCT

It was 1974, and Robert Noyce was on top of the world.

The 47-year-old was already a living legend, and now chairman of the board of Intel. The company single-handedly led the digital revolution of the 20th century. Intel had breakthroughs in microprocessing as regularly as the changing of the seasons. It had amplified the powers of computers by a factor of 100,000. Its miniaturized processors made the Apollo missions possible, redefining possibilities for space travel.

Noyce could have rested on his laurels and spend the rest of his life on executive boards, playing golf and yachting. But he was not content to merely change the scientific world. Now he wanted to change the business world.

In his new role as chairman of the board he became a spokesman for Silicon Valley. It was an easy role for him to fill: Noyce essentially built Silicon Valley with his development of the semiconductor and microchip. Nearly every tech company in the valley was founded by a former employee of his first enterprise, Fairchild Semiconductors. They all adopted his ethos of egalitarianism, where the lowest designer could pitch ideas directly to the owner and even *argue* with him – both fireable offenses in the East.

His radical democracy at Intel was already legendary. Noyce in his tenure as CEO shunned corporate cars, reserved parking spaces, office furnishings, and private jets. His secretary had a better desk than his scratched metal workspace. His office space was in the same open area as any other worker. This lack of hierarchy permeated the culture of Intel, and it became embedded in the DNA of the emerging Silicon Valley. Noyce became the model for the next generation of CEOs, paving the way for today's Silicon Valley start-ups, staffed by dozens of hoodie-clad programmers, led by a boss who dresses no differently.

Noyce was an elite innovator, but he did not have an elite background. Although he earned a doctorate in physics at MIT, Noyce's story begins at Grinnell College in Iowa.

Unlike other famous figures from small towns, he never disparaged his humble origins later in life. Noyce hated journalists and authors who described his hometown with Dickensian colorings, making Iowa something for him to overcome before he could get on with life. Quite the opposite – Noyce credited his creativity and problem-solving abilities with his humble Midwestern upbringing. In a small town, one had to be an engineer, tinker, and technician, all rolled up into one.

"In a small town," Noyce said, "when something breaks down, you don't wait around for a new part, because it's not coming. You make it yourself."

This Midwestern mindset followed Noyce to California and stayed with him throughout his career. He was among the richest men in Silicon Valley by the latter part of the 20th century, and the most celebrated, winning the National Medal of Science in 1980 and induction into the National Inventors Hall of Fame in 1983. Despite these accomplishments, Noyce lived an understated life. He loved sports cars and mansions, but he hid his cars in garages and his estate behind an enormous wall of trees.

Noyce, in his mission to flatten corporate hierarchy at Intel, eliminated the notions of management all together. Beyond him and co-founder Gordon Moore there were only strategic business segments, which were highly autonomous. They were run like a separate corporation. Middle managers, many in their mid 20s, had more power than vice presidents of corporations back East, who spent their days locked in bureaucracy and labor-management battles. This allowed for the capacity to move quickly from product planning to product production. At meetings everybody was an equal. A young engineer who disagreed with Noyce could speak up and correct him. Such behavior at a New York firm could get an associate banished to the mailroom.

Workers could also dress as they pleased, a shocking innovation to the Mad Men-era office culture of the 1960s. Most came to work in a coat and tie, but they came off when the lab coat came on. Gone were the double-breasted pinstripe suits of Harvard business school graduates.

The origins of Noyce's value system, and Silicon Valley's value system by extension, start in the Midwest, but they aren't merely small town values. Nor were they the religious values of his family, although their Congregationalist church did reject hierarchy and thought every Christian his or her own pastor, a self-starter mindset that was widespread at Intel. Nor were they the values of his lower-middle class background, in which his family lived in a rented house off the main street of a town of 7,000.

The strongest of Noyce's influences was the peculiar breed of Midwestern universities that he attended as an undergraduate. These schools believed in the odd notion that higher education should connect to one's future profession. While providing a good technical education, they did not have the polish or curriculum of classical instruction that Ivy League universities offered. Iowa's university system was respectable in the 20th century but not thought important. But by the end of the century, its ambassadors such as Noyce spread across the United States, Europe, and capitals of the developing world.

Few understood how far-reaching the system's influence was. Iowa's higher education system – which didn't exist in 1850 – became the template for the planet's university education system by the late 20th century.

THE MODERN UNIVERSITY SYSTEM AND ITS MIDWESTERN ROOTS

No matter where you go in the world, the university system is set up in the same way. There are engineering, mathematics, and other hard sciences programs, along with history, philosophy, literature, foreign languages, and other social sciences and humanities. These degree programs are directly or indirectly connected to a future job. The relative wealth of a university in Gambia is starkly different than its counterpart in America, but the curricula of both is largely the same. Why is this? Because most new universities in the world are based on the same American model.

Initially, American universities were rooted in elitism. Universities with any practical career-focus did not exist until the very recent past, not even in America. If a young person attended a university in the late 18th or early 19th centuries (which only about 1 or 2 percent of the population did due to the high social and academic bar for admittance) he typically hailed from the elite society of northwestern New England.

He (and it was almost always a he) would study subjects with only the loosest connection to a future career. The aspiring lawyer or businessman would take courses in Greek rhetoric or Latin even if he never used the information ever again. For most families, sending a child to college was more about social status than it was about education.

The entrance exam to elite universities of the past would be incomprehensible to all but today's elite students. Harvard's undergraduate entrance exam from 1869 expected the prospect to know things few doctoral candidates would know today. For example, students were required to translate into Latin the following sentence: "Who more illustrious in Greece than Themistocles? Who when he had been driven into exile did not do harm to his thankless country, but did the same that Coriolanus had done twenty years before." Then the student would have to give the Latin grammar rules for the subjunctive after *dum, cum, quominus* and whether or not *ne* or *ut non* follow *restat* and *monco*, respectively. Following this were similar questions about the Greek language. The history and geography sections were no simpler. Students were asked the chief rivers of Ancient Gaul and Modern France and whether France was larger or smaller than Transalpine Gaul. To wrap up, they would describe the significance of Leonidas, Pausanias, and Lysander, with no leading questions that might offer directional clues for their answers.

Amazingly, at the time some suggested these standards were *too low*. In 1869 The New York Times wrote critically that university education was a "buyer's bazaar," because classified ads from Columbia, Harvard,

Yale and others fought for students from a limited pool of qualified candidates.

As this entrance exam shows, only elites attended higher education before the mid-19th century, which totaled only 63,000 students, or 1 percent of the American 18- to 24-year-old population. Of this number even fewer finished their programs. Only 21 percent of those who attended were female. Today about 33 percent of all 18 to 24-year-olds are in college. More than 50 percent of college students are female.

Practical concerns pushed early shifts in curriculum. Historian Kenneth Wheeler notes that people started questioning whether translating the ancient Greeks and Romans was the best way to acquire a decent education. More schools started allowing elective courses to respond to this criticism. They also did so to accommodate an explosion of scientific knowledge in the 19th century. Universities tried to grapple with things like scientific agriculture and new discoveries in medicine. Soon there was a shift toward the modern academic emphasis that people take for granted in collegiate university coursework.

Then a new fad in education popularized practicality. One early factor that supported the trend away from traditional education was the Manual Labor Movement. It was a fad in the 1820s and 1830s in which students and professors worked on a college farm for hours each day. The Manual Labor movement came out of Europe, in which reformers such as Swiss educator John Heinrich Pestalozzi and Phillip Emanuel von Fellenberg believed that manual labor would reinforce hierarchy and class structures. They supported denominational and charitable institutions where orphaned and low-income boys could earn their education. In America it was adapted so that teachers and students worked equally. The concept was connected with abolitionism and eliminating any distinctions between racial or class groups. (Abolitionists tried to level social hierarchy while the Europeans wanted to structure it.)

American manual labor programs came to Connecticut in 1819, Maine in 1821, and Massachusetts in 1824. Following these the Oneidas Manual Labor Institute came to New York, emphasizing daily activity in workshop and fields, with the rest of the day devoted to classroom work. The program structured itself as training the whole person, both mind and body. Religious instruction was also kept in the mind of every branch of study to feed the soul, a common part of university instruction at the time. The Oneidas Institute stated in a list of its core values that it would provide a system of education to train in habits of industry, independence of character, and originality, greatly diminish the cost of education, do away with distinctions in society, and "render prominent all the manlier features of character."

Such programs did not last long in the East because of lack of interest and opposition from existing universities. But when these programs were transplanted to the Midwest, they found ideal growing conditions. The student body there was already familiar with manual labor, compared to East coasters from a more pampered background. Midwesterners wanted a mental, moral, and physical education instead of a purely abstract one. For example, at Western College, faculty and students worked together on the college farm each day. It was an egalitarian system where professors and pupils mucked out the stalls and planted corn.

Practical concerns generated technical problems. The Manual Labor movement died out by mid-century, but in its place came growing demand for vocational instruction. By the 1820s and 1830s, American politicians realized that the developing country needed more roads, bridges, dams, and waterways, and large plantations in its Western frontier. Harvard could produce plenty of seminarians or lawyers, but it couldn't produce engineers or crop scientists.

New schools were set up specifically for this purpose. The military academy at West Point was established in 1802 to provide special training to military officers and engineers – mostly civil engineers – how to use artillery correctly and manufacture weapons. They did not teach classes beyond this specialized instruction until 1817 or develop a full curriculum until the 1820s. This and Rensselaer Polytechnic Institute were the only engineering programs in the East until the 1850s. Everything else was small workshops, manual labor institutes, or apprenticeships, which were looked down upon by the gentry.

The new colleges in the Midwest took on the character of their settings and thrived in their new environment, free from such class snobbery. There was no aristocracy in the Midwest. Iowa, Illinois, and Missouri were sprawling lands settled by humble farmers and small businessmen, if they had any population at all. New colleges followed suit, establishing hands-on technical programs that reflected the hands-on culture.

"The mistake has sometimes been made to transplant eastern

education systems without any modification to the West," said Oberlin College professor J.H. Fairchild in 1860. He believed universities were an outgrowth of their society, and a successful "Western" system must have a connection with Western society and reflect that place. Schools in the Midwest, therefore, were located in small towns instead of cities. Colleges barely existed in cities like Detroit or Cincinnati in the 1850s but sprung up in towns with 2,000 inhabitants or less. Their catalogues claimed that such locations were ideal for university study – away from the vices of the city and conducive to building intellectual and moral character. These schools had a genuine belief that their community was something like a monastic community, with the university as the center of town life.

COLLEGE FOR FARMERS: WASTE OF TIME OR FULFILLMENT OF THE AMERICAN DREAM?

The spark that really set off the Midwestern university revolution was a piece of legislation that passed in the 1850s. At this time a U.S. Senator Justin Morrill Smith argued for the government to make changes to America's system of higher education. Morrill was a self-taught businessman who had bootstrapped his way through life. He believed in the Jeffersonian philosophy that America would be a nation of active educated farmers, even though this dream had not come to fruition more than seventy years after America's founding.

Morrill had a more practical worry. Agricultural output of U.S. farms was declining, and American farmers were behind the curve in adopting the latest advances in crop science. European farmers were becoming more sophisticated in their use of crop rotation to improve per-acre output. Morrill knew that a nation could grow only as much as it could be fed. He advocated for a new kind of college that would be specifically aimed at educating farmers. The senator emphasized the notion of industrial colleges that would focus on mechanical arts, which became engineering.

This was a controversial idea. The concept of agriculture or engineering as a subject of university study didn't exist at this time. The mechanical arts were considered to be a craftsman's job, akin to the work of a cobbler or carpenter. Elites recognized mechanical technicians as a necessary part of society. But many thought that including these professions as a part of university study was as out of place as teaching coursework on trash collection. The ancient European bias against manual labor lived on in the East. To many, engineering was considered another form of manual labor with a thin veneer of science. Pure sciences of the likes of Newton were still respected, but engineering was a form of labor ranked below that of businessmen, lawyers, military captains, or doctors.

But advocates of Morrill noted that out of 100 American workers, society needed just five employed in professional jobs like lawyers, politicians, or doctors, but 95 to work industrial class jobs. They needed better education to produce better technology.

What came next led to the birth of agriculture and engineering colleges. In 1856 Morrill implemented a scheme that would create colleges for farmers. Tuition would be free; taxpayers would cover all bills. In arguing for the plan Morrill believed an investment in Americas farms would be similar to the country's investment in railroads, harbor improvements, and coastal surveys. To fund these schools, the federal government would give states wide swaths of federal land that they could sell to raise money to fund these new land grant colleges. There would be at least one per state.

The bill passed in 1859, but President James Buchanan vetoed it. He believed that the proposed colleges would be unsuccessful, and that agriculture and mechanics weren't legitimate fields of study. It finally passed in 1862 with Abraham Lincoln as president, but opposition remained from critics who thought that farmers should be working in the fields instead of idly sitting in front of a blackboard.

The fear of farmers slackening in the agricultural output was so sensitive an issue that when land grant colleges started out they required that students should be engaged in several hours a day of routine manual farm work for fear they would be educated out of their jobs. This was the case at Iowa State College when it was established in 1858 and incorporated into the Land Grant Act in 1864. It offered agricultural and technical training. The first building on campus – which still stands today as a historical museum – was a massive farmhouse. It became the home of the superintendent of the model farm and later years other deans of the school. On this site farm tenants could conduct agricultural experimentation, testing the crossings of crops to improve yield and using early forms of factory-designed farm implements.

It wasn't easy to convince farm families to send their children to college either. Even though tuition was free, farmers did not understand the purpose of a university education for their children. "We can train them in a shop or on the farm; why do we need to send them off to school?" they asked. University recruiters and government officials structured their programs to answer these objections. Schools only ran from March to October so that students could go home to plant in the spring and harvest in the fall.

Instructors skipped over the routine aspects of farming that students already knew. They focused on the industrial possibilities of a large farm and changed their pupils' understanding of a farm as a stubborn piece of land that required sweat, blood, and endless toil into thinking of it as a lucrative business.

An influx of farmers grew the market for education. Farmers were trained to produce more food in specific soil types and climates to feed a growing and hungry nation. Iowa State established institutes, small workshops and county extensions to train new farmers arriving to the Midwest in the 1860s. Many came at this time. Almost any American not fighting in the Civil War joined the Western exodus due to Congress passing a whole slew of acts that incentivized immigration. They included the 1862 Homestead Act, which gave an applicant ownership of farmland at little or no cost as long as the applicant never took up arms against the United States, was 21 years old or older, or the head of the family. Politicians believed it would fill the nation with what Jefferson called "virtuous yeomen" and give new lands to independent farmers rather than wealthy planters with platoons of slaves as seen in the South. At no other time in the history of the world did a lower-class farmer have such an opportunity to claim a large tract of his own land. It spawned a global immigration push to the United States.

Other acts that year included the Pacific Railroad Act, which promoted the construction of a transcontinental railroad across the United States. The government issued bonds and grants of land to railroad companies to build a railroad and telegraph line from the Missouri River to the Pacific Ocean. The line was finished in 1869 and made travel to the Midwest from the East coast a pleasant day-long ride rather than a multi-week journey through empty prairie. Passenger carts were filled with idealistic farmers, ready to plow the land and transform virgin soil into a productive, lucrative harvest. Historians credit the Transcontinental Railroad as having as much economic and social impact on 19th-century America as the moon landings did on 20th-century America.

Midwestern universities arguably had a greater effect. In 1870, only 1,200 students attended the land-grant colleges in Iowa, Michigan, Nebraska, and Wisconsin. The number shot up to 5,000 by 1880. Two decades later over 40,000 students attended land-grant schools, with 18,000 studying agriculture or engineering. The University of Nebraska had over 2,000 students by 1900 even though it was located in a barely-populated farm state, with little visible change from its frontier days. Midwestern engineering departments had the largest attendance levels in the nation, lagging only behind Cornell University and MIT. Only 48 engineering students graduated from Rutgers in 1899, 44 from Yale.

Engineers became more than glorified tradesmen. Historian Paul Nienkamp, who received his doctorate from Iowa State, notes in his dissertation that the growth of Midwestern land-grant institutions permanently altered the demographics of America's pool of formally-trained engineers. It also shaped the nature of Midwestern culture and professionalism for middle-class Americans in frontier states. In the late 19th century, university faculty lobbied for better laboratories and modern equipment. This along with gifts from wealthy businessmen allowed programs to professionalize. Engineers changed from skilled mechanics to educated professionals. The public no longer considered the practical application of scientific knowledge to be the domain of tinkerers or farm boys. Even high schools now began to separate the educational spheres of mechanical arts based on trade skills from professional engineering programs.

Schools in America that had the highest percentage of baccalaureates getting their PhDs in the hard sciences were clustered in the Midwest. Of the top 50 colleges in the country, it was small colleges in Iowa such as Simpson and Grinnell that were putting out top-tier scientists, not the Ivy League. In 1900, four times more engineers graduated from Iowa State University, the University of Wisconsin, and Michigan State University than all engineering students from the East Coast combined. Nebraska State University graduated more engineering students in 15 years, over 2,000 graduates, than all southern university students combined.

While there was good scientific instruction on the East Coast, most people didn't see a career in the hard sciences as a pathway to a high level of respectability in society. Most young men went into business or law. Science simply wasn't sufficiently bourgeois. The farm mindset, in contrast, went hand-in-hand with engineering. It respected hard work and perseverance. It did not look down on mistakes but respected those who overcome problems with ingenuity, whether fixing a broken harvester on the spot or working through the night to repair a tractor engine on the eve of harvest season. This outlook differed sharply with the more traditional East Coast outlook that favored conformity, a prestigious family name, and membership in the right church.

Modern engineering and science-based education in American schools was solidly underway, and it did not come from the industrialized East. It came from the educational philosophy and practices of 19th-century Midwestern colleges. A love and respect for science flourished in the Midwest long before it did in other parts of the United States. The Manual Labor Movement of the early 19th century translated into the late 19th-century scientific endeavor. These professors and administrators developed a culture of technical knowledge that changed how America viewed science.

THE RELIGIOUS, GENDER-INCLUSIVE, CULTURALLY INCLUSIVE HERITAGE

The Midwestern can-do culture made for good scientists, but it was also deeply religious.

In the 19th century there was not a clash between religion and science as most in the 21st century assume. The egalitarian culture of this period was still heavily tied to a Protestant worldview that saw nature as God's creation and understandable by rational inquiry and investigation. The local church was still the hub of social activity, and communities pressured local businesses not to open on Sundays. (still a thorny issue in towns such as Pella, where nothing outside franchise stores are open).

Religious groups funded numerous colleges. Small denominational schools had as much influence in the Midwest as state universities and technical schools. In Iowa, Congregationalists, Presbyterians, and

Methodists built schools at every crossroad; state legislatures in the Midwest freely handed out collegiate charters to nearly any religious group that asked. In contrast, South Carolina would not charter any denominational colleges until the 1850s; it preferred a state university put together by government class. The old guard of the East coast only gave charters to the denominations that had roots in its region – Massachusetts favored Congregationalist colleges, Maryland favored Catholic schools. But there was no established church in the Midwest, so little colleges sprang up, funded by small denominations such as the Swedenborgians, the Universalists or the Free Will Baptists.

Such a mix of denominational schools reflected the religious diversity of the region, as opposed to the South, which at the time was sharply separated between the Methodists and Baptists. The Midwest was no-holds-barred in terms of denominational diversity and competition. Methodists were the first to arrive in the state, following in the wake of circuit riders who travelled on horseback throughout settled portions of Iowa in the 1840s. Each rider typically had a two-week circuit in which he provided sermons for the local congregations and visited families. These riders attracted hundreds of converts. Following this Methodist wave came Catholic immigrants, many of whom moved to the settlement of Dubuque along the Mississippi River. Congregationalists arrived in the 1840s, led by a group of 11 ministers whose motto was "each a church; all a college."

These and other denominations built universities soon after building churches. By 1900, Methodists and Catholics had each created five colleges. They included Marycrest, Saint Ambrose, Briar Cliff, Loras, and Clarke by the Catholics; and Iowa Wesleyan, Simpson, Cornell, Morningside, and Upper Iowa University by the Methodists. Congregationalists established Grinnell College in 1900, which became known as the Harvard of the Midwest. (Today its endowment is second only to Harvard, due in large part to its early investment in Noyce's Intel). Other denominations followed suit. Presbyterians established Coe and Dubuque Colleges; Lutherans established Wartburg and Luther; Baptists established Central College; and the Disciples of Christ established Drake College.

These were religious, yet female friendly. Small denominational schools were the first in the United States to offer co-education. Elite schools in the East Coast at the time did not allow females into their universities. They thought such a practice was only suitable for high schools or academies, and admitting women could damage their brand.

Midwestern schools had no such worry. The Christian colleges were more interested in the moral development of students regardless of gender. A word that appeared often in the discussion of student development was "usefulness." The word was used frequently in a 19th-century debate at Grinnell College on whether to admit nine female students from Davenport, Iowa. One administrator argued in favor. He said the college needed to be co-educational from the start. If they didn't develop the character of both young men and women, *useful for society*, then "the devil will get us all into his net." Ultimately the board agreed. They hoped to produce more useful Christian citizens with the benefit of a university education.

At Midwestern public schools women had opportunities that did not exist in the East, much as they did at smaller denominational schools. Iowa State University had the first home economics program in the United States. The first president, Adonijah Strong Welch, told the first female students, "We offer, then, to the young women who shall resort to this College, a scope for scientific progress and research as unlimited and free as that which we offer to the other sex." His wife Mary Beaumont Welch developed the "ladies course" for female students.

For females, the freshman year curriculum was identical to the men's course in agriculture. In their sophomore year women studied botany, chemistry, physics, with the option of Latin and French, English Literature, or Music and Drawing. Such coursework continued the next two years, with smatterings of history, psychology, geology, and other sciences. Mary Welch believed that women could learn the sciences in a laboratory-like setting because it mirrored running a large, well-organized home. Women should also learn economics, she believed, because they often ran the business and accounting aspects of farm management from behind the scenes.

Working as lab assistants, women made several important but unrecognized contributions to research science. Some ended up marrying their professors, but others made startling discoveries that are only beginning to be recognized. When James Watson and Francis Crick discovered the DNA double helix in 1953, the data and research of Rosalind Elsie Franklin was critical in determining the structure. However, her images of x-ray diffraction, which confirmed the helical structure of DNA, were shown to Watson without her knowledge or approval, so recognition was denied her.

Despite snubbings, the land grant university opened career paths to women that were once closed. Iowa State Teachers' College – now the University of Northern Iowa – was founded in 1876 to train teachers for the state's public schools. Many women became public school teachers after World War I. Before this time the profession was dominated by men, mostly due to university academic calendars of the time. Male university students took courses in the spring and fall and taught public school courses in the winter. As men left these jobs to fight in the war overseas, women filled in the gaps. Midwestern universities educated these new female workers. They slowly broke down the notion that men work outside the home, women do not, and the two shall not mix.

Even minority students had new opportunities in the Midwest that were unavailable in much of the rest of the country. Many of today's historically black colleges and universities were established as land grant universities. Minorities were also admitted into the flagship land-grant schools.

One notable alumnus of Iowa State University is its first black student and its first black faculty member, George Washington Carver. The renowned botanist was accepted into the school in 1891. As a faculty member, he revolutionized the uses of the peanut. His research into the promotion of this alternative crop, along with soybeans and sweet potatoes, helped aid in nutrition for farm families.

Carver wanted poor farmers to grow alternative crops both as a source of their own food and as a source of other products to improve their quality of life. Until the 1930s the peanut was mainly a garden crop and used for animal stock. He utilized this cheap crop in ways never imagined. Carver developed and promoted over a hundred products made from peanuts useful for farmers and their homes, including cosmetics, dyes, paints, plastics, peanut butter, gasoline, and nitroglycerin.

A SEEDBED FOR TECHNOLOGY

Along with Carver's work, technological innovations from Iowa State included a curiosity known as the digital computer. It was built by mathematics and physics professor John Atanasoff and engineering student Clifford Berry from 1937 to 1942. It was a monstrosity that could do much less than today's average smart phone. But at the time it could do binary arithmetic and parallel processing, which were revolutionary for the time.

Universities around the globe began to copy the model of the land grant institution. While there are ancient universities in Europe and the Middle East that predate America's by centuries – notably Al-Azhar university in Egypt, which has taught theological coursework for over a thousand years – nearly all universities built in the 20th century copy the American model. Take the example of Turkey. The country of 70 million has built dozens of universities in the last decade. Turkish administrators have copied the American model down to the letter. Nearly all have the exact same programs as a land-grant school: a college of engineering, business, life sciences, humanities, and social sciences. There is no difference in these programs from their American counterparts except in small areas (for example, Turkish history replaces American history). The similar program of study across the globe makes student exchanges and international study abroad programs possible since equivalent courses exist around the world.

Midwestern science and technology universities continue to influence the world, mostly in terms of foreign graduate students. Any engineering, mathematics, physics, or chemistry department lab is largely staffed by graduate students from India or China. They come to the United States from an Asian model of education that rewards compliance, respect for order, obedience, and heroic levels of memorization. After their stay in the United States of two to five years, they return home with American education models. If their education included a PhD, they run their laboratories and classrooms on the same models as the lab in which they were trained. At these labs, traditional Asian models of education are used less than models that prefer critical thinking and open dialogue between professors and students.

American professors may want foreign students in their labs for their dedication and focus, but these same students are usually not the ones setting up the experiments in the beginning. It is the Western-trained students who come up with creative solutions. A technology writer observed, "When you look at the production of phones and laptops and gadgets we use, the production is going on in China. They have the workforce and political structure that makes it cheaper. We don't produce these things in the U.S. anymore. But we consume them so that the beginning and end of this economic structure are still in the U.S. This goes back to the ideas of the older state universities that were focused on critical thinking and how we approach problems."

In discussing the impact that Iowan universities have had on the course of history, it would be wrong to discount other schools outside of Iowa State. The University of Iowa, founded in 1847, has consistently ranked as one of the best public universities in the nation. It has a distinguished record as a university focused on the social sciences and the humanities. Probably one of the most well known programs the Iowa Writer's Workshop. This graduate-level creative writing program has arguably had more impact on American literature than any other institution. Over its history its faculty have won numerous national book awards and other literary honors. Six U.S. Poets Laureate have graduated from the workshop, and faculty and graduates have won 28 Pulitzer Prizes. Alumni include Flannery O'Connor and current Poet Laureate Charles Wright.

HOW MIDWESTERN VALUES CREATED SILICON VALLEY

Of course, no discussion of the entrepreneurial spirit of Iowan colleges is complete without a closer look at the life of Robert Noyce.

As we saw earlier, his technological accomplishments rival that of Thomas Edison. Born in Burlington, Iowa in 1927 and educated at Grinnell College, Noyce co-founded Intel Corporation in 1968, invented the integrated circuit, and was dubbed "the Mayor of Silicon Valley" for his personal mentoring of dozens of the next generation's CEOs. Steve Jobs idolized him for creating the open source spirit of Silicon Valley. Jobs thought his mentor to be a rebel against the status quo, a mutation in the body of American business. What Jobs didn't know is that Noyce merely brought the Iowan spirit of education and business to California.

Noyce was the son and grandson of Congregationalist clergymen. His mother was a graduate of Oberlin College and dreamt of being a foreign missionary before she married. From an early age Robert put together inventions. He built a radio from scratch and attached a motor to his sled, using a propeller and parts from an old washing machine. Noyce then graduated to building a small aircraft. When he was 13, Robert came across an illustration for a glider that he found in *The Book of Knowledge*, a multi-volume encyclopedia, for building a glider. He and his brother pooled $4.53 to buy materials. It included bamboo spindles for the frame from a furniture store and cheesecloth to cover the wings. A girl on their block sewed the cloth to their frame. When finished it was four feet tall and stretched 18 feet. They tied it to a neighbor's car and managed to launch the glider a few feet above ground. A few years later Robert rode it off the roof of a barn. He flew for three seconds before crashing to the ground. Thankfully he avoided injury.

Noyce's community may have disliked his eccentricities, but it never looked down on him or his poor family. Grinnell was fiercely egalitarian and rejected class division. Although his family lived in a house owned by a local church, there was no stigma attached to not owning one's own house. Thomas Wolfe argues in his essay "The Tinkerings of Robert Noyce" that Grinnell's Congregationalist roots made the town reject the idea of social hierarchy as fiercely as a religious hierarchy in the Catholic or Anglican churches. The Congregational Church was a breakaway from the Church of England in the sixteenth century. Each congregation of the Congregationalist Church was autonomous. Their rejection of a church hierarchy reflected their hatred of a British class system divided into royalty, aristocracy, yeomen, and peasants. A minister led by teaching, not by using the threat of excommunication. Each church member was supposed to learn moral teachings and be his own pastor in dealing with God. As a result, divisions weren't marked by the rich or poor in the Midwest; they were divided by those who were devout, educated, and hardworking, and those who weren't. Being poor wasn't a social gaffe. Taking tennis or riding lessons instead of working an odd job was.

Noyce was accepted by the community, but he was an irascible student and got into frequent trouble. When a university student at Grinnell, he stole a 25-pound pig from the town's mayor. He and his friends roasted it at a student luau, a popular event in the years following World War II when soldiers returning from the Pacific Theatre brought Polynesian culture back with them. The mayor wrote a letter to Noyce's parents, reminding them that in Iowa stealing livestock was a felony that demanded a minimum sentencing of one year in prison and a fine of $1,000. The crime went deeper than that, however. To a Midwesterner, livestock was both a livelihood and a primary source of food. Stealing it was a crime against the whole person and demanded fierce punishment. The issue resolved only when Noyce's physics professor, not wanting to lose a star pupil, intervened and compensated the mayor.

Noyce was still a college student in Iowa in 1947, but at this time he began working on state-of-the-art technology. The transistor had just been invented at Bell Labs in New Jersey. One of the co-inventors was John Bardeen, college friends with Grant Gale, Noyce's physics professor. He read about the breakthrough in the newspaper and asked Bardeen to send him technical writings on the transistor. The invention performed the same function as a vacuum tube (invented by another Iowan, Lee De Forest) which amplified specific electrical signals such as a radio wave. But it was fifty times smaller and did not require glass tubing, a vacuum, or a plate. Gale got a hold of the two first transistors ever made in the world, which he showed to his eighteen physics students in Grinnell. He wasn't interested in its technological applications. Gale merely thought the transistor might be a good teaching device to show the flow of electrons through a solid.

Noyce, one of the lucky few to see the technical curiosity, was fascinated. He saw the future potential of this device and threw himself into his physics studies, graduating Phi Beta Kappa in 1949 (although not before leaving with the Brown Derby Prize, which recognized the senior who earned the best grades with the least amount work).

On the recommendation of his professors, Noyce applied to MIT's physics doctoral program in 1949 and finished 1953. When he first arrived in Boston, some of his professors had never heard of the transistor. They couldn't be blamed for this ignorance – Noyce was doing academic research at Grinnell, the only place in the world outside of Bell Labs where one could study the transistor. But they could be blamed for dismissing the full potential of the transistor. Many thought of it only as a novelty developed by a telephone company, with little commercial potential. To his annoyance, Noyce found that MIT was behind Grinnell College when it came to adopting new technology.

Following graduation, Noyce joined 11 other electrical engineers with doctorates to work for William Shockley, a future Nobel Prize winner in physics who understood the digital possibilities that could be unlocked by the transistor. He formed the startup Shockley Semiconductor Laboratory in 1955. Shockley proved to be a poor manager, so seven engineers, Noyce included, defected to start their own semiconductor company. The "Traitorous Eight" – whose leaving Shockley described as a "betrayal" – established Fairchild Semiconductor Corporation in 1957. They began in a humble two-story warehouse in Mountain View at the northern end of Santa Clara Valley. At the time Mountain View was still full of apricot, plum, and pear orchards. Nearby companies such as IBM and Hewlett-Packard were already up and running. Both were trying to develop the electronic computer.

Fairchild was perfectly positioned to offer the semiconductor to these manufacturers. With the Soviet Union launching Sputnik the same year, the dawn of the space race made large companies clamor for more computing power. The government in particular wanted small computers that could be installed into rockets to provide onboard guidance, which was impossible in the age of vacuum-tube-powered monstrosities. Transistors could shrink computers to such a size. With Noyce's invention of a solid-state circuit using silicon, he created the industry standard for the integrated circuit, or microchip. Miniature computers were now possible, and the possibilities were endless. Robots, complex computing, and even rockets to the moon were no longer science fiction. He parlayed his success into founding Intel in 1968.

Noyce started the company with Gordon Moore and Andrew Grove. Noyce was the visionary, Moore the technological genius, Grove the management scientist who pushed Intel's laid-back company culture. Grove was a Hungarian-born Jew who avoided the Holocaust and escaped the communist country at the age of 20. His early-life experiences made him appreciate a business climate of democracy and collaboration. Grove was dubbed "the guy who drove the growth phase" of Silicon Valley.

But it was Noyce who ultimately drove the egalitarian spirit at Intel that he learned in Grinnell. Even after becoming rich from his integrated circuit discovery, he opted to stay in the modest Mountain View rather than move to a wealthy part of Palo Alto. He rejected the social hierarchy found in the East Coast and all the social markers of wealth, CEOs with their oak bookcases, leather-bound books, and carved paneling. There were no reserved parking spaces at Intel; manager and secretary fought for the same spots. Everybody began the work day at the same time – eight a.m. – and their were no office suites for the executives. There was no dress code, except for the unwritten expectation that workers dress modestly. Wolfe describes the clash between these mindsets when Fairchild CEO John Carter came to visit Noyce's office:

> One day John Carter came to Mountain View for a close look at Noyce's semiconductor operation. Carter's office in Syosset, Long Island, arranged for a limousine and chauffeur to be at his disposal while he was in California. So Carter arrived at the tilt-up concrete building in Mountain View in the back of a black Cadillac limousine with a driver in the front wearing the complete chauffeur's uniform: the black suit, the white shirt, the black necktie, and the black-visored cap. That in itself was enough to turn heads at Fairchild Semiconductor. Nobody had ever seen a limousine and a chauffeur out there before. But that wasn't what fixed the day in everybody's memory. It was the fact that the driver stayed out there for almost eight hours, doing nothing. He stayed out there in his uniform, with his visored hat on, in the front seat of the limousine, all day, doing nothing but waiting for a man who was somewhere inside... People started leaving their workbenches and going to the front windows just to take a look at this phenomenon... It wasn't merely that this little peek at the New York-style corporate high life was unusual out here in the brown hills of the Santa Clara Valley. It was that it seemed terribly wrong.

Noyce renounced such hierarchy with the ferocity of Martin Luther at a papal court. He was the young CEO of the company and not afraid to give incredible levels of responsibility to new hires, even those fresh out of graduate school. There were no layers of staff and management between the top and bottom of the company, a shocking contrast to legacy companies such as GM or GE, which in the mid-20th century employed hundreds of thousands, separating them with management levels as hard as sedimentary rock layers. Noyce preferred quick movement instead. Any functionary could make a large purchase. Back East, it would take the approval of one or two superiors, and the request could take weeks. At Intel, only one request form was necessary.

Defectors from Noyce's company started dozens of their own companies, all supplying microchips. Fruit trees were uprooted and replaced with office buildings housing hi-tech start-ups, with cultures inspired by Noyce's ethos of informal codes of conduct and no social distinctions. They embodied the California spirit of the 1960s, with casual surfers, political protestors, and hippies that defied any social convention imaginable, and even a few unimaginable. Yet their laid-back exterior belied and incredible work ethic, another trait that the Midwesterner Noyce bequeathed to the new business community.

Noyce became a patriarch of this newly-minted Silicon Valley. He was a father figure to the next generation of Silicon Valley giants. After leaving daily management at Intel in 1975 he mentored Apple co-founder Steve Jobs and imbued the energetic young entrepreneur with his vision of business. Their relationship may have also influenced Jobs' 2005 decision to transition to Intel processors, which it still uses today. Jobs later recounted the influence that Noyce had on his career, teaching him both how to think and how to act:

> Bob Noyce took me under his wing. I was young, in my twenties. He was in his early fifties. He tried to give me the lay of the land, give me a perspective that I could only partially understand... My observation is that the doers are the major thinkers. The people that really create the things that changed this industry are both the thinker and doer in one person. And if we really go back and we examine, did Leonardo have a guy off to the side that was thinking five years out in the future what he would paint or the technology he would use to paint it? Of course not. Leonardo was the artist but he also mixed all his own paints. He also was a fairly good chemist. He knew about pigments. [And] knew about human anatomy. And [combining] all of those skills together, the art and the science, the thinking and the doing, was what resulted in the exceptional result.

Noyce was a thinker and a doer. He had the theoretical knowledge of a physicist and the practical ability of a craftsman. He was a secular Protestant saint, a worker who did not isolate himself like a Vatican bishop or New York CEO but was a hands-on laborer who walked among the cubicles. Although he abandoned the simple moral light of his childhood and left the church later in life, Noyce brought a different form of this light to Silicon Valley. Wolfe said three decades ago that Noycisms are still repeated in Silicon Valley like a holy catechism: "Datadyne is not a corporation, it's a culture," or "Cybernetek's assets? Its assets aren't its hardware; they're the software of the thousand souls who work there." Those phrases are still repeated today. They are Midwestern folksy truisms transformed into 21st century corporate speech.

Noyce was his own man, but he was also the product of the global university revolution that started in the Midwest. In the 19th and 20th centuries, education at the university level was democratized for the masses. It left the hands of a small number of Northwestern New England elites and spread throughout the Midwest. Here the values of egalitarianism, experimentation, and hard work were internalized. From this solid beginning, higher education spread throughout the rest of the globe, forever eclipsing the Harvards, Oxfords, and other old, stuffy institutions obsessed with status and family heritage. These values spread to California soil and took root in the business community like corn transplanted to virgin Iowa soil, returning a hundred-fold harvest.

These universities believed in building something out of nothing: coming to an empty field and building a school that could provide technical instruction for otherwise uneducated farmers. The graduates went on to create companies that believed a few tiny gold wires and bits of silicon could transform the global economy.

A final story from Noyce sums up this very Midwestern ethos of creating opportunity where none existed before. Andrew Grove would ask at employee meetings, "How would you sum up the Intel approach?"

"Many hands would go up," Wolfe writes, "and Grove would choose one, and the eager communicant would say: 'At Intel you don't wait for someone else to do it. You take the ball yourself and you run with it.' And Grove would say: 'Wrong. At Intel you take the ball yourself and you let the air out and you fold the ball up and put it in your pocket. Then you take another ball and run with it and when you've crossed the goal you take the second ball out of your pocket and reinflate it and score twelve points instead of six.'"

CHAPTER TWO

MENNONITES, TRANSCEDENTALISTS, AND UTOPIAN COMMUNES: WHY IOWA IS THE MULTICULTURAL CAPITAL OF THE WORLD

Every day at 5 p.m., 1,700 residents of Fairfield, Iowa file into the Golden Domes, a twin set of buildings that look like flying saucers sprayed with polyurethane foam. The number of residents is carefully dictated, chosen for its sacredness, as it is one percent of America's population divided by its square root. But the 1,700 aren't there to argue mathematics. They are there to take flight.

Each of the residents puts themselves in the lotus position. Then they propel themselves in the air using only the force of their buttocks. Smiling serenely, they start to bounce higher and higher. This is the first stage of yogic flying, a "natural extension" of Transcendental Meditation. The second stage, adherents claim, is floating in the air. The final stage is taking flight. While the second and third stages have not yet been reached – although mediators have been optimistic for decades that a breakthrough is around the corner – levitation isn't in the only benefit of this technique. According to Yogic Flying Club for Students, other effects appear when sufficiently large numbers of people practice the technique.

"This coherence-creating effect, termed the Maharishi Effect, neutralizes stress and negativity in the innermost fabric of the nation. The crime rate drops. Sickness and accident rates drop. Inflation and unemployment decline and the economy improves. Even terrorism and open warfare have been reduced or stopped and the superpowers have become friendlier."

The mediators explain this technique with difficult-to-capture technical jargon. "The latest scientific discoveries" or quantum mechanics are frequently mentioned. Additional validation is offered in the form of photos of yogic flyers appearing to hover in air.

These transcendentalists have been in Fairfield since the 1970s, yet traditional Iowans consider Fairfield to be an anomaly, a weed growing in the cracks of the state's cultural asphalt. What most Iowans don't know is that utopian communities like Fairfield are not an aberration in the state's otherwise vanilla-plain identity. They are hard-wired into the state's character.

In the last chapter we looked at the entrepreneurial spirit of Iowa and how its egalitarian approach to business created the culture of Silicon Valley. This risk-taking spirit had remarkable influence on the business world. But new arrivals to Iowa did not restrict this spirit to business or work life. They also applied it to religion and government. For this reason, idealists and socialists built many experimental communities in Iowa.

The abundant land, freedom, and privacy allowed any group from around the world with more than a few dozen adherents to come, purchase a sizable acreage, and conduct their social experiments. They came with wide-eyed enthusiasm and believed that their community would bring the next stage of human progress. Out of their experiments a New Man would emerge, free from poverty, social strife, or greed. While most of these experiments ended in failure – and they usually failed, ironically, over money – they stand as a testament to the multicultural nature of the state.

Descriptors like "multicultural" tend to be assigned to places like California, not Iowa. In 2010 I worked for the U.S. Census Bureau in California conducting door-to-door interviews. Part of the questionnaire asked residents their ethnic make-up. Though most fell into the main categories of white, black, or Latino, there were endless mixes and matches thrown in. They were one-fourth this, one-half that, a bi-racial grandmother here, a pan-racial father there. Some residents even reported ethnic backgrounds that were mathematically impossible. One man said he was one-third Japanese, one-quarter Guatemalan, and half white. (I don't know if he was irritated at my presence or genuinely confused with his lineage, but the work of the census drone is to report, not argue, so I logged the results without comment.)

You will not encounter nearly as much ethnic diversity in Iowa. In some communities a mixed marriage is still thought of as a German-background person marrying a person of Danish or Swedish descent. Spanish speakers are few except in Iowa's larger cities. To paraphrase an article in The Onion, "White Family Moves To Town," diversity in Iowa means that whether someone is of Irish, English, German, Italian or Swedish background, we are all the colors of God's white rainbow.

Iowa may appear to lack ethnic diversity, but a quick survey of town names in the state suggest a far more complex cultural diversity. Des Moines and Dubuque have French names, befuddling visitors to the state who attempt to pronounce them. (Is it "Dey Mwah" or "Dah Moyne"?). The names point to the brief French control of the state. Iowa was the sight of considerable French exploration, fur trapping, and basic industry when France owned much of the continental United States prior to selling it to the United States in the Louisiana Purchase of 1803. They were the first European visitors to Iowa.

In 1673, Father Jacques Marquette, a studious 35-year-old Jesuit, and Louis Jolliet, a 27-year-old philosophy student-turned-fur trapper, went west of the Mississippi, thought to be the first two white explorers to see Iowa. After surveying the area, they commented in their journals that Iowa appeared "lush, green, and fertile" – as did immigrants who came to Iowa two centuries later to farm. The French and Spanish governments established trading posts along the Mississippi River over the next century, but American settlement didn't begin until after the War of 1812. The U.S. government encouraged settlers to come after strong-arming Indian cultures to leave through forced population movement. The Sauk and Meskwaki tribes were pushed out altogether in 1846 after Iowa gained statehood. But in the 1850s the Iowa Legislature allowed the Meskwaki to purchase land in the state, an unprecedented move. There is still a large Meskwaki reservation in Iowa today.

The number of foreign-born settlers in Iowa remained small prior to the Civil War. It increased shortly after when active recruitment for immigrants began. The state printed a 96-page book in 1869 called *Iowa: The Home of Immigrants.* The booklet provided educational, social, physical, and political descriptions of Iowa. It was published in English, German, Dutch, Danish, and Swedish to attract any would-be immigrant groups. Iowans welcomed northern and western European immigrant groups to fill out the sparse landscape, considering these groups to be "good stock."

Germans were the largest immigrant group, settling in every county in the state. Most were farmers but others became craftsmen and shopkeepers. They published German-language newspapers, opened schools, and managed banks. Other European groups included Swedes, Norwegians, Dutch, Danes, and various groups from the British Isles. Schwieder notes that they usually occupied the same corner of the state. Norwegians settled in Story County; Swedes came to Boone County; and Danes settled in southwestern Iowa – there the "sen" suffix of last names dominates. Later immigrant groups included Italians and Croatians, who were poorer and often lacked vocational skills to do work other than hard manual labor. They turned to coal mining, which was the simplest but most physically intensive work available at the end of the 19th century. Italian immigrants usually came to America with the financial support of his family or friends. Laborers worked in the coal mines to pay back their travel loans, then saved to bring over their wives and families. For two generations Italians dominated the Iowa coal industry until it began to decline in the 1920s. It all but disappeared by the 1950s.

Immigrants typically traveled in groups of a few dozen and formed towns with a specific ethnic identity. Such towns that popped up in the early 1800s were Pella, a Dutch town; Elk Horn, which is primarily Danish; or Melrose, which is Irish. These groups often came for reasons of religious persecution. Pella was founded as a unit of eight hundred Dutch immigrants who were one congregation of a dissident minister. They travelled to America with all their savings in a large iron safe pulled by a team of oxen and guarded by a group of burly Dutchmen. They found a new site in Iowa to locate their new town and construct a planned community. The Hollanders purchased the land and began to build their settlement. The community was united by common ideals, and the settlers built the town with a common plan and purpose. The name Pella was a biblical term meaning "city of refuge."

Other less mainstream groups also settled in Iowa. In the late 19th and early 20th centuries, many Russian Jews came to Sioux City. The city had at least a half-dozen synagogues. At the turn of the century Sioux City had a cosmopolitan luster and appeared poised to become another Chicago, a midwestern cultural and commercial hub that attracted immigrants from across the world. These Jews were part of a massive wave of Russian and Eastern Europeans fleeing Russia's pogroms. They came to Iowa for its farms, meatpacking plants, and coal mines. Many of them also joined communist groups and supported the Bolshevik Revolution. The most famous – or infamous – figure to emerge from this community is George Koval. He was a scientist who became a Soviet Spy and infiltrated the Manhattan Project. Historians believe he accelerated Russia's nuclear program by years, making the Cold War and Soviet-American mutually assured destruction a possibility in the 20th century.

DREAMS OF A COMMUNIST MIDWEST: IOWA AND THE UTOPIAN EXPERIMENT

A much more interesting trend in Iowa's immigrant history is its many communist colonies. From the beginning of the state until 1900 several utopian communities were founded in Iowa. These groups had different ideologies, but most were fleeing economic misery or political/religious persecution in Europe. They were attracted to philosophies like communism that spoke of empowerment for the lower classes. They also came with nothing, so they had nothing to lose – why not take a risk and try to build a perfect society from the ground-up?

Most communities ended in failure shortly after their founding: Abner Kneeland, a pantheist, started Salubria in Van Buren County in 1839, but the community folded five years later after he died.

Hungarian refugees founded New Buda in 1850 after fleeing the Hungarian Revolution of 1848. Economic difficulties forced them to abandon the town three years later and move to Texas. Followers of French socialist Charles Fourier established Phalanx in Mahaska County in 1844, but it folded two years later. Fourier believed that a society that shared all its resources could eradicate poverty and vastly improve its production levels. His social structure called for farmers to feed a community of artisans, craftsmen, and intellectuals. Eventually all creative activity including industry, craft, and agriculture would arise from a liberated passion. It didn't work. Sharing resources was a difficult task among farmers, many of whom barely produced enough to feed their own families, let alone other members of the community.

Although most of these communities failed after a few years, the idea of utopianism took hold in the American psyche during the 18th and 19th centuries. Utopian communities were based on the idea of achieving religious or social perfection based on communal living. According to Robert V. Hine, author of *California's Utopian Communities*, the definition of a utopian community "consists of a group of people who are attempting to establish a new social pattern based upon a vision of the ideal society and who have withdrawn themselves from the community at large to embody that vision in experimental form."

Over 250 communal groups formed in the United States before the mid-20th century. The communities were small, sometimes only numbering a few dozen. Other groups attracted a larger following. Perhaps the most well-known are the Shakers, which had 6,000 members at its peak in the mid-19th century. They were a group of dissenting Quakers under the leadership of Mother Ann Lee. They came to America in 1774 and received their name for their ecstatic behavior during worship. Mainline Protestants frowned at their dancing, whirling, and clapping in a church building. They were more mystified by the Shaker insistence on celibacy. New members came from converts or adopting children.

Iowa, however, held a special attraction for utopianists. "Iowa had a very large number of communal groups, at least a dozen in the mid-19th century. That's a larger number than you'll see farther west and in the south," said Peter Hoehnle, president of the Communal Studies Association, in an interview with Iowa Public Radio.

The early settlement of Iowa coincided with utopianism reaching its high point in the 1830s and 1840s. Iowa was open ground, known to be good farm land, but also isolated, which is attractive when trying to establish a new order. It had good connections to the Mississippi River and wasn't totally unreachable, but empty enough to build whatever the community wanted to build. "It was a rich canvas on which the utopian picture could be painted," Hoehnle said.

The idea of community life in which members held all things in common existed for two thousands years in Christianity, with monastic groups living out the principle of first-century Jerusalem in which believers "held all things in common." (Acts 2:44). The idea became popular among secular thinkers in the 1800s, who fashioned themselves as the heirs of classical Greek thought. Plato put forward the concept of a human utopian society in *Republic*, in which he wrote of a fictional Greek city-state with communal living among the ruling class. Thomas More, the 16th-century English statesman, developed Plato's ideas in his book *Utopia* in 1516, describing an idyllic political and social system on a fictional island. Few readers realized that the world "utopia" means "no land" in Latin, a play on words that suggests Thomas More thought such a place to be unworkable.

Nevertheless, 18th-century European rationalists believed in empiricism and creating new political orders. They thought that a well-organized society could be free of poverty, greed, ignorance, and any forms of immorality. French Enlightenment thinkers such as Jean-Jacques Rousseau believed that vice and sin came from external forces. But if man could return to a state of nature – free from social conditioning that put him in conflict with his neighbor – then a new, perfect social order could emerge. Thus utopian movements and their communities were formed.

It is easy to judge harshly such experiments today because we sit on the other side of history and know that they did not work. From our 21st-century perspective, we think of these colonists as wingnuts, willing to follow any charismatic leader, and not too different from a religious cult. But we have to take that time in history in to consideration. In the 18th and 19th centuries, social changes were happening that had never happened before. The French Revolution overthrew France's king and queen. That part is not remarkable, as plenty of monarchs had been overthrown over thousands of years. But what is remarkable is that they did not *replace* their rulers with anyone.

The French called for unity, equality, and brotherhood, and the utter alien notion that all members of society deserved the same rights and were liable to the same laws. Under this new system, a king could receive the same punishment for lawbreaking as a peasant. Many found it absurd.

The French Revolution failed, but the equally radical American Revolution succeeded. The rebel American colonists managed to install democracy as their operational government model. What had only been a strange ruling practice by the Ancient Greeks was now the guiding principal behind a massive new nation. It was a time in which startling changes were happening across the globe.

The future seemed limitless. If a country could rule itself without a king and queen, some thought, why couldn't it rule itself without any ruler at all? Many utopian thinkers asked themselves that if one Greek form of government, democracy, could be dusted off after thousands of years on the shelf, then why not try other discarded ideas? Perhaps the time had come for Plato's vision of a utopia.

From the 1830s to 1850s, charismatic leaders formed groups of 50 to 100 Europeans who followed a basic ideology or religious denomination and set up communist communities in Iowa. As we saw earlier, most experiments failed after a few years. These towns were distant from cities and the community members were forced to pursue farming, even though few had any experience in agriculture. Wide-eyed utopianists could articulate the values of communism, but they couldn't translate this enthusiasm into working a plow. They struggled to learn on the job, but their early harvests were barely large enough to feed the community, let alone accrue any capital. As a result, the town's mortgages and land purchases were never paid. Debt accumulated until the towns went bankrupt.

CORNING: A UTOPIAN CASE STUDY

But a few towns stabilized in their early years. A few even lasted for decades. One of the greatest utopian success stories in Iowa was Corning, founded by the Icarians. They were a French-based utopian socialist movement inspired by Étienne Cabet, a French philosopher who wanted to replace capitalist production with workers' cooperatives. Cabet was a radical politician who played a leading role in the Revolution of 1830, which returned a constitutional government to France. Later conflicts forced him into a five-year exile in England. Upon his return he wrote a novel *Voyage to Icaria*, which explained his economic and social ideas.

Cabet appealed to European artisans of the early 1800s who were being priced out of the market by cheaper goods churned out of European factories. A blacksmith who could not compete on the cheap costs of metal factory goods was suddenly out of work. Immigrating to America with like-minded fellows and joining a society free from poverty and social strife seemed like an attractive proposition.

Cabet called for mass migration to the United States to put his ideas into action. He believed that 20,000 working men would immediately heed his call, with numbers soon reaching a million as news of the colonies' success spread across Europe. Wide enthusiasm greeted his appeal. Donations of money and farm equipment came pouring in. Cabet even contracted with a Texas land agent to obtain a title for 1 million acres of land, as long as it was colonized by 1848.

Critics thought of Cabet as an effete thinker who preferred academic speculation in a comfortable house to the hard work of actually building such a community. Years after Cabet's dream communities had become a reality, researcher Charles Nordhoff visited the community. He praised his followers but dismissed their petty leader: "One cannot help respecting the handful of men and women who, in the wilderness of Iowa, have for more than twenty years faithfully endeavored to work out the problem of Communism according to the system he left them; but Cabet's own writings persuade me that he was little more than a vain dreamer, without the grim patience and steadfast unselfishness which must rule the nature of one who wishes to found a successful communistic society."

The conditions upon arrival were definitely grim. An advanced guard of 69 Icarians left France for Texas and arrived at the port of New Orleans. To their discouragement, they found the land grant was only for 10,000 acres, and it was much poorer soil than promised. To make matters worse, the plot was not a contiguous piece of land. Parcels were cut up in a checkerboard fashion, making large-scale farming or community development impossible.

Despite these difficulties, other colonists came. They set up communes in California, Missouri, Illinois, Texas, and Iowa. The Illinois colony was ironically purchased from Mormons who were leaving for Utah, anxious to sell or rent their buildings. One utopian community handed its resources to another.

The shining star of the Icarian movement was the Iowa colony in Corning. It lasted for 46 years until it ultimately disbanded in 1898, making it the longest-lived secular commune in American history. The Icarians purchased 3,000 acres of land in Iowa in 1852. Immigrants from the failed colony in Nauvoo, Illinois joined them in 1860 after it fell apart due to factional battles and financial difficulties. The Nauvoo residents donated all their worldly goods to the community and passed a probationary period of four months before they could join the Corning settlement.

The French-speaking settlers arrived, greeted with nothing but mud hovels. Unlike the Nauvoo colony, the land had never been farmed before. Settlers had to break the sod for the first time, making the initial year full of backbreaking labor. But communal living was there from the onset. To ensure that everyone lived equally, they built modest log cabins for each family. Larger multi-purpose buildings were used for laundering, dining, and other activities. By 1874, they built up the community to include a two story, 1,200-square foot dining hall and school, along with a dozen houses to accommodate the 11 families. They ate all their meals at the community halls; partly out of custom, but also out of necessity since there were no kitchens in any of the houses. Work was divided by gender. Women were ironers, seamstresses, and cooks; men were blacksmiths, shoemakers, mechanics, masons, and tailors. After a few years the Icarians produced enough to sell their goods to nearby towns. They sold cattle, hogs, and wool, which was a prosperous venture during the Civil War.

Corning's political and social life stayed faithful to communist principles. The group governed itself through weekly meetings every Saturday. The colony elected a president as its formal head each year, but officers were elected each week for the conduct of meetings. There were no formal religious observances in the community. Most rested on Sunday, with some electing to go hunting or put on a musical or theatrical production for the amusement of the other colonists.

The child-rearing practices also reflected their unique way of life, and it strongly resembled the daycare system in the United States and Europe today. At the age of two all children went to the nursery. There they were cared for by older women. Schwieder notes that all toys were held in common, and children were instructed to think of others at all times. Mothers, who were not tasked with watching their children, were free to work in the garden, laundry, kitchen, or sewing room. The usage of helpers to raise one's children was an alien practice at the time for all but the wealthy, so this daycare model was revolutionary.

Charles Nordhoff visited the colony while preparing his book *The Communist Societies of the United States.* He spoke positively of Corning's commitment to education and equality among all members. Everyone was free from servitude and promised an education, which was a major priority in the commune. The library in their former colony of Nauvoo had over 4,000 books. This is a paltry number today, but it was quite a collection at the time, especially among laborers and craftsmen. Much of Europe was still mired in rigid class structures, with aristocrats hoarding resources and denying lower classes a formal education. Russia had only liberated its serfs a decade before. America had done the same with its black population, but perpetuated a de facto slavery in the form of emerging institutions such as sharecropping. Universal public schools were not yet common. Equally among all regardless of class status was a promise in the Constitution, but its full application was still a work in progress.

Nevertheless, Nordhoff noted that their living conditions were spartan and dull:

> The living is still of the plainest. In the common dining-hall they assemble in groups at the tables, which were without a cloth, and they drink out of tin cups, and pour their water from tin cans. 'It is very plain,' said one to me; 'but we are independent — no man's servants — and we are content.'"

Over the years, ideological splits developed. They soon threatened to break apart the small community. In the 1870s colonists were split over allowing women the right to vote. Thirty-one colonists opposed the measure; 17 supported it. Those 17 left the community and moved to a new site a mile down the road, naming it New Icaria. The two groups divided up the land and property. The citizens of New Icaria were older members of the original group and found it difficult to continue supporting their community. They could not perform arduous physical labor and had to hire outside help. Nor could they produce children for the next generation of Icarians. This daughter colony disbanded in 1878 due to bankruptcy.

The original community, Old Icaria, limped on until 1895. The younger members believed that their parents had forgotten the ideals of the community and wanted to bring in new members. They also wanted to bring in new businesses, expanding the ideas of the movement beyond its limited reach. Integration with society tempted many to leave altogether, particularly those who had a better handle on English than their French-speaking parents. Some members decided to abandon Iowa for California, but even in their new home the group did not stay together.

Those that remained behind in Iowa disbanded voluntarily, assimilating into nearby communities. Some returned to France, while others stayed near Corning as individual farmers.

ALL THINGS IN COMMON: THE AMANA COLONIES' VISION OF A SHARED SOCIETY

No discussion of utopian societies in Iowa is complete without mentioning the Amana Colonies. Founded by the Inspirationalists, a German dissident movement against the Lutheran Church, the Amanas were a network of seven villages on 26,000 acres in eastern Iowa. The villages were settled by an initial wave of 700. It is perhaps the most successful and longest-lasting experiment in communism in the United States. All the more ironic for its intense focus on Christian piety.

Thousands of settlers lived in the religious community, which was based on peace and prayer. All residents were provided free housing, education, health care, and three large meals daily. Families lived in one of four 15-by-15-foot bedrooms in each home. They worked in common shops, factories, or gardens, and they attended at least 11 church services a week. The all-things-in-common structure lasted from 1855 until 1932. It was only brought to a final end due to fires in the flour and woolen mills and economic hardship from the Great Depression.

The Inspirationalists began in the 1700s as a breakaway movement. They sought to reform their religion and worship in a simpler way than the formal practices of the Lutheran church, much as Martin Luther had done with the Catholic Church. The German government forbade them from purchasing property. The group came to America for land and religious freedom.

They also became socialists there. The Inspirationalist communal movement began in Ebenezer, New York in 1842 on 5,000 acres of land. Christian Metz, the leader, rejected capitalism and national markets, embracing a cooperative economic system. Due to their past problems with the state, Metz believed that the community must separate itself from outsiders or government reliance, becoming completely independent. They desired to build a self-sustaining economic system, a town with its own flour mills, factories, farms, wineries, furniture shops, schools, and saw mills. American currency would be replaced with bartering. Members would dress in plain clothing without differentiation or embellishment.

The movement was initially successful, so successful, in fact, that 5,000 acres was not sufficient for their needs. In 1855, the first members immigrated to eastern Iowa and purchased 30,000 acres of land in Amana. Over the decades they built seven self-sustaining communities. Each adult was required to work in the colonies. Most moved from job to job – men cared for animals, worked in the fields, or toiled in the factories. Women tended the gardens, did the laundry, and worked in the kitchens. Older women looked after the children.

Meals were always held together in the dining hall, taken in groups of 30 to 45. Communal kitchens produced the meals, making the whole affair resemble a university dorm cafeteria, except for conversation being discouraged at the dinner table, as meals were not considered social affairs. Menus were largely standardized to promote equality, but they all consisted of standard German fare: pork sausages, boiled potatoes, streusel, and boiled beef. The practice of communal dining continued until 1900, as the community grew and commitment to communism ebbed. Families began to eat alone, taking food from

43

the communal kitchen to their own homes, which, like the Icarians, they did not own.

HAPPINESS IN THE SPIRIT(S)

Marriage and children were frowned upon and seen as a sign of weakness. Celibacy was celebrated as total commitment to God. Weddings were rather stern affairs where the "happy" couple was reminded of their difficult responsibilities ahead. To even receive permission to marry required the groom to be at least 24. The couple had to wait a year after receiving permission from the council before they could wed. Marrying anyone from outside the colony was grounds for expulsion, even if the outside partner wished to join.

The definition of happiness in the Amana Colonies was based on a peaceful life and being filled with the Spirit of God. Pious living came from avoiding the evils of the outside world, such as anger, impatience, and desire. The colonies adopted twenty-one rules to guide their daily living. Some of these rules are as follows:

I. Study quiet, or serenity, within and without.

V. Abandon self, with all its desires, knowledge and power.

VII. Do not disturb your serenity or peace of mind - hence neither desire nor grieve.

VIII. Live in love toward your neighbor, and indulge neither anger nor impatience in your spirit.

XI. Be honest, sincere, and avoid all deceit and even secretiveness.

XV. Have nothing to do with unholy and particularly with needless business affairs.

XVI. Have no intercourse with worldly-minded men; never seek their society; speak little with them, and never without need; and then without fear and trembling.

XVII. Therefore, what you have to do with such men do in haste; do not waste time in public places and worldly society, that you be not tempted and led away.

XX. Dinners, weddings, feasts, avoid entirely; at the best there is sin.

The last ordinance encouraged moderation. It worked – feasting and merry-making was as rare as Haley's Comet in the Amanas – but it also made for dull living. Not that there was much else to do in the villages outside of work. Everybody labored long hours. Men and women arrived back at their homes exhausted each night from chopping the wood, plowing fields, fixing machines, or cooking for three dozen. Even children in the Amana Colonies were kept incessantly busy. Children attended school six days a week, year-round. The program continued until the age of 14, when boys took a job on the farm or began their craft apprenticeships. Such professions included tailoring, blacksmithing, and shoemaking, printing, milling, or wool-weaving. Girls worked in the gardens or communal kitchens.

Not to say that there weren't ways for the colonists to enjoy themselves. As Germans they could not say no to a good drink, no matter their level of piety. The colonies once featured five breweries, until they were closed in 1884 due to Iowa prohibition laws. Colonists reopened the Millstream Brewery after national Prohibition ended in 1933. It remained Iowa's only brewery well into the 1990s.

With beer out of the picture, wine production remained a popular activity in the late 1800s among the Amanas, who were largely immunized from the Temperance movement. Most homes featured grapevines on trellises along the sides of the four-square brick houses. Popular varieties included wines made from dandelion, blueberry, cranberry, raspberry, plum, and local grapes. Wine was piped directly from presses to church cellars.

Each resident had enough wine to drown a horse. Men received 20 gallons of wine annually, and women 12 gallons, working out to 120 wine bottles per family per annum. That is not to say the Amanas were a colony of alcoholic pietists. They obeyed Prohibition when it became national law in 1920. Residents dumped 19,000 gallons at once into the Iowa River and according to legend, the fish had hangovers for a week.

The success of the Amana colonies would have pleased any communist. Nobody received any wages for their labor. Profits were spread among the community. The only leadership was a board of trustees. Property was recognized legally as collective, and each family received the same wage. Individuals were given $25 to $50 each year. This money was spent at village stores. Mismanagement of funds was grounds for expulsion from the community.

When labor shortages occurred, hundreds of hired laborers were brought on from surrounding communities during the agricultural season. Due to the productivity and efficiency in their endeavors, the colonies became financial successes. They were even contracted for mechanical work when the first refrigerator was invented in Iowa City. The refrigeration company "Amana," which is now a subsidy of Whirlpool, was formed when the company hired their craftsmen.

"The motto was 'Alles muss Genaues sein' – everything must be exact," explained Barbara Hoehnle, librarian for the Amana Heritage Society. Amanans were systematized, hard working, and organized. They built their goods to exact specifications. Houses were also designed with the same table, clock, bureau, and rocker. They were so similar that anyone could go into any house blindfolded and find his way around.

Of course, no communal society could completely be an island unto itself. Interaction with the larger American public was necessary, even if the colony bylaws threatened expulsion if a member cavorted too much with Americans. In order to deal with the outside world, Amana set up controlled entry points for trade. Each village had an exchange center where all goods were purchased. Raw materials and manufactured goods such as grease, raw wool, oil, pipes, and fittings came in; manufactured goods, handicrafts, and simple machinery went out.

Despite the Amana aversion to worldliness, the colonies were known for their hospitality. Any homeless person or traveler passing through on train could be temporarily taken in by the colony and fed. They could work for wages and would be provided with shelter for the length of their stay. These workers supplemented the seasonal help hired each year to do agricultural and industrial jobs. The colonies were likely an important stop on the national hobo railway circuit.

In spite of its successes, not even the Amana Colonies could escape the national demise of utopian communities in the 19th and 20th centuries. All other communities had died out decades ago or assimilated into wider society to avoid total ruin. The Amana Colonies did this in 1933, when they abandoned cooperative living. The Great Depression wreaked havoc on the colonies, which were not able to earn the minimum revenue necessary to house, feed, and clothe its members. Residents voted to abandon communal life in 1932 and reorganize the colony based on the principals of capitalism. Each member received stock in the new community corporation. Dollars came into the colony the next year.

The failure of the Amana Colonies raises many questions. Is communal living ultimately destined for failure? Were the pious colonists hopelessly behind the times? Could they have done anything to save their community from falling apart and forcibly integrating into American society? These questions are more difficult to answer than they appear. Lanny Haldy, executive director of the Amana Heritage Society, said in a 1993 interview with The Seattle Times that the colonists were both backwards and forward-thinking.

"They were taking the Chicago Tribune and Scientific American - they were very much in contact with the outside world. They had telephones 10 years after the outside world did. They sent students to college to become doctors in the 1860s. The colonies lasted for three generations - it's remarkable they lasted as long as they did."

But as time passed, Haldy noted, many of the young people were no longer committed to pietist socialism. And it was harder to live differently than the rest of the world in 1932 than it was in 1882. Radio programs, roads, the automobile, global war mobilization efforts, and higher population densities made the outside world more intrusive than ever.

Not that the colonies passed without their mourners. Elsie Caspers, a former clerk at the Ehrle Brothers Winery who was born in 1933, said the changes bothered her grandparents, who missed the old way of life.

"There was camaraderie, but hard work too," she said. "The women had to get up so early to go to the kitchens."

The descendents of the Amana colonists still live in the villages.

They still go to church and practice a 21st-century version of the trades that their great-grandparents did. Many residents still speak High German and a dialect known as Amana German. But meals aren't held in dining halls anymore and nobody threatens excommunication for talking with outsiders. Amanans couldn't avoid outsiders if they wanted to – the colonies get over a million outsiders in the form of tourists each year, who visit the independent shops, crafts stores, and family-style restaurants.

There are those who keep the original dream of the German Inspirationalists alive. Some argue that the colonies didn't even fail. The end goal of the Society of True Inspiration was never communal living – this was merely a means to an end to their true goal of faith, piety, and a simple expression of worship. The committee members voted to embrace capitalism in the 1930s because they believed incorporation with society was a better means of achieving this goal than communal living, which had outlived its purpose. Many of the current residents of the Amana colonies, who still make church and piety the centerpiece of their lives, would agree.

A MUSLIM FREEDOM FIGHTER'S NEW HOME IN IOWA

It wasn't just European immigrants who made Iowa's culture interesting in the 19th century. Iowa was home to one of the earliest Arab immigrant communities anywhere in the United States. In the 1880s and 1890s Christian Arabs first arrived, mostly from Syria. Arab Christians arrived before Muslims because they were more connected to Western culture, and there was no religious gap between themselves and their new neighbors. The first arrivals were Tom Bashara, a Syrian from Damascus, and the Lebanese brothers Charles and Sam Kacere.

It is not clear why they chose Iowa, but the most likely reason was agriculture. Another reason is that they likely met Iowans when they still lived in the Middle East. If a Syrian Christian were considering a move to America, he would ask the nearest American where to move. This would almost definitely be an American missionary. American missionaries traveled to the Middle East by the thousands in the 19th century. There they built hundreds of schools, hospitals, and orphanages in Lebanon, Syria, Egypt, and Anatolia. And many of these missionaries were from Iowa. They couldn't help but recommend their home state to an America-bound Arab.

Muslims came to Iowa shortly after Arab Christians. In 1888, Haji Abbas Habnab emigrated from the Ottoman Empire and settled in Fort Dodge. His reasons for choosing Iowa are unknown, but his three brothers Musa, Yusef, and Ali joined him over the next seven years. They and other immigrants spread out from northwest Iowa into Sioux City and Sioux Falls, South Dakota.

The new Muslim arrivals received support from the Arab Christian community. Sam Bashar, a Syrian from the same region, had established a general store warehouse and supplied the newly-arriving men. Others began to trickle into the state upon hearing that a Muslim community existed there. In 1907, Haji Yahya William Aossey heard about Bashar while on a ship outbound from Brazil. An American he befriended on the ship said that he had come across Arabs in Iowa. Aossey arrived at the port in New York then boarded the first train for the Midwest. He got off in Iowa and met the Christian Arab brothers, who welcomed him warmly.

Aossey began his new life in Iowa. He first worked as a peddler, selling small goods across the state. He walked nine or ten miles a day, spent nights in barns, churches, schools, and the occasional farmer's home. Aossey eventually married one of Abbas Habhab's daughters and settled in Cedar Rapids.

From the early 1900s to the 1920s, Cedar Rapids became the home base for these young Syrian merchants. According to Saudi Aramco they formed the first and oldest Muslim community in the United States. By the 1920s there were several dozen Muslim and Christian Syrian-Lebanese communities in Iowa. Most Iowans failed to distinguish Arabs according to their religion. They tended to lump them together as "the Syrian peddlers." Religious distinction became sharper after 1914, when Arab Christians completed the St. George Syrian Orthodox Church in Cedar Rapids. The Ottoman Empire also joined the Axis Powers in World War I, and to some residents any Middle Easterner was an enemy Turk. In one instance Aossey was chased away at gunpoint when he revealed his religion to a farmer whose dinner he had been sharing.

The Cedar Rapids Muslim community continued to expand. Some converted a rented hall into a mosque. In 1934, they built a permanent structure and called it the Mother Mosque of America, which is still in use and is America's oldest mosque in continuous usage. The original building bore no resemblance to a typical domed mosque. The members did much of the work themselves and drew upon the architecture style of Iowa. The building could be mistaken for a prairie-country schoolhouse or even a local church due to its white clapboard exterior and stark lines. The only adornment to distinguish the building as a mosque was a small dome sitting atop the protruding entrance with a crescent-topped spire. Signs in English and Arabic welcomed visitors.

In 1948, Yahya William Aossey donated 12 acres of land in Cedar Rapids to establish the First National Muslim Cemetery in North America. In 1971, a new Islamic Center was built in Cedar Rapids. The original building is now on the National List of Historic Buildings. Governor Terry Branstad recognized this heritage. He instituted Muslim Recognition Day in 1992.

One famous Iowan Muslim was Abdallah Igram, a World War II Army veteran who had the chance to meet President Dwight D. Eisenhower in 1953. He asked the president a novel question – why didn't the military recognize the religion of American Muslims as they did Protestants, Catholics, and Jews? Why was there no symbol for Islam on a Muslim soldier's dog tags so he could be given appropriate burial rights if he was killed in action? Good question, Ike answered. The president, at Igram's urging, pushed to have the symbol "I" stamped on the ID tags of Muslim soldiers.

It is strange to imagine Muslims coming to Iowa in the 1890s, settling in the midst of cornfields, which looked nothing like the arid landscape of their homes in the Middle East. But in one sense they might feel like they were getting a warm reception. Two counties over from Cedar Rapids there was a little town with the name of Elkader. They soon realized, to their delight and astonishment, that this spelling was an English transliteration of *el-Kadir*, an Algerian religious scholar, Sufi, and guerrilla leader who fought against the French colonial invasion of the mid-19th century.

How did a town in Iowa become named after a Muslim militant?

The story is strange, but it originally came as a tribute to the fighter. In 1845, when land developer Timothy Davis prospected a site along the Turkey River for a flour mill and settlement, he looked for a name of the town that would convey its future values. Davis wanted to name the city after a nationalist patriot across the ocean. It was a common practice in Iowa – Kossuth County was named after Lajos Kossuth, the president of Hungary after the 1848 revolution. Davis ultimately settled on Abd el-Kadir after reading about his fight against the French in American press accounts. He thought of him as a "valiant Arab chieftain."

Many other Americans thought the same. Because Abd el-Kadir saved the lives of 12,000 Christians during the Damascus uprisings in the 1860s, Abraham Lincoln sent him a special commendation and a gift of Colt pistols. Napoleon III, Pope Pius IV, and Queen Victoria showered him with praise as a humanitarian statesman. When Abd el-Kadir died in 1883, a New York Times obituary praised him as "one of the few great men of the century."

The memory of Abd el-Kadir lived on in the town for a few decades after its founding . A local college named its student newspaper "The Arab Chieftain." He was then forgotten for nearly a century. Today Elkader is a small town of 1,200 nestled in the Turkey River valley. Its inhabitants are mostly of German and Scandinavian background. It is quaint beyond belief, lacking a single traffic light. It is known mostly for its sandstone arch bridge over the Turkey River and having America's oldest grocery store west of the Mississippi.

El-Kadir would have likely remained forgotten if not for an Algerian liason at the American Embassy who discovered the town in the 1980s. The liason, Benaoumer Zergaoui, established a sister city relationship between Elkader and Mascara, Algeria – the birthplace of the emir. For the last six years it has welcomed a delegation of Arab dignitaries that celebrate this connection between the United States and the Islamic world.

"Our audience is the people who are compassionate already," said Kathy Garms to The New York Times in 2013. She is the driving force behind the Abdelkader project, a movement to restore the historical memory of El-Kadir. "But there are so many people who are ignorant or scared or even hateful. We just hope that once they get across the starting line they will listen."

Ties continue to strengthen in this unlikely alliance between Iowa and Algeria. In 2008, Garms visited Algeria, talked with government leaders, and visited el-Kadir's grave. When the Turkey River flooded two weeks later, destroying thirty homes and causing $8 million in property damage, she learned that the Algerian government was interested in sending money for disaster relief. She expected a few thousand dollars. The amount turned out to be $150,000. Today, there are matched sets of poles with the word "peace" in French, Arabic, and English that stand in Mascara and Elkader.

There's even a restaurant that serves Algerian food. Schera's Algerian American Restaurant is run by the town's only Muslim, Frederique Boudouani. In an even more unlikely twist, he is an openly gay man who runs the restaurant with his partner, a native Iowan. The two have been largely accepted into the community and the restaurant has its regulars, even if many locals politely decline to come.

Boudouani said that he feels as though he has become a member of the community. Although some locals still treat him as the official spokesman for Islam in the event of terrorist attacks.

"If there's a bomb in a nightclub in Bali people come and feel compelled to ask me why did that happen, can you explain it to us. I turn into this sort of weird spokesman for the whole faith," he said to PRI.

The town of Elkader is a testimony to Iowa's multiculturalism, even if Iowa is not considered diverse according to the calculus of 21st-century American racial politics. Admittedly it does not have as large a heterogeneous population of black, Latino, and Asian residents as Texas or California. Despite this, Iowa still has many multicultural feathers to put it in its cap. Like the utopian communities of the 19th century, it is still a place where people come in groups to start a new life. Here they conduct experiments in social living with the hopes that they can improve the world by changing it on the local level. Others – like the Transcendental Meditation movement – strive to go one step further and change the world on a quantum level.

SILICORN VALLEY: FAIRFIELD AND THE TRANSCENDENTAL BUSINESS BOOM

In the 1970s the Transcendental Meditation movement decided to make a new home for itself in Fairfield. It is in many respects a normal Iowa town, with a population of slightly over 10,000, rolling farmlands, and a quaint town square with characteristic Midwestern brick buildings. Here there are small diners where corn and cattle farmers breakfast, discussing the futures market, and complain about the city manager. Fairfield remained quiet and predictable for much of the 20th century.

All that changed in 1974, when the Maharishi Mahesh Yogi, an international celebrity who popularized meditation in America, directed his followers to move from their headquarters in California and make a mass exodus to Iowa. They relocated to Fairfield and began to build their organization. It is now a $300 million-dollar empire.

The Maharishi taught millions of people his meditation techniques during a set of world tours from 1958 to 1965. According to his teachings, through meditation a person could enter his own consciousness and join with other invisible fields in the universe to improve one's life. His technique consists of closing one's eyes for 20 minutes while repeating a mantra to create deep relaxation, attain clear thinking, and eliminate stress. His technical presentations of meditation became popular among celebrities, including the Beatles, Clint Eastwood, and Mia Farrow. Among his disciples were Deepak Chopra, who has taken his teacher's business approach and built his own multimillion-dollar network.

The yogi parlayed that fame into a heavily endowed worldwide network of Transcendental Meditation (TM) centers to promote unorthodox views of medicine, science, politics, and economics. He founded the Maharishi International University (MIU) in 1971 in Goleta, California. At this time his popular influence was at its height. Famous musicians and actors consulted him. He was honorarily dubbed one of the "fifth Beatles" after the band began studying with the Maharishi at his Himalayan retreat in northern India. His techniques gained respect in the medical world for reducing stress-related ailments. The school thrived in the West Coast.

But directors of the university decided to move it to Iowa anyway. This decision was based on two reasons. First, they believed in the Maharishi Effect, a theory that if a significant number of people practice TM at they same time, they could affect their natural and spiritual environment. Enough people practicing at the same time and the same place would be greater than the sum of its parts and increase "life-supporting trends." These positive unity force fields could reduce the world's crime rate, ease global tensions, raise the stock market, and even reduce traffic accidents. According to the Maharishi, using a complex array of charts, graphs and barely intelligible mathematical formulas, all of the world's problems could disappear if only 7,000 people would meditate together daily. Group leaders realized that thousands of meditators practicing in the geographical center of America could send out positive energy like a radio transmitter to the four corners of the nation. Iowa was perfectly located.

The second reason was simple economics. MIU was able to purchase Fairfield's bankrupt Parsons College – dubbed "Flunkout U" by one publication – at the fire sale price of $2.5 million. MIU was established with the philosophy of Transcendental Meditation in mind. Its principle was to develop the "full potential of the individual, realize the highest ideal of education, improve government achievements, solve the age-old problem of crime and all behavior that brings unhappiness to the world, bring fulfillment to the economic aspirations of individuals and society, maximize the intelligent use of the environment, and achieve the spiritual goals of humanity in this generation."

The new college kept up a high profile in popular culture. In 1978 the Beach Boys, which had embraced the spiritual elements of the Baby Boomer generation, recorded their album *M.I.U.*, named after the university, on campus. Andy Kaufman, the eccentric actor, was a dedicated practitioner of Transcendental Meditation. One scene of his biopic *Man on the Moon* takes place at the school, where he is asked to leave because his public image and private behavior did not match that of an enlightened person. The university awarded Jim Carrey, who played Kaufman in the film, with an honorary Ph.D. in 2014 due to the actor's own interest in meditation.

The integration of an eastern spiritualist movement with a quaint farm town has had its bumps. At first the locals merely stared at the West Coast transplants walking down the street. They did more than stare when the group hosted the Maharishi Mahesh Yogi in 1984. Over 7,000 followers descended on the town. In order to accommodate all the visitors, MIU erected two major buildings and brought 200 mobile homes from Indiana in the short span of the Christmas and New Year holidays. The university ordered 8,000 blankets, 1,200 cots, and a trailer-load of pasta for the festival.

Some residents disliked the more outlandish claims from the TM practitioners. M.I.U. administrators stated that due to the massive assemblage of meditators at the conference, hospital admissions had fallen, U.S. relations with other nations were improving, and the stock market was rising. Other residents were less optimistic of the meditative effects: "A lot of people just wish these wackos would go home," said Charles Barnett, then-member of the Chamber of Commerce.

Further friction points came when Mayor Robert Rasmussen received a call from the Federal Aviation Administration. The Maharishi had put in a request to close down the town's tiny municipal airport for a week to have a laser light display of the Maharishi's bearded image on the clouds over the whole town. It was more than the mayor, who earned an honorary $300-a-month salary, could handle.

"Why me? Why here? Why now?" he asked in exasperation.

A few years later over 5,000 devotees descended on Fairfield for the "Heaven on Earth" assembly. After meditating en masse twice a day, attendees claimed that international tensions had eased and an upsurge of positivity and progress in world consciousness.

"Did you see the paper today?" asked Patty Schneider, public affairs director of M.I.U., who described to The Los Angeles Times the real-world effects of their meditation. "In East Germany they apologized to Jews for the Holocaust and a couple of days ago those hostages were released in the Mideast. You can't tell me this stuff doesn't work."

The town and its new arrivals have been able to smooth relations over the years. A large part has to do with the economic shot in the arm that the new arrivals have brought to Fairfield. Major Maharishi festivals and events meant hundreds of thousands of dollars flowing into the local economy. Some events attract thousands, requiring several temporary structures to be built in a short amount of time. Local construction companies and sub contractors get weeks, or even months, of overtime pay. Fairfield also has an airport for corporate jets and a new 522-seat Stephen Sondheim Center for the Performing Arts.

The Maharishi have developed Fairfield's economy in other ways. Thanks to the university's business school, the town has attracted entrepreneurs from around the United States. Some of the startups springing from these cornfields of Southeastern Iowa have become multi-million dollar businesses. Fairfield has been called one of the state's economic superstars and received multiple entrepreneurship awards. Oprah Winfrey visited here in 2012 to produce an episode of her TV show *Oprah's Next Chapter* on Fairfield's meditators. In honor of the more than 40 software development and telecom companies, locals call their town "Silicorn Valley."

Many of the Maharishi believers already had business experience when they came to Iowa from the coasts. One of them, according to a 1998 New York Times profile of the town, was Cliff Rees, the co-owner of an oil company, who came to Fairfield in 1985. He launched the telecommunications company Telegroup. It became the 13th largest telecommunications company in the United States in the late 90s, with revenue of $337 million and more than 600 employees.

Rees credited meditation for his business success. Sitting cross-legged in his office, he said it was "a great business tool that clears my mind and allows me to focus on detail." Some locals would point out that Fairfield already had a business legacy that predated the arrival of Maharishi University. But once the groundwork was laid, it was easier for their new companies to develop, creating a ripple effect of new business creation.

VEDIC CITY

The most visible mark that the TM movement has left on Iowa is the Maharishi Vedic City, a square-mile-sized town of 259 designed with Vedic architecture, located just outside of Fairfield. Disciples incorporated the town in 2001. Designers hope for the population to swell to 10,000 as word spreads of the town's symmetry and harmony.

Maharishi Vedic City is the new North American capital of the Global County of World Peace. Its ancient Indian system of city planning and architecture is said to promote happiness and peace. All buildings are designed according to precise Vedic proportions. Rooms are placed according to the movement of the sun. All buildings face east, have a central "quiet space," and are topped with a golden dollop called a *kalash*. Building houses to such a specific code is expensive due to consulting fees from designers with a highly specialized body of knowledge. Prices run from $200,000 to $800,000, a princely sum for a small-town midwestern house.

The town features an outdoor observatory with ten, 6-foot-tall, white, concrete-and-marble astronomical instruments. Its designer claims that each is perfectly aligned with the sun, moon, and stars, and can calculate their movements in order to create tranquility and physiological balance.

That is not to say that perfect social harmony has been reached among all members of the community. Along with its non-permanent residents are 1,000 Indian pandits – a Hindu scholar and a teacher – who have come to the United States on a religious visa program. The program does not lack controversy, as many of the pandits have "disappeared" in the past, presumably to work illegally in the United States. Further controversy erupted in March 2014 when the Jefferson County sheriff was called in to investigate a protest over the deportation of a popular pandit. The sheriff arrived at the compound only to have his car damaged after being mobbed by 60-70 pandits.

Nevertheless, the city has mostly lived up to its ideals. Since 2002 the city council passed an ordinance that banned the sale of non-organic food within its borders and the use of synthetic pesticides. In 2005, it became the first all-organic city in the United States. Vedic City's organic grocer looks like it belongs in a college town or a hipster portion of Brooklyn – except for its bulletin board advertising guru services. The city has received federal grants to develop renewable energy sources and recycling programs. The city's 160-acre organic farm runs on wind turbine energy, which was developed from a federal renewable energy grant. It sells 50 varieties of fruit and vegetables produce to restaurants in Iowa City, Des Moines, and Chicago, and retailer outlets such as Whole Foods.

The color pink dominates the town. Citizens wear it. Rooms and buildings are painted with it. Even the private plane that first spirited the Maharishi Mahesh Yogi to Iowa in 1971 was done up in it. The name of the town's trailer park is Utopia Park, located near Taste of Utopia and Heaven streets.

The aesthetic of an Indian-style city in the Midwest is still jarring. Some critics have said that it transplants an eastern architectural style into the heartland without bothering to incorporate local elements, like a strip mall in an open field. Immediately outside of the town is a landscape dotted with cornfields, red barns, and small farm houses. Such a move comes across to some observers as brash. Carina Chocano, a reporter for the Los Angeles Times, came to the city in 2006 for a profile. She said it "displays all the architectural characteristics of a new exurban development: gaudy, over sized construction that has no stylistic relation to the environment but instead vaguely alludes to a theme-park version someplace sort of magical and far away."

Ironically, the spread of meditation across the United States since the 1950s might be the undoing of Fairfield's unique culture. Practitioners of TM came to Iowa as part of a utopian movement, but meditation has been absorbing into mainstream culture ever since. It also does not help that much of the leadership is still from the Baby Boomer generation, most of whom are well into their 60s or older. Young blood continues to course through the university, but college-age members of the TM movement do not consider it as revolutionary as their parents. Americans have practiced yoga and meditation for decades; millions do it without signing up to the Maharishi Mahesh Yogi's brand of philosophy.

To some, the TM movement's relentless talk of positive energy permeating the conscious has devolved into an infomercial pitch like a commercial for a Snuggie or Showtime Rotisserie. Chocano notes this irony – this Eastern utopia may have been an alternative lifestyle 40 years ago, but now it is just another marketable lifestyle product. It is an "entropic mix of spirituality and materialism; self-betterment and self-absorption as a cure for all of humanity's ills; consciousness-expansion as a way to building wealth and saving the world. For the not-so-low price of $2,500 [for a three-day meditation seminar] you're offered inner peace, world peace, reduced blood pressure and the sense of yourself as a maverick pioneer, a 'cultural creative.'"

All this proves, she writes, is that the early 21st century may be looked back upon as a time when it was made clear that money, good PR, and an honest banality have the power to normalize anything. Constantly quoting a study from the National Institute of Health or findings in prestigious medical journals on the powers of the meditative effect only resulted in severe scientific proof fatigue.

The story of new arrivals to Iowa in the 20th century is not only that of the Maharishi. In the late 20th century, new waves of immigrants came to the state, primarily in the form of refugees. In the 1970s, turmoil in Southeast Asia led to the emigration of the Tai Dam. They are an itinerant people that once lived in China, then North Vietnam, then in Laos. When communists captured their new home, they fled to Thailand for fear of their property being confiscated. From Thailand, some came to Iowa. Dorothy Schwieder writes in *Iowa Past to Present: The People and the Prairie* that like earlier groups of immigrants, the Tai Dam families have brought along their crafts and culture. At different events in Des Moines they presented native dances and prepared special food.

Other groups of recent immigrants escaping war-torn countries include Bosnians and Sudanese. Bosnians began to arrive in the mid-90s, with the outbreak of war in the Balkans and the Serbian ethnic cleansing of Muslims. More than ten thousand Bosnians lived in the state by 2001, with at least six thousand living in Des Moines. They have opened restaurants, food stores, and coffee bars in the capital and Waterloo. Sudanese refugees arrived at the same time, also due to a civil war between the largely Muslim north and the Christian south.

But the story of Fairfield and its transcendental meditation is still unique. The Maharishi Mahesh Yogi founded MIU based on his wide appeal and fame as the Beatles' onetime spiritual leader. He may be dead, but his movement, his university, and its Golden Domes of Pure Knowledge still remain. So does the dream of coming to Iowa and launching a global ideological revolution.

POSTVILLE: WHERE THE MIDWEST MEETS ULTRA-ORTHODOX JUDAISM MEETS RURAL MEXICO MEETS SOMALIA

Postville is a town of 2,227 tucked in the northeast corner of Iowa. The county hugs the Mississippi River and features topography found in few other parts of the state. The high stone bluffs, abundant creeks, and deep valleys owe to the last Ice Age not flattening this part of the land. For this reason some affectionately refer to the area as the land the glaciers forgot.

Everything changed in 1987. The town was still reeling from the Midwest Farm Crisis, when land values dropped by one-third, thousands of farmers were forced into bankruptcy, and soaring interest rates crippled everyone else. In this year Aaron Rubashkin, a Hasidic butcher from Brooklyn who was born in Russia, purchased an unused meat-rendering plant in Postville. He transformed it into a state-of-the-art center for producing glatt kosher meat, which must be prepared under strict conditions to meet orthodox Jewish dietary standards. He moved to Iowa to take advantage of the proximity to livestock and the lack of unionization in the Midwest. The economic investment put a new lease on life for the struggling town. His company Agriprocessors was born.

Rubashkin's purchase was not remarkable in itself. What was remarkable were the hundreds of Hasidim who moved with him to Postville to help manage and operate the facility. They arrived wearing their traditional garb and practicing their customs. Groups of bearded men walked down the street in full black dress, with tassels hanging from their shirts and *shtreimel*s, large hockey-puck-shaped fur hats, on their heads. Such garb would barely raise an eyebrow in New York. It could cause a car crash in rural Iowa.

Over 100 Hasidic families moved to Postville. They opened schools for their children and a synagogue. As their numbers increased, business at Agriprocessors grew. The slaughterhouse became the largest owned and operated by the Lubavitchers in the world. By 1996, it processed 13,000 cattle, 225,000 chickens, 700 lambs, and 4,000 turkeys a week. The plant shipped kosher meat all over the United

States and even to Jerusalem. Postville now had the highest concentration of rabbis of any American city.

Author Stephen Bloom chronicles the challenges of inter-communal harmony in his book *Postville: A Clash of Cultures in Heartland America*. Hasidic Brooklyn and rural Iowa could hardly be more culturally different. The mutual suspicion of the Hasidim and the locals, most of them of Lutheran background, was hardly to be avoided: "Clearly there was a culture clash of the strongest magnitude between two groups, both born-and-bred Americans, who rarely had the opportunity to clash. Here was a kind of experiment in the limits of diversity and community, the nature of community, the meaning of prejudice, even what it means to be an American. Postville seemed like a social laboratory, perhaps a metaphor for America."

Bloom found that both communities were insular and suspicious of strangers. He wondered whether the Iowans were prejudiced or the Lubavitchers simply unbearable. Bloom ultimately sided with the local Iowans as being more open and friendly. They recognized that Postville might have fallen into ruin if not for the financial injection that the Jewish manufacturers brought to the town. They opened the community to the newcomers. Bloom, a secular Jew who taught at the University of Iowa, attacked the Hasidim for their "closed-off" nature and suspicious attitude towards all non-Jews. He criticized them for maintaining their Jewish Eastern European culture regardless of the society around them. Even in their piety they had an ulterior motive. In one scene Bloom described them visiting a dying man and praying for his soul, perhaps with an intrusive missionary intention.

The Lubavitchers, he writes, were not interested in mingling with the locals. They considered the quaint Lutherans as fundamentally inferior and treated them in rude ways. They inhabited a Manichean worldview, where total good is in conflict with total evil. The New York butchers haggled with local merchants, which is not a custom of rural Iowa culture. They took any personal disagreement or opposition as a form of anti-Semitism. Over time, conflict grew between the two groups.

"Ultimately, I discovered, carrying on a conversation with any of the Postville Hasidim was virtually impossible. If you didn't agree, you were at fault, part of the problem. You were paving the way for the ultimate destruction of the Jews, the world's Chosen People. There was no room for compromise, no room for negotiation, no room for anything but total and complete submission."

Bloom narrated the conflict as a showdown, but relations between the locals and the Hasidim were never this tense. They couldn't be – Postville has had to accommodate other groups besides the Orthodox Jews in recent years and approach a flexible mindset to foreign cultures. Many came to work on the slaughterhouse's floor. Russians and Ukrainians first worked at Agriprocessors when it opened. Over time, Mexicans and Guatemalans moved to the town to take up jobs. By the 1990s Postville was split largely into three cultural clusters: Central American, Hasidic Jewish, and Midwestern. The town, in addition to its Methodist churches, now had a synagogue and Catholic churches with services in Spanish.

But the Latin American men were different than the Hasidic arrivals. The Hasidim came in family units. Even though their lifestyle was different, they found a place within the rural, family-centered Midwestern social fabric. The Latino newcomers, in contrast, were largely single men, causing locals to worry that crime would follow them. It didn't, and the single men returned home and brought wives with them. Many now lived as families, but marriage did little to integrate the Latino community into Postville. They did not rely on public assistance, social programs or the Family Investment Program. Their independence prevented a strain on social services, but it isolated the Latino arrivals from the larger culture.

Most of the immigrants did not plan on staying in Iowa indefinitely. In the meatpacking world, if a better job offer comes along, a worker will take it, even if it involves moving to another state to earn a dollar or two more an hour. Others returned to their homeland after earning enough money. Even for those few who planned to reside long-term, family life came first in the Hispanic households, before jobs or community. This view made for stable family units, but also led to self-segregation.

Over time community members fell into a pattern. Different groups found a way to co-exist, even if they did not freely mingle. A 2012 account from the New York Times described the public schools' K-12 bilingual program as integrating immigrant children into Iowan culture. A Mexican restaurant and grocery store appeared on the main street, along with a Guatemalan restaurant. Workers dropped by these stores to wire money back home and purchase Spanish-language DVDs. In 2005, a Guatemalan factory worker took over the local bakery and transformed it to a place where farmers could sip coffee while Latinos could purchase *pan dulce* and tostadas. Aaron Goldsmith, an Orthodox Jew, even won a seat on the city council.

THE POSTVILLE RAID

Postville's holding pattern collapsed on May 12, 2008. The Department of Homeland Security raided Agriprocessors. Nearly 400 immigrant workers were arrested, the largest single raid of a workplace in U.S. history. The move was made to pressure companies with an illegal workforce and make an example out of Agriprocessors. The plant had already been under investigation since 2006 for complaints of workplace safety issues, unsanitary conditions, and violations of workers' rights. The meatpacking industry is dangerous even in the best of times and often draws desperate immigrants willing to work long hours where mistakes on the line lead to injury. But Agriprocessors failed to meet even this low standard. Workplace accidents led to broken bones, hearing loss, and even mishaps resulting in amputations. No compensation came to these illegal workers since they had no contractual rights.

Foreign workers were ultimately charged with document fraud, identity theft, and the use of stolen Social Security numbers – the first time that government officials used felony charges to prosecute workers instead of immigration law. Over 300 workers were convicted of document fraud within four days. Many served a five-month prison sentence before being deported. The owner, Aaron Rubashkin, escaped charges, but the plant's chief executive, Sholom Rubashkin, was convicted of bank fraud and sentenced to 27 years in prison.

David Strudhoff, the superintendent of Postville's schools, said to the Washington Post that the sudden incarceration of more than 10 percent of the town's population of 2,300 was "like a natural disaster – only this one is manmade."

The raid sent tremors through the town. The next day, half of the schools' 600 students were absent, nearly all of them Hispanic, because their parents had been arrested or were hiding. Businesses saw a drop in revenue by at least 50 percent. The Mexican grocery store closed down, along with the Guatemalan restaurant. Tax revenues for the town took a steep dive. A small number of arrested workers that were allowed to stay in Postville after being processed had to wear ankle bracelets while awaiting trial.

Agriprocessors quickly scooped up replacement workers wherever they could find them. Other immigrants or residents of homeless shelters and treatment facilities took their place on the factory line. Groups came and went, whether a Native American contingent from Nebraska or students from Kyrgyzstan. Ads even appeared in newspapers and on telephone poles in Guatemala City that advertised meatpacking jobs for $8.50 an hour in Postville, "a technologically developed town with a friendly atmosphere, pretty green areas, public schools and family recreation areas."

The Postville raid has led to a new multicultural chapter in the town's story. Mark Grey, an anthropology professor at the University of Northern Iowa, said that government raids on meatpacking plants in the Midwest has resulted in them steering away from hiring Latinos. They fear government scrutiny. So they instead recruit African and Burmese refugees and other non-Latino immigrants. The workforce for a Midwestern plant in a small Iowan town is even more ethnically diverse, even if they are hired legally.

Shortly after the raid, Agriprocessors recruited 170 people from the Pacific island of Palau. They traveled 8,000 miles on plane and buses, adorned with flip-flops and brightly colored clothes. In 2008, Agriprocessors even recruited Somali refugees from Minnesota to work at the plant. They were promised a hiring bonus and a month of free housing. These Somali Muslim workers form the backbone of the plant today. Many leave Postville on Saturday – when the plant is closed due to the Jewish Sabbath – and travel to Minneapolis. There they enjoy the company of the city's large Somali population, purchase halal meat butchered to an Islamic standard, and buy Somali tea.

Oddly enough, some local residents felt more kinship with the illegal Latino groups of 10-20 years ago than the new African workers today.

"People can scream about the illegal work force, but a legal work force will also be more ethnically diverse," he said. "In these towns, I have people whispering in my ear, 'I miss my illegal Mexicans.' "

Postville is in a perpetual state of cultural adjustment. Its historical population of white Lutherans has been forced to accommodate different races, religions, and languages. But its story – along with other stories of Iowa's immigration history, whether German pietists, French utopianists, transcendental meditators, Muslim traders, or Somali meatpackers – speak of an untold diversity in Iowa's history. While the state may not win diversity awards anytime soon, it has far more multicultural merits than most suspect.

Each ethnic group has contributed something to Iowa, continually altering its identity and leaving a mark on its cultural tapestry.

CHAPTER THREE

HOW IOWA SAVED BILLIONS OF LIVES IN THE 20TH CENTURY BY AVERTING A GLOBAL FAMINE

Norman Borlaug had only recently arrived in Mexico, but he had already lost his temper. A local bureaucrat argued with Borlaug about his intention to go out into wheat fields himself to conduct crop research and show farmers how to cultivate stronger strands of wheat.

"Dr. Borlaug," the official said, "we don't do these things in Mexico. That's why we have peons. All you've got to do is draw up the plans and take them to the foreman and let them do it."

The tall, scrawny Iowan had had it. He came to Mexico in 1942 to launch an attack on hunger. The country already imported half of its wheat, its second most-important food source, at a cost of $21 million per year. Per-acre yields were half of those in the U.S. And whole harvests could be wiped out from wheat rust.

If solutions couldn't be implemented soon, starvation would set in. Borlaug wasn't about to let a pompous official stop him.

"That's why the farmers disrespect you!" he shot back. "If you don't know how to do something yourself, how can you possibly advise them? If the peons give you false information, you wouldn't even know. No, this has to change. Until we master our own efforts, we will go nowhere with this project."

Thanks to his brute determination, Borlaug did go somewhere with the project. He spent the next two decades in the fields of Mexico under the burning sun. Clothed in his checkered shirt, brown pants, and work boots, he spent his days coated with dust as he laboriously analyzed wheat samples.

Billy Woodward recounts Borlaug's remarkable stamina and ability to conduct monotonous research over enormous stretches of time in *The Biggest Lifesavers of the Twentieth Century*. In one hand Borlaug held a pair of needle-nosed tweezers. The other calloused hand encircled a head of wheat containing the tiny fleck of grain. With surgeon-like precision he plucked each tiny starmen – the male part of the plant – from the flower. He then slid a small glassine envelope over the wheat head, folding over the top and sealing it with a paper clip. He returned to the same plant five days later, removed the paper clip, and slipped in the starmen of another type of wheat. With each of these crossings, Borlaug made wheat that was marginally better at resisting fungal diseases and thriving in poor soils.

After thousands of these crossings and twenty years of work, Borlaug stopped a famine in Mexico. After tens of thousands more, he saved a billion lives around the world from starvation.

Seventy years later, in March 2014, the U.S. Congress honored Norman Borlaug by adding his statue to the Capitol's Statuary Hall to honor his 100th birthday. U.S. Senator Mitch McConnell said this unlikeliest of revolutionaries helped create a world with less misery and more hope, and he did all this with a grain of wheat. Others heralded him as the best proof that humans are the ultimate resource against hunger.

He is credited with saving over a billion lives in the 20th century and helping global poverty decline by 80 percent since 1970. And his "Green Revolution" hasn't ended. In 1980, 47 percent of the children in the developing world had stunted growth because of malnutrition. By 2000, the number had dropped to 33 percent.

However, Borlaug did his work with little support from the broader society that he could succeed. By the 1960s experts of the time had already decided that humanity was doomed to mass starvation.

In 1968, Paul Ehrlich published *The Population Bomb*, a book that argued rates of population growth would always rise compared to the rates of food production growth. A catastrophic worldwide global famine was inevitable. The battle to feed all of humanity was over.

Ehrlich looked upon humans as irresponsible breeders and called for compulsory sterilization, abortion on demand, and even a federal Department of Population and Environment which would regulate procreation. He encouraged heavy taxes on baby carriages to send a message of official disapproval toward child rearing. In an Orwellian move, Ehrlich called for photos of large, happy families to be removed from the print media. To him, unwanted or excessive births were a cancer on the planet. He explained, "A cancer is an uncontrolled multiplication of cells; the population explosion is an uncontrolled multiplication of people."

Such a mindset influenced a genre of 1970s dystopian science fiction in which humanity scrambled for dwindling resources of an overpopulated earth. Examples include Charlton Heston's 1970s camp classic *Soylent Green*. The plot involves the U.S. government harvesting the citizenry of a futuristic New York with 40 million residents as food to feed itself. Episodes of the original *Star Trek* took up this plot, along with the British sci-fi film *ZPG* from 1972, which featured a number of British A-listers including Geraldine Chaplin and Oliver Reed.

The trend even extended into the 1990s. The eco-friendly cartoon *Captain Planet* ran episodes that warned its child viewers not to have too many children, less they risk sucking the planet dry of resources and killing Gaia, the Spirit of the Earth.

None of this happened, all thanks to Borlaug and crop researchers like him. Much of his success can be credited to his farm roots.

Borlaug was born in Saude, Iowa on his Norwegian grandparents' farm. He helped with farm work from age seven onward, tilling the fields, feeding livestock, and splitting wood. Borlaug walked over a mile to school in the winter in blowing snow to a one-room schoolhouse. His grandfather Nels admonished him to get an education rather than ease into a farm life. "You're wiser to fill your head now if you want to fill your belly later on," he said. Borlaug heeded his advice and attended Cresco High School, 15 miles away.

He then attended the University of Minnesota, where he learned a lesson about hunger that stayed with him during his decades in

Mexican and Indian wheat fields.. Borlaug was a star on the wrestling team and frequently binge fasted to compete in his weight class. On one occasion he fasted five days, only drinking a little water and spending hours in a steam box. He was shocked at the anger and short-temper that overtook him. Normally peaceful and soft-spoken, Borlaug lashed out at another wrestler and had to be pulled away by onlookers before punching him in the face. He realized that hunger had a dehumanizing effect. He would later observe, "You see, it wasn't me at all. It was primitive, rudimentary. I can't explain how hungry I was. I was starving, and I found out that a hungry man is worse than a hungry beast."

Borlaug's career began in the early 1940s. He was fresh off his Ph.D. from the University of Minnesota in plant pathology and genetics. He was then employed as a microbiologist at DuPont where he led research on industrial and agricultural chemicals such as preservatives, fungicides, and bactericides. With the onset of World War II the U.S. government converted his lab into a research facility and assigned the task of developing technologies that would aid the Americans in the Pacific Theatre. The DuPont lab developed camouflage paint, aerosols, and chemicals to purify water. One particularly tricky request was to develop a glue that could withstand the South Pacific's warm salt water and not disintegrate so shipping containers providing supplies to troops in Guadalcanal would hold together. He and the other researchers developed a solution within weeks.

Borlaug's career took an important turn when the Rockefeller Foundation sent him to Mexico in 1944 to aid their Ministry of Agriculture in boosting Mexican wheat production, a project intended to indirectly support U.S. economic and military interests. The project's ultimate goal was to train Mexican scientists on modern farming techniques so they could run crop experiments and not have to depend on America.

In all, Borlaug worked with four other researchers as a plant pathologist over the course of 16 years to help Mexico develop adequate agricultural infrastructure to feed its own people without handouts from the United States.

The early years of the project were difficult. The team lacked scientists and equipment to deal with consecutive years of poor harvests. There were no irrigation supplies, gasoline, trucks or tractors.

The rural landscape was depleted after the war effort. Worst of all, farmers were experiencing catastrophic crop losses from stem rust, a fungal infection that affected cereal crops by lowering the plant's seed count or killing it. The fungus could infect a healthy crop three weeks before harvest and reduce it to a black tangle of broken stems and shriveled grains. It was the stuff of nightmares for Mexican farmers, who could see a year of work disappear before their eyes.

Borlaug labored in loneliness in those early days. He had left behind his pregnant wife Margaret and 14-month-old daughter when he flew to Mexico City to lead the program as geneticist and plant pathologist. His family later joined him, but they rarely saw him because of his long hours in the Mexican wheat fields. Also, farmers in the wheat fields were initially distrustful and cold to him. A large cultural gap separated them and this American college graduate who was giving them untried new technologies but didn't speak their language.

Borlaug persevered, mostly due to his rural background and seeing Mexican cultivators as fellow growers in need of a hand. He learned Spanish. More importantly he got his hands dirty. Richard Zeyen, a professor of plant pathology at the University of Minnesota who knew Borlaug for decades said the idea of improving the Mexicans' quality of life attracted him. "He had that small town farmers-help-each-other spirit. He was strong and he knew he was strong and he knew he could use his strength to help others."

Borlaug first sought to speed up the breeding of wheat in the highlands of Texcoco by taking advantage of the two growing seasons of the country and utilizing a process known as shuttle breeding. He bred wheat in the highlands, then took the seeds to the lower altitude region of Yaqui Valley in Sonora. His superiors vetoed the plan because agronomists of the time wrongly believed seeds needed a rest period after harvest to store energy for germination. His colleague George Harrar thought Borlaug's plan was ridiculous. "It makes no sense to risk a round trip of 2,500 miles through that country," he said, thinking of the broken roads and inaccessibility of most areas. "You could lose everything – and for what? The guts of our problem are here in the poverty areas."

Borlaug recounts in his biography that he knit his brows, thrust out his chin, and before responding, took a stance he had learned in his days as a wrestler.

"Don't try to discourage me, Ed," he said. "I know how much work is involved. Don't tell me what can't be done. Tell me what needs to be done – and let me do it. There's one single factor that makes the Yaqui effort worth a try, and that's rust. Breeding two generations a year means beating and staying ahead of the shifty stem-rust organism. If I can lick that problem by working in Sonora, then we've won a victory. To hell with the extra work and strain. It's got to be done, and I believe I can do it."

His plan was eventually approved. The results were startling. The double wheat season produced a faster crop. The plant generations produced at different altitudes and environmental conditions allowed the production of wheat varieties that fit a larger range of ecologies. The project would not need to produce wheat that was specific to each geographic region in Mexico. Borlaug could assault the country with the planting program. He could also supercharge the process of determining which wheat varieties were the best, rather than plant a crop, wait for it to grow, and see which varieties survived.

His accomplishment with wheat surprised some because he had spent his childhood in the cornfields of Iowa. Vice President Henry Wallace commented on this disparity when he visited the project in the 1940s. "What's a good Iowa boy like you doing working on wheat?" he said jokingly.

Borlaug continued to strengthen the wheat varieties through the processes of dwarfing and backcrossing. Dwarfing meant shortening the tall, thin stems of wheat into shorter stems, which can support the extra grain produced by the wheat grown in the nitrogen fertilizer that Borlaug introduced into the thin Mexican soil. Backcrossing is the crossing of a hybrid with one of its parents to achieve genetic identity closer to the plant's parent. This allows an elite genotype to be recovered and allowed Borlaug to transfer various disease-resistant genes to a single parent. Soon his crop lines were resistant to common pathogens.

By 1956, his work was bearing fruit. Borlaug's new wheat varieties allowed Mexico to achieve self-sufficiency. By 1964, Borlaug's semi-dwarf wheat was planted in 95 percent of Mexican wheat fields. The once-famished country was now a wheat exporter. Each year it released different high yield varieties of wheat. Output was six times higher than when he arrived. Farmers who were once at risk of watching their crops fail and falling into terrible poverty watched their incomes rise year after year.

Borlaug was now an international celebrity for his successes, but he did not rest on his laurels. The Indian Agricultural Research Institute had heard of Borlaug's success with crop production in Mexico, and requested that he visit the subcontinent to develop varieties of dwarf spring wheat strains. During the early 1960s, India and Pakistan were at war and the U.S was sending millions of tons of grain to the region to avert famine. He arrived in 1963 and oversaw the planting of 220 pounds of seed from four promising strains in test plots in India.

Paul Ehrlich had used India as a prime example of a third-world nation unable to cope with the challenges of feeding its massive population. He and other intellectuals wrote off the subcontinent as on the brink of an unavoidable starvation. He declared, "I have yet to meet anyone familiar with the situation who thinks India will be self-sufficient in food by 1971... India couldn't possibly feed two hundred million more people by 1980."

Borlaug had already been hard at work for years when Ehrlich made his prediction, and was proving Ehrlich wrong. Borlaug's team imported tons of semi-dwarf seed to Pakistan and India, working with war raging in the background and artillery flashes lighting up the sky. Despite damage to the seeds in a Mexican warehouse, they produced an initial yield that broke South Asian records. Though Pakistan continued to import thousands of tons of wheat in 1966 and 1967, at the same time the country launched a vigorous program of planting Borlaug's dwarf varieties, covering 1.5 million acres of wheat land. The harvest saw yields so high that storage space quickly ran out. Government agencies had to use any municipal building it could to hold the harvest. Local schools were temporarily closed to hold the grain.

By 1968, Pakistan was self-sufficient in wheat production; by 1974, India was self-sufficient in cereal production. In a rebuke to Ehrlich, both nations produced wheat faster than population growth. Borlaug helped per-acre wheat output increase so much that over a hundred million acres of land did not need to be converted into farmland.

In India, the national gross yield of wheat rose from 12.3 million tons in 1965 to 20 million in 1970. The numbers continued to rise throughout the century. In 1999, India harvested a record amount of wheat, 73.5 million tons, an increase of 11 percent over 1998. The nation's population has more than doubled, its wheat production tripled, and its economy octupled. Ehrlich's prediction has proven embarrassingly wrong – so much so that he quietly omitted the prediction from later editions of *The Population Bomb*. Borlaug's revolution spread to much of the rest of Asia, when his colleagues at the Consultative Group on International Agricultural Research developed similar forms of high-yield rice varieties.

Fame caught up to him. In 1970, Borlaug's wife Margaret pulled up to the Toluca station in Mexico in their beat-up car. Borlaug, standing in a plot of wheat in his mud-splattered clothes, boots, and baseball cap, feared that one of their children had been hurt. He dropped his wheat samples and asked what happened to them.

"Nothing," Margaret laughed. "You've won the Nobel Peace Prize, that's all."

He refused to believe it and went back to work. Borlaug came around 40 minutes later when the press descended on him.

At his acceptance speech in Stockholm, Borlaug reflected on all the progress that had happened since the 1940s. The third world was feeding itself and the specter of famine was disappearing. But he spent most of his speech reminding the elite audience not to forgot the majority of humanity that they had likely never seen:

> It is a sad fact that on this earth at this late date there are still two worlds, "the privileged world" and "the forgotten world." The privileged world consists of the affluent, developed nations, comprising twenty-five to thirty percent of the world population, in which most of the people live in a luxury never before experienced by man outside the Garden of Eden. The forgotten world is made up primarily of the developing nations, where most of the people, comprising more than fifty percent of the total world population, live in poverty, with hunger as a constant companion and fear of famine a continual menace.

He tried to retire in the 1980s, but third-world officials coaxed him back to work. (Not that he ever really could retire; Borlaug was an Iowan farmer at heart who would have preferred to die laboring in the fields rather than ever stop working). This time, Borlaug traveled to Africa to bring the Green Revolution there. He came despite protests from environmental groups, which so opposed inorganic fertilizers in

Africa that they had persuaded Western European governments to stop supplying fertilizer to the continent.

However, the Japanese shipping magnate Ryoichi Sasakawa personally funded a project to ease famine in sub-Saharan Africa. The 72-year-old Borlaug began implementing his research in Ghana in 1984. By 1991 the area was producing all its own food and began exporting to other countries. The key to this success was a new form of corn called Quality Protein Maize (QPM), a grain packed with nutrients. Once again, Borlaug averted a famine. Once again, he helped a nation record the largest harvest of major crops in history.

Borlaug was a universally respected figure, but he was not afraid to tackle controversial issues. Many developing nations at the time required their farmers to accept only half of world market prices so these governments could pacify the urban populations with low food costs. These unfairly low payments to farmers resulted in underproduction of crops and hoarding. Borlaug used his international prestige to persuade Pakistan and India to eliminate these policies and pay poor farmers the standard global rate for their grain.

IOWA: THE CRUCIBLE OF AGRICULTURE BREAKTHROUGHS

Taking a step back from the life of Norman Borlaug, it is important to understand his contribution in the context of his upbringing. He is not a wholly self-made man but a product of the agricultural ingenuity of Iowa. How do we make sense of the entrepreneurial spirit of this state that formed his values? To do so, we need to take a detour through Iowa's agricultural history.

A first step is to consider Iowa's landscape. If you have ever driven through Iowa, you would notice that farms are everywhere. A forest, a cornfield, or a soybean field covers any stretch of rural land. These crops contribute significantly to the state's economy. They are also the primary reason that America dominates global agriculture.

Oddly enough, neither corn or soybeans was preferred by the Iowa Territory's first settlers, who first appeared in the 1830s. As farms spread across the Midwest during the 19th century, the first big cash crop was wheat. Wisconsin, Iowa, and Minnesota are thought of as corn country, but they were all wheat producers first, quickly supplanting the Mid-Atlantic States in terms of its production. Corn was common but bulky and tough to transport for profit. Farmers consumed it at home as Johnnycakes, a cornmeal flatbread, rather than sell it. The rest was distilled into spirits, which could be better transported at a higher economic value. It was not until corn was adopted wide-scale as animal feed that its value was truly recognized. Instead of letting animals feed on prairie grass, farmers hauled feed to animals, allowing them to be raised in smaller confines and requiring less pastureland. (Animal rights activists and grass-fed beef lovers likely do not celebrate this development, but raising livestock was now simpler and cheaper than it would have been without this development.)

Iowa was ecologically destined to be an agricultural center of the world. Its massive production capabilities have to do with its environmental conditions, which are perfect for corn production. It has hot humid summers, many hours of daylight, a long growing season, and optimal rainfall. Those factors make it a good area for raising a crop like corn that has a tremendous biological payoff in terms of mass. A corn kernel is no bigger than a fingernail. But when planted and harvested it produces far more kernels when compared to wheat. There is a greater payoff in terms of plant material fiber, or cellulose, which is important for feeding livestock and raising thousands of hogs and cows. The seed is a high sugar, high calorie product and necessary for converting feed into flesh.

Iowa's role as the agricultural hub of the United States came with the expansion of settlers with the 1833 Black Hawk Purchase. Many of these settlers, which came in family units, arrived from New York, Indiana, Kentucky, Virginia, and Pennsylvania. There they found endless prairie that contrasted with the heavily timbered homes back East.

These settlers had to be hardy folk. For one thing, the land appeared bleak and desolate, compared with the homes they had left behind. Historian Dorothy Schwieder quotes an account of a woman settling in Iowa from New York State who announced to her husband she would die without any trees. To some new settlers this threat of death was a literal truth – prairie fires were common in the dense tall grass and it took the help of all family members on a farmstead to keep the flames at bay. Iowans slept with one eye open for fire until the first snow fell.

Early farm machinery was just as dangerous as nature. Entrepreneurs had steam-powered threshers dragged from town to town, threshing farmers' crops for a fee. One spark from the boiler could shoot out and set the whole prairie on fire.

But underneath the prairie grass rested some of the richest soil on earth. Much of the state was settled by the 1860s with immigrants who dreamt of lucrative work in farming. Railroads came into the state in the 1860s from Chicago, bringing thousands of settlers eager to homestead and claim their own land. Council Bluffs became the eastern terminus of the Union Pacific Railroad in 1867. By the 1870s family farms covered the state. They kept busy year round. In the winter farmers butchered livestock, mended fences, and chopped wood; in the summer they sheared sheep, hayed, and threshed; in the fall they harvested.

Women were just as active as men and often had the same chores. An account of a Midwestern farm wife in 1900 from the book *The Life Stories of Undistinguished Americans as Told by Themselves* describes her role on the farm:

> No man can run a farm without someone to help him, and in this case I have always been called up on and expected to help do anything that a man would be expected to do. I began this when we were first married, when there were few household duties and no reasonable excuse for refusing to help. I was reared on a farm, was healthy and strong, was ambitious, and the work was not disagreeable, and having no children for the first six years of married life, the habit of going whenever asked to became firmly fixed, and he had no thought of hiring a man to help him, since I could do anything for which he needed help.

Tough-minded pioneers like these took to farming rich soil, forming an Iowa asset that lasts to today. Farmers moved from the East Coast brought with them short-season 90-day corn, well adapted to New England; those coming from the South came with the 120-day gourd seed corn variety. People began to deliberately or accidentally cross those varieties. The result is the grandfather of our modern-day dent corn. Farmers discovered cattle and pigs could relatively easily digest this cross-pollinated variety. This discovery helped encourage a shift from pasture feeding to feed lots.

When the United States entered World War I in 1917 and transformed into a wartime economy, farmers saw their profits increase dramatically. Federal officials urged farmers to increase production, so they purchased more land and raised more livestock. A ready market existed, because the U.S. Army bought whatever they produced making many farmers rich.

Another Iowan, Herbert Hoover, made use of this expanded agricultural output to feed Europe at the end of the war. He was in charge of the American Relief Administration, an American outreach to Europe after World War I. The multi-million-dollar program was funded by Congress, and the organization saved millions of lives throughout Europe and Russia by averting a massive famine.

U.S. agriculture lagged after the war and collapsed in the Great Depression. Farmers had little relief until another Iowan, Henry A. Wallace, Franklin Roosevelt's Secretary of Agriculture, went to Washington to design a new farm relief program. He crafted the Agricultural Adjustment Act in 1933, which paid farmers to curtail their agricultural production and withhold land from farming. Wallace, former editor of the leading farm journal of the Midwest, *Wallace's Farmer*, hoped to return prosperity to the sector.

Wallace challenged the cherished belief that it is good to make two blades of grass grow where one grew before. This was an idea deeply embedded in the mindset of farmers, and continues to be so today, with their obsession on total crop yield and productivity. Instead, Wallace basically paid farmers not to farm. His federal farm programs restricted too much production and offset price decline in crops. This price control mechanism was arguably successful. But it lived on for decades after its original expiration date, ballooning into a program that today costs billions of dollars.

Keeping all this history in mind, how has Iowa contributed so much to the technological advancement of agriculture? After all, technology does not come from the organic effort of crop cultivation and soil tillage. It comes from scientific research. Most of this innovation has come from Iowa State University. It was founded in 1858 as the Iowa Agricultural College and Model Farm. The modest farm was a testing ground for new agricultural methods such as crop planting, crop growing, cross-pollination, disease resistance, and drought resistance.

At the time European scientists were making startling advances in biology. Gregor Mendel presented a paper on hybridization in 1865 and Louis Pasteur developed a cure for anthrax in 1881. Charles Darwin popularized the idea of evolution of plants and animals in 1859 with his book *On the Origin of Species by Means of Natural Selection, or the Preservation of Favoured Races in the Struggle for Life.* But it was at such research programs as Iowa State University that these ideas were put into practice.

One of the most influential research wings of Iowa State was its mechanical arts department. Here engineers and designers worked on more efficient farm implements. Their discoveries coincided with technological breakthroughs happening around the world.

In 1837 John Deere developed the cast-steel plow. Before this invention, most farmers used wooden or iron plows that stuck to the Midwestern soil. The smooth steel plow solved this problem, cut through the soil, and aided the massive migration to the American Great Plains.

In 1892 John Froelich produced the first gasoline-powered tractor., built to replace the bulky, dangerous mobile thresher. He replaced the hazardous steam engine with a one-cylinder gasoline engine on his steam engine's running gear. It worked; the new machine could move at a blistering three miles per hour. Now 26 gallons of gas could provide power to thresh more than a thousand bushels of grain a day. As a result, a farmer could easily acquire more power to do work than animals pulling the machines could have ever supplied.

Farms became mechanized with the application of gasoline engine technology to threshing machines and reapers. Tractors came and quickly grew in size. The early models were rated at 15 horsepower on the drawback and 30 on the belt, compared to a modern-day John Deere 9400, a tractor rated at 425 horsepower and costing nearly $200,000. Early tractors were little more than mechanized draft animals, pulling implements such as the grain binder formerly drawn by horses. Over time, the machines were built to accommodate tractors. The tractor and corn picker were designed together and made into a self-propelled machine: the combine.

The pace of evolution was startling: corn farmers of the 19th century used a single-row, horse-drawn planter, which was replaced by the tractor-pulled two-row planter. Then came the four-row; then the 12-row; and now the 24-row planter. Combines today are self-propelled and self-leveling to accommodate uneven terrain.

Tractors had a side effect of reducing the number of people in the state who actually farmed. With mechanization came a reduced need for laborers and the consolidation of small plots. Larger farmers started to accumulate more wealth and gobble up properties next to them.

Tractors increased in number from 1.6 to 3.4 million from 1940 to 1950. Horses were literally put to pasture and kept only for recreational purposes. Today farmers feel affinity for their tractors in the way that their great-grandfathers felt for their horses. For example, it is not uncommon to see a farm family decorate their infant son's room in John Deere green and yellow.

With mechanization came enormous gains in efficiency. According to the book *The Agricultural Revolution of the 20th Century*, if a farmer from the Old Testament were dropped in American in 1900, he mostly would have recognized the implements being used: hoes, harrows, rakes, and plows. But if he came in the 20th Century, he would think he was on a different planet. The changes that occurred during the previous century exceeded all changes that had happened during the 10,000 years since humans first began cultivation of crops during the Neolithic Revolution. In 1939 the per-farm average value of land, buildings, and equipment was only $6,000. By 1996, the sum increased by a factor of eighty.

In 1910, it took approximately 70 minutes of labor to earn a dollar of farm income. By 1980, only four minutes were required. In 1900, it took a farmer 81 minutes to produce a bushel of corn. With the use of mechanical power, today it takes less than two minutes. Due to this massive growth in productivity far fewer farmers are necessary to grow crops. Nearly 30 million Americans were involved in agriculture in 1900. This number fell to less than 5 million by 2000. Farmers constituted nearly 39 percent of the population in 1900; they were less than 1.5 percent in 2000.

The productivity gains are so great that farmers, despite constituting a fraction of the total population, have long ago set their sights beyond merely feeding the American population. They now consider how to feed the rest of the world, and feed them toward better health. They seek to rid the world of nutrition-related diseases such as scurvy, goiter, rickets, and pellagra.

With an explosion in agricultural technology, biotech, and high-tech farm equipment came the mindset of industrialization. Farms used to be the simplest, most granular part of an agrarian society. They were now part of the global industrial economy. Farmers accepted the idea that agriculture requires scientific expertise, not merely hard work or experience working the land, using knowledge passed down from generation to generation. In the 20th century it capital requirements for farming were so great that farmers needed financial systems in place. Buying hundreds of acres and million-dollar combines took enormous bank loans backed by federal financial securities and national programs.

Farms morphed from household operations to small businesses and even miniature factories. Along with this came professional accounting practices. A typical farmer's ledger before World War II did not pay much attention to cash flow – if he was buying some nails or hardware, he didn't bother to compare the true expenses of repair and maintenance versus buying new equipment or housing. But after the war, the U.S. government took a more direct role in agriculture and forced farmers to pay income taxes. Farmers had to know how much money they were making since they paid taxes based on their revenue. That imposed an accounting system on agriculture.

Iowa ignited the global explosion of agriculture, which sent ripples throughout the rest of the world. Previously untouched areas such as Argentina or Australia saw an expansion of cash crops. In 1905 Western Canada was a desert; in 10 years Canadian Pacific Railway actively promoted agriculture and put millions of acres into tillage. Agriculture expanded not just in the United States but everywhere. The growth of the global crop market made food prices drop across the industrialized world.

Lower food prices changed the diets of average Americans, whether a Midwestern farmer or a New York banker. As early as the 1880s and 1890s, tailors began talking about how proportions of the male body were starting to change; better nutrition meant the average man was no longer rail thin. The size 38 or 40 jacket had to be cut differently to accommodate the larger frames of the male populace.

It also meant the creation of the middle class. Most of the world's population worked in agriculture up until World War II because the prices of food were so high that all but the relatively wealthy could only get by if they grew their own food. In the early 1900s, over 25 percent of a family budget was spent on food; in 2000 it was less than 14 percent. Families now had more money to spend more on consumer goods, clothing, and housing. Family cars were affordable, along with track housing. And those houses wouldn't be complete without toasters, ovens, refrigerators, and Zenith televisions. For the first time in history the middle class became a majority of society's population.

And change keeps happening. Researchers estimate that in 20 years the output of an acre of fertile Iowa farmland could produce 300 bushels of grain, double what is currently produced now. Some even estimate it could get to the 400 or 500 level mark. While the new generations of Paul Ehlrichs have come along to preach a gospel of starvation due to overpopulation and depletion of natural resources, a new generation of Norman Borlaugs is rising up to answer their call, ready to feed the planet and continue growing the global economy.

A NEW GENERATION OF NORMAN BORLAUGS

Borlaug brought productive agriculture to the third world, but his work remains unfinished. Vast swaths of farmland in Africa, Asia, and the Americas are barely productive enough to support a farm family, let alone the surrounding community.

A lack of agriculture will permanently cripple a poor nation's future. Global development leaders such as Allan Savory say that agriculture is not crop production as popular belief holds. It is the production of food and fiber from the world's land and waters. It is also the fulcrum on which any kind of social, cultural, and political development turns.

He has said, "Without agriculture it is not possible to have a city, stock market, banks, university, church or army. Agriculture is the foundation of civilization and any stable economy."

Fortunately a new generation of Iowan farmers and researchers are rising to the challenge of feeding the world. They are creating new farming technologies to increase yields and make crops grow in the developing world. Their research is generations beyond diesel tractors or plows. They are blending farming with genetic engineering, robotic harvesters, and satellite-guided tractors.

The idea that farmers are utilizing such advanced technology may sound surprising, but that is only true for those who believe Midwesterners do subsistence farming and barely live above the poverty line. This may have been true three generations ago. But a modern farm is more akin to a multimillion-dollar business than a quaint family operation with a red barn and one tractor. Today a top-line tractor is smart phone-controlled and can be steered via GPS. Intelligent sensors know exactly how much fertilizer to spray. They collect massive amounts of data, enabling farmers to continually boost crop yields. Farms use hybrid specific GPS and a digital map of the field to maintain pinpoint accuracy.

Clay Mitchell of Geneseo, Iowa is a Gorlang-style pioneer. Using satellite navigation, computer piloted tractors, and thousands of sensors, Mitchell pushes the limits of technology to re-create farming. His autopilot-controlled John Deere crop sprayer uses different nozzles to apply the right amount of pesticide down to the drop. This is a far more exact science than altering spray pressures along the field, and the droplets coat leaves more effectively, saving money on pesticides and keeping chemicals on the field. "Environmentally, drift is a big issue," he said in a profile with *Wired* magazine. "If the entire outside edge of the field gets a sub-lethal amount, then it's a sure thing that it's only going to take a couple of years for some weeds to develop resistance."

He is one part Pa Wilder, three parts Tony Stark

In this future world of agriculture, farm tools act with as much precision as insects extracting nectar from a flower. Although farm mechanization is a process that has gone on for at least a century, traditional implements such as threshing machines and seed drills are blunt and imprecise. Mitchell's new tools are anything but. He has installed a fixed GPS receiver on his land and programmed it to broadcast coordinates to farm vehicles to spontaneously account for errors while working on his fields. This allows him to inject the soil with fertilizer in rows and come back a few months later to place a seed on top of each granule, determining each position by using lasers and cameras. His efforts to increase productivity have paid off – he reaps approximately 750 bushels a hectare a year, compared to the average of 75 bushels a hectare a century ago.

Mitchell is the embodiment of an intelligent but down-to-earth Midwesterner. He was born on the Geneseo family farm and helped his father build much of the farm equipment. When in high school he wired the grain bin's storage screws with electrical inputs and outputs. After graduation he studied biomedical engineering at Harvard.

Mitchell returned to the family farm in 2000. He installed his own RTK system after reading about it in a farming magazine, which was originally designed for horticulture. He personally overhauled his tractor with RTK auto steering, then his seeders and fertilizer machines.

John Deere now funds many of his experiments. Mitchell controls them from his computer station set up at the back of his barn, near a fridge full of Red Bull. He computer shows a color-coded map of the field that displays plants with nitrogen placed at different distances from the seed.

Mitchell is not the only Iowan transforming agriculture with technology. Dave Dorhout, an entomologist who graduated from Iowa State University dreams of planting an entire field with an army of robots that are modeled on insects. Dorhout, an amiable researcher who once dreamt of opening a pizza shop, has designed a hexapod robot named Prospero. He built it to control farming on a plant-by-plant, seed-by-seed basis. It will operate in a swarm of planting, tending, and harvesting, running on the principle of game theory behavior algorithms to operate on the fly. To him, this is not a bizarre, Isaac Asimov take on the future of farming. Rather, it is agriculture assuming its proper role as the traditional early adopter of new technologies.

"Looking back at history agriculture seems kind of quaint," Dorhout said to *Popular Science*. "But I realized growing up around a farm in Iowa that rather than being one of the last industries to adopt technology, agriculture is one of the earliest adopters." He pointed to innovative technologies like genetic engineering, statistics, and the diesel engine, all used early on by farmers to squeeze out more productivity per acre.

Prospero is the opposite of a massive tractor. Smaller is bigger, and according to Dorhout, hundreds of little robots can do far more work than one massive one. It's the same concept as a huge lawn mower versus millions of micro-mowers: a massive mower can cut down hundreds of grass blades a second. But millions of micro-mowers that each cut down one blade in five minutes will finish sooner. Prospero is an off-the-shelf robotics platform that is simple, costs less than ten dollars, and is equipped with sensors such as photo resistors and an LED, along with a fertilizer sprayer and a seed hopper. The robot communicates with other robots with a weak radio signal. It walks around the field and only bothers to detect what is directly beneath it. If there is no seed planted in the soil below, or immediately around it, then Prospero drills a hole, deposits a seed, sprays an exact amount of fertilizer, covers the seed, and marks the spot with some paint that other robots can detect. The "paint" is similar to a pheromone mark that insects leave to communicate with each other.

The degree to which the robots look and act like insects is creepy: They operate in a swarm pattern and do not bother to plant the field in straight rows, but instead with optimized seed spacing for whatever shape the field might take. Prospero robots "talk" to each other like drones in an ant colony. If a robot detects a large swath of soil with no seeds, then it signals other robots to come to the area and get to work, much like ants working in unison to drag a leaf back to the colony or protect a queen in danger. The swarm method's purpose is to cut down on expensive data crunching because each robot does not have to know the exact position of each other robot.

All of these futuristic prospects are exciting, but the modern industrialization of agriculture hasn't come without its controversies. This is particularly true in considering the power imbalance between rich Western agriculture companies and poorer farmers in the developing world. Borlaug's motives in feeding the third world were pure, but his legacy of a wide-scale approach to farming has put new burdens on third-world farmers. The wheat varieties that Borlaug and others developed required more fertilizer applications than local varieties due to the poor local soil. A farmer who used his new types of dwarf wheat could expect a better harvest but had to buy expensive imported fertilizer.

Unanticipated consequences resulted. Farmers across the world, whether in Iowa or the poorer parts of Mexico and Ethiopia, now rely on synthetic fertilizers. Countries that once relied on subsistence farming must now practice input-intensive farming. They now have the IV drip of global agribusiness injected into their economies and are dependent on international companies like Monsanto that offer combined seed and chemical packages. It forces an agenda of U.S. corporations onto poorer, weaker countries to create an uneven food distribution system. Money flows up from the poorest farmers to the richest CEOs, a practice that critics call "farming the farmer."

Industrialization has also presented environmental challenges both inside and outside the United States. Aggressive farming results in soil erosion, which, if not controlled, renders land useless. This is a dangerous prospect in Iowa, in which soil is likely the state's most precious commodity; what coal is to West Virginia, fried cheese to Wisconsin, or lawsuits to California. To reduce the threat of soil erosion, minimum tillage was developed, along with the farm machinery to implement it. More advanced machines used laser-guidance to lay plastic tile with the desired gradient through an undulating surface. But concerns remain.

Lastly, the industrialization of farming threatens to eliminate the most American of all institutions: the family farm. In the early 20th century, farming was be a family enterprise. This was true throughout history, and a reason that farmers preferred large families in order to create more workers.

Today the total value of an average farm, including land, equipment, and buildings, exceeds half a million dollars. Other than a few wealthy families, the only true "owners" of farms are corporations or banks. The average Iowa county had hundreds of independent hog farmers prior to the 1990s. But when pork prices plummeted later that decade, the number was reduced to less than a dozen.

The family farm can survive into the 21st century, but only with great difficulty. To do so, it must redefine itself. Don and Philip Paarlberg argue in *The Agricultural Revolution of the 20th Century* that in the original idea of a family farm, the farm family supplied all forms of production, whether the land, labor, capitol, or management. However, due to the enormous investments required, one person cannot supply all these different factors of production. External factors must enter into the equation. These include borrowing money, earning off-farm income, contracting with integrating firms, hiring labor, and reducing the amount of decision-making power of the farm operator.

Borlaug acknowledged these difficulties before his death in 2009 at the age of 95. He admitted that while the Green Revolution had been a net positive, it had not transformed the world into a utopia. He also worried that future potential for land expansion and cultivation of crops would not be as simple in the 21st century as it was in the 20th, even though demand for more crops would continuously rise. The world food supply needed to be doubled by 2050, with up to 85 percent of the growth having to come from lands already in use.

Nevertheless, Borlaug dismissed most of his critics of the Green Revolution and its "shotgun wedding" between first-world agribusiness and third-world farming. With Midwestern lack of pretense, he blasted those critics as pampered elites more concerned about abstract environmental threats than the very real threats of third-world starvation. In 2008 he said, "Some of the environmental lobbyists of the Western nations are the salt of the earth, but many of them are elitists. They've never experienced the physical sensation of hunger. They do their lobbying from comfortable office suites in Washington or Brussels. If they lived just one month amid the misery of the developing world as I have for fifty years, they'd be crying out for tractors and fertilizer and irrigation canals and be outraged that fashionable elitists back home were trying to deny them these things."

To Borlaug, the threats to future food security were not issues with production. The real threat was a pervasive but camouflaged bureaucracy strangling the global supply chain. Environmental activities and international agencies could interfere in biotechnology and crop cultivation to the degree than a man-made famine was possible, a ghastly repeat of Stalin's man-made famine triggered in Ukraine in the 1930s. Barring such interference, Borlaug remained optimistic that scientific breakthroughs would continue to boost crop production to meet the demands of 2025, in which the global population is expected to reach 8 billion. Before his death he predicted that the world could feed up to 10 billion if policy makers stayed attuned to rural development.

Borlaug's greatest achievement, and those of other Iowans who helped feed the world in the 20th century, was to prove that modern agriculture could be made to work in fast-growing developing countries where it was needed most, even in the small farms removed from cities. He proved that the greatest asset for any hungry country is human ingenuity.

Borlaug's legacy literally covers the Earth. Gary H. Toenniessen, director of agricultural programs for the Rockefeller Foundation, calculated that half the world's population goes to bed every night after consuming grain descended from one of the high-yield varieties developed by Borlaug or his colleagues.

"He knew what it was they needed to do, and he didn't give up," Toenniessen said to The New York Times in Borlaug's obituary. "He could just see that this was the answer."

His answer was to feed the planet. The unassuming Iowan and other farmers like him conquered the world. They conquered not with a military campaign like Alexander the Great or plundering campaign like Genghis Khan. They won with but with something far more important: food.

CHAPTER FOUR

HOW IOWA STANDARDIZED
AMERICAN ENGLISH

Lynn Singer's therapy sessions have changed her clients' lives, but the change hasn't come without suffering. Some clients burst into tears when sessions begin. Others have taken years to overcome their past. One client has come to her Manhattan office weekly for more than 11 years.

Their problem? All have a New York accent and want to speak with neutral English. That is, they want to speak like an Iowan.

Singer sits across from her clients and looks at their mouths closely. She works with the sounds that they have the most trouble pronouncing. Improvement techniques include enunciating vowels that use the back of the tongue and conscious sound substitutions that replace their swallowed vowels. The process – as described in a New York Times profile – can take years. But the payoff is worth it. New York accents have been rated as the most disliked style of speech in the United States.

Her clients drop r's in their words (doctor becomes doctuh, water becomes wawtuh). Actresses complain of not being cast in movies because their accent makes them sound ignorant. Corporate execs worry they are not understood by clients or stereotyped for their speech patterns. Their speech pigeonholes them as tough guys or mafia members. Every word sounds like a line from *The Sopranos*. The New York accent – a mix of German, Irish, Yiddish, and Italian – is among the most stereotyped of all American dialects.

The worst among working class New Yorkers sound like the chorus of a 1946 song by Bobby Gregory: "Who is de toughest goil in dis whole woild/Moitle from Thoidy-Thoid and Thoid."

But no such speech therapists exist in Iowa. Nobody tries to lose their Iowan accent. Why? Because there isn't one. The language spoken in American films, national news, commercials, radio programs, and TV series is the natural language of a farmer in Decorah or banker in Marshalltown. This is the preferred accent of broadcasters across the nation. You won't hear a CNN reporter use a Southern twang in which a one-syllable word becomes three. Nor will they use a Northeastern accent in their description of a "pahty platah of clahm chowdah."

General American English is found in its native habitat only in a tiny chunk of the Midwest. Maps of the accent place it in a swath that begins in central Illinois, moves west to cover the lower half of Iowa and a tiny portion of northern Missouri, then ends in the western third of Nebraska. The full spectrum of the accent, however, likely includes Ohio, Missouri, and Kansas, with parts of Michigan and Wisconsin thrown in. But the epicenter of standard American English, if one wants to be precise, is in Iowa.

Today English learners around the world are learning to speak with an American accent, and by default, an Iowan accent. The omnipresence of Hollywood films and popular television dramas make the U.S.-style of speech easier to understand and learn than British-style English. Global media exposes more citizens to it, giving the American accent more cultural capital. Learners in Asia say it makes them sound more contemporary and a better fit within the international business world.

American accent schools are flourishing in places such as Hong Kong. Parents send their children there with the hopes that a North American accent will increase their employability, particularly with a U.S. firm. There, students as young as nine recite speeches by U.S. politicians, enunciating each word with perfect American diction.

In the school Nature EQ, Charlotte Yan goes to the front of her class, where a giant American flag hangs on the wall. She recites a 2008 campaign speech by Hillary Clinton in front of dozens of fellow students.

"Make sure we have a president who puts our country back on the path to peace, prosperity, and progress," she says, opening her mouth wide to pronounce her phonemes correctly.

Yan is one of many Hong Kong language students who are learning the accent. Children as young as five chant words in unison and memorize Robert Frost poems. Teachers quickly correctly any enunciation error. Although Hong Kong is a former British colony, her family prefers the accent to the more common English-style speech.

Many others believe the American accent is more relevant in the globalized world than British English. The boom in accent schools reflects this belief – wealthy Chinese mainlanders are crossing into Hong Kong and filling these programs. Nature EQ was set up 17 years ago with 40 students. Today 350 attend. Nearby another school hosts an American English workshop. It enrolled 180 students in its first year.

"I intend to send my sons to America for further study so I chose an American accent for them," said Victor Chan to Agence France-Presse. "I think having an American accent is better for their employment [prospects] in Western countries."

What all of these accent learners don't realize is that they are mimicking the speech of Iowans. General American English is modeled off of Midwestern English. General American English has become the global standard for accent. To complete the syllogism, Midwestern English is now the global standard. Few know this. A Chinese college student would be shocked to learn that the template for "correct" English is an insurance salesman in Des Moines or feed lot operator in Keokuk.

The story of the Iowan accent becoming the template for the General American accent is an accidental history. Nobody planned for it to happen. The speech trajectory of America could have very well gone in a different direction. Perhaps in an alternate reality, Asian schoolchildren and broadcasters try to speak like Minnesotans (let's get on the fishing boot, *eh?*). Why did it happen this way?

Language evolution is a complex and ongoing process. It happens faster in certain places than others and sometimes doesn't happen at all. Isolated immigrant communities in America have managed to retain the accent of their homeland. One noteworthy group are the Tidewater communities around Chesapeake Bay in Virginia. They are descendants from settlers from Somerset and Gloucestershire in the West Country of England. To the delight of linguists and tourists everywhere, they still speak the Victorian English of their predecessors. More extreme examples are Mennonite communities that speak a dialect of German called *Plautdietsch* (Low German), due to the perpetuation of their culture from their pietist roots in Germany.

Dialects persist in smaller regions, but every nation has a standard form of its speech. A British gentleman or lady prefers to speak the Queen's English. Most French citizens do their best to mimic a Parisian accent, which itself came from the royal court and French aristocracy of centuries earlier. Even in Turkey, most residents prefer to copy the Istanbul accent, with its steady flow of harmonized vowels, rather than the clippier speech of the Black Sea or Anatolian hinterlands.

This story is repeated across Europe – as nations began to consolidate in the 1700s and 1800s, schools were built and teachers sent to staff them. In this new universal education system, one dialect came to dominate all the others. These dialects were typically associated with the aristocracy, the upper class, or the monarchy and made the standardized version of speech throughout the rest of the nation.

The spread of radio broadcasts in the early-20th century further entrenched these accents. In 1917, English researcher Daniel Jones introduced the concept of Received Pronunciation, which is a standardized form of the Queen's English, or BBC English. This archetypal accent spread to the masses, even though only about 1 in 50 residents of England spoke this way at the time. Centuries-old dialects soon died. The original accent of Shakespeare, which sounds like a hybrid of Gaelic, Irish, and working-class English, diminished to the point of irrelevance. This was a great loss, as many of the rhymes in his original plays were rendered meaningless when reproduced in the Queen's English.

America followed a different path in its language standardization. There is no "President's English." Nobody tries to mimic his speech, except in a Saturday Night Live skit. Many U.S. presidents have had a strong regional drawl, such as Jimmy Carter, Bill Clinton, and George W. Bush. John F. Kennedy's speech style has become the go-to accent for over-the-top Northeastern speak ("ahsk nawt what yah cahntry cahn doo fohr yoo...").

Nearly all American broadcasters speak with a Midwestern, Iowan accent. Unlike European nations, they do not speak with the accent of the powerful (a New York accent) or the aristocratic (New England). We all know this is not how it is, but why is it not like this? Accents in other parts of the world gravitate to the center of wealth and power. Those from the hinterlands mimic those in the capital. Why shouldn't an Iowan hoping to become a film or television star mimic a New York accent? Why doesn't he or she practice in front of a mirror how to say "the baseball battah got to thoid base"?

To answer that question, we need to look into the history of American English. The story takes on unexpected twist and turns. It would have to – how else could the standard for American English come to reside in Iowa?

THE HISTORY OF AMERICA'S ACCENTS

Early American colonists spoke with a British accent. They did so for the simple reason that they weren't Americans – they were British subjects. It only evolved into General American English through centuries of immigration.

Language is a mutable force. It does not conform to exact weights and measurements. It is not like the kilogram, which was and still is based on a small piece of metal in the town of Sèvres, France, created in 1889 as the International Prototype Kilogram. In order to preserve the integrity of the metric system of weights, it is kept in an environmentally-controlled chamber and protected by three bell jars that can be opened only by three keys from three different people. It is taken out once every 50 years to compare to six sister copies, used as a model for 34 replicas around the world.

Language doesn't exist in such controlled conditions – it is shaped by its environment and society. As settlers pushed further West into

America, the language evolved from its English roots. A standard variety of American English formed in most of the country by the 19th century. It was based on the dialect of the Mid-Atlantic states, with notable features being a flat "a" and a strong final "r."

Not that the Founding Fathers didn't want to control the evolution of a new, standard American accent. They knew of the heavy class divisions in England and discrimination against lower-class workers due to their manner of speech. Language aficionados such as Benjamin Franklin, John Adams, and Noah Webster wanted to spread a neutral English that was free of such regional dialects. Although America never made English its national language, unlike Australia or England, the idea continued to germinate in the following decades.

The spirit of language reform and standardization began with Benjamin Franklin, who went so far as to call for the abolishment of "unnecessary letters" such as 'c', 'w', 'y' and 'j.' John Adams continued this reform movement. He proposed in 1780 that Congress establish an "American Academy for correcting, improving, and ascertaining the English language." Adams dreamed of establishing a public authority to fix and improve the language, as many of the nations of Europe had done. He spoke highly of the academies in Spain, France, and Italy, and their great successes in standardizing their own languages. It was to the shame of England that although many learned men had proposed a similar institution, the government never imposed it in such a manner. As a result, there was no standard dictionary that carried any public authority. Spellings of words were so widely divergent ('jail' could be spelled 'gaol' or 'goal'), that meaningful communication between two parties was unnecessarily complex. If the United States could standardize its language, the nation could achieve unbounded levels of success:

> The honor of forming the first public institution for refining, correcting, improving, and ascertaining the English language, I hope is reserved for congress; they have every motive that can possibly influence a public assembly to undertake it. It will have a happy effect upon the union of the States to have a public standard for all persons in every part of the continent to appeal to, both for the signification and pronunciation of the language. The constitutions of all the States in the Union are so democratical that eloquence will become the instrument for recommending men to their fellow-citizens, and the principal means of

advancement through the ranks and offices of society" *(The Words of John Adams, Second President of the United States.... by his Grandson, Charles Francis Adams:* Boston, 1852).

Noah Webster went further in his effect on standardizing and simplifying American spelling. His dictionaries and reference books sold like wildfire throughout the colonies, with his "The American Spelling Book," a fixture as common in schools as the Bible in a church. He is credited with unique American spellings different from British English, with *theater* and *center* instead of *theatre* and *centre*. He also made the British 'u' (colour, flavour, honour) fall out of fashion. He is the one who is credited with creating American Standard English.

But new waves of immigrants to America threatened this project. In 1813, Thomas Jefferson saw the influx of Irish and Scottish immigrants to the young country and worried of a cultural clash with the newcomers and America's established residents. A common identity unique to America needed to be formed, and this included the manner of speaking: "The new circumstances under which we are placed call for new words, new phrases, and for the transfer of old words to new objects. An American dialect will therefore be formed."

Jefferson believed that American English would evolve into a completely different language from English. At the end of the 19th century, English linguist Henry Sweet predicted that in 100 years, "England, America, and Australia will be speaking mutually unintelligible languages, owing to their independent changes of pronunciation." Obviously this didn't happen – Brits and Americans understand each other perfectly well, even though they both snicker at the others' accent.

Global communications have mitigated these changes, but they haven't eliminated them altogether. American English developed many of its own words, thanks to pioneers pushing west and coining terms to describe new lands with new flora and fauna. The Lewis and Clarke Expedition introduced over 500 new words to American English, many taken from Native American terms themselves. But they also gave us some of their own words. When they talked of the strange qualities of the "outlands" beyond the Mississippi River, it evolved into the term "outlandish."

Other explorers with a plucky spirit and a sense of humor created new colloquialisms. Figures such as Davy Crocket made their own quirky neologisms – such as riff-raff, hunky-dory, skedaddle, lickety-split, rambunctious, rip-snorter, humdinger, and shenanigan. Although these words are no longer used outside of aunts who cook pot roasts in linoleum-tiled kitchens, other phrases from the American frontier are more common in everyday English. They include knuckle down, go whole hog, kick the bucket, face the music, sitting on the fence, a chip on the shoulder, barking up the wrong tree, stack the deck, horse sense, stake a claim, and two cent's worth.

That is not to say that the East Coast aristocratic society did not contribute its own terms to American English. Perhaps the most universal utterance of Americans, and the phrase that foreigners immediately latch onto when they are speaking English with an American, is "OK." This term comes from the 1830s. Its origins are obscure and debated, but the most interesting theory is that it comes from the presidential campaign of eighth president Martin Van Buren. He was born in the village of Kinderhook, New York. The 20th-century etymologist Allen Walker Read argued that the wide usage of the phrase OK started during Van Buren's presidential campaign and subsequent presidency as an affectionate way to refer to "Old Kinderhook."

Today there are approximately 4,000 words that separate British and American English, such as tap/faucet, bath/tub, biscuit/cookie, and bonnet/hood. The difference became apparent enough that by the early 1900s, George Bernard Shaw quipped that "England and America are two countries separated by a common language." The reasons for the changes were many, but one reason is the English preference for comportment and erudition, and the American preference for reform and simplification.

Beyond this diversity in Transatlantic accents, differences linger in the hundreds of American dialects and sub-dialects. They can be as small as a Minnesotan pronouncing "boat" as "boot," and other features borrowed from their largely Scandinavian heritage. A Southern Pennsylvanian might use the long 'o' in words like "goat" or "go." Missourians might even call their home state "Missour-a" instead of "Missouri" (a sin many Iowans are guilty of as well).

Accents can really go off the rails in the Upper Midwest, which was made famous by the film "Fargo." This speech style is only heard in rural North Dakota or Minnesota, and rarely spoken as thickly as the characters in the film, but still has a distinct musicality. If you ask somebody about their pet goat, they'll look at you quizzically and then respond with, "Oh, you mean my pet gawwwt?"

Western American accents diverge even more sharply. The use of 'like' as an emphatic statement or signifier of indirect speech (He was like, what are you, like, doing here?") dominates. My wife is a Californian, and although her English is excellent, she has friends that use "like" more than "the."

The emergence of General American English came with industrialization and the Civil War. With new lands in the Midwest opening up to homesteading, railroad lines, and factories, America's economic center of gravity moved west. The eastern port cities and cotton regions of the American South, which still had strong economic ties to England and preferred their pattern of speech, passed the baton to new manufacturing centers of Cleveland, Chicago, Detroit, and St. Louis. Americans had been slowly discarding the British accent for over a century, but this process accelerated as British influence on America diminished.

The Midwestern dialect becoming the basis of General American English is often attributed to the mass migration of Midwestern farmers to California or the Pacific Northwest. Most of the settlers were of German, Scots-Irish, or North British descent, producing an amalgamation that largely resembled standard American English today. Rhoticism was a dominant feature of this accent, which means that speakers pronounce the 'r' in words such as hard, instead of the BBC-preferred 'hahd.' Many of the new European settlers spoke with this accent; their settling in the Midwest fortified it. Industrialists of the Midwest began to eclipse their brethren back East, and non-rhotic English lost its luster, dying out in the United States.

But the standardization of Iowan English would not have been complete without the help of Hollywood.

IOWA'S INFLUENCE ON HOLLYWOOD

Famous TV personalities spend much of their early career working to eliminate their regional accent. Stephen Colbert, a South Carolina native, spent hours a day eliminating his draw, because he knew that Southerners were depicted as unintelligent on television. Decades of shows like *The Beverly Hillbillies* left their mark. It would not have benefited his current career as a satirist, skewering the unintelligence of the American journalistic and political classes. Linda Ellerbee, a long-time reporter for NBC News, strove early on to eliminate her Texas accent. "In television, you are not supposed to sound like you're from anywhere," she said.

But early television and film stars were from somewhere, and that somewhere was Iowa. It was the role of Iowans on the silver screen that confirmed their accent as the standard American dialect. During the Golden Age of Hollywood (late 1920s-early 1960s), when film dominated the American consciousness in a way that it never did before or never has since, the screen was full of Midwesterners who took their accents to the masses. At this time America saturated its nation with movie theaters. After World War I, nearly 40 percent of the world's theaters were in America. It produced more films than any other nation, filling the world's cinemas with American films. "The sun, it now appears, The Saturday Evening Post wrote in the mid 1920s, "never sets on the British empire and the American motion picture." And the American motion picture was filled with Iowans.

Film goers across the nation may have been under the impression that this was the "correct" way to speak. Who could blame them? John Wayne strutted his ruggedness and calm demeanor across three decades of cinema. The native of Winterset, Iowa appeared or starred in over 170 films from 1926 to 1976. He was a marquee star whose name was displayed in small town theaters across the United States. Wayne's profile rose further during World War II, in which the 34-year-old toured U.S. bases and hospitals in the South Pacific from 1943-1944.

Wayne desperately wanted to fight in the war, but his studio was too afraid of losing him and prevented his status from turning into draft eligible. The actor reportedly carried guilt for decades for failing to serve in the military. His widow later suggested that he atoned for this "dereliction" by crafting an image of a super patriot in films throughout the rest of his life. He became an American cultural icon who symbolized traditional values, individuality, ruggedness, and integrity.

Other iconic Iowans emerged at this time. Two of the first superstars of television, which began to grow in popularity among middle class Americans in the 1950s, were George Reeves, the star of *The Adventures of Superman*, and Jerry Mathers of *Leave it to Beaver*. Reeves was born in Woolstock, Iowa. In 1951, he was offered the roll of Superman, even though he was reluctant to take it. Reeves considered television unimportant, much like an actor today appearing in a web-only series. The budget for *Superman* was tight. At least two half-hour episodes were filmed every six days. Multiple scripts were filmed simultaneously in order to save money by taking advantage of the standing set. Many scenes of Clark Kent talking with newspaper editor Perry White were shot back-to-back.

Despite the show's low budget, Reeves quickly became a superstar. Young fans planned their day around the show, gathering around their humming cathode ray tube screens. Reeves was aware of this status and worked to avoid public vices, such as smoking where children could see him. Although he had many extra-marital affairs – a typical practice for Hollywood stars during the Golden Age – he kept secret a relationship with a married ex-showgirl that was eight years his senior. Reeves maintained his Midwestern, down-to-earth nature throughout his career. A sign on his dressing room said "Honest George, the people's friend."

Donna Reed, the co-star of *It's a Wonderful Life*, was literally a farm girl that didn't consider acting until she was selected beauty queen at her high school in Denison. Today the welcome sign to her hometown still boasts of itself as "Home of Donna Reed." She moved to California and began her acting career at the age of 20, signing herself over to MGM studios at the height of the studio system. She received stardom for her Best Supporting Actress Academy award for her role as the prostitute Alma in *From Here to Eternity* (1953). She then moved to television and hosted *The Donna Reed Show* from 1958 to 1966.

Jerry Mathers, one of the first child stars of television, also took a large role in the American pop culture consciousness. His show, *Leave it to Beaver,* is the program most associated with idyllic American life. It was not an immediate hit. Leave it to Beaver was cancelled in its first season in 1957, ridiculed by critics for its uber-quaint take on American life, and never made a dent in nightly ratings. ABC picked up the show from CBS and ran it for another five years, but the show failed to gain traction.

It found a second life in syndication and grew in popularity. Over the decades it has proven to be the most enduring of any television show from the 1950s and considered the most purely-distilled form of mid-20th century American life. The Cleavers are the quintessential American family: two brothers who have various hijinks but never get into any real trouble, a father who works a stable job and can afford a suburban house, and a mother who vacuums while wearing a pearl necklace. The show is much parodied today for its heavy-handedness dictating the requirements for a proper middle-class life in such stifling terms.

Other prominent Iowans that dominated America's television sets included Johnny Carson, host of *The Tonight Show* from 1962 to 1992. The Corning, Iowa native was the most universally recognized television figure during the turbulent years of the 1960s to the 1980s, providing a comic, carefree escape from social tensions challenging the cohesiveness of American society. He also launched the careers of future sitcom stars and talk show hosts including Jerry Seinfeld, Roseanne Barr, David Letterman, Jay Leno, Jeff Foxworthy, and Tim Allen. He even introduced the game Twister to the world when he played it on TV in 1966 with actress Eva Gabor.

But despite his fame, Carson was reserved in nature. He avoided most large parties, considered "the most private public man who ever lived," and preferred the quieter aspects of life. Carson also had the Midwestern tendency to avoid controversy and stirring up division. Unlike 21st-century comics, who overwhelming skew to the political left and have made their beliefs known with increasing volume in recent years, Carson explicitly avoided mentioning his views on the Tonight Show. None of them were earth-shattering – he was against criminalizing extramarital sex and favored racial equality – but he did not want to be pinned down to any ideological group or alienate audience members. He said it would "hurt me as an entertainer, which is what I am... in my living room I would argue for liberalization of abortion laws, divorce laws, and there are times when I would like to express a view on the air. I would love to have taken on Billy Graham. But I'm on TV five nights a week; I have nothing to gain by it and everything to lose."

Other famous media personalities spent significant stretches of their career in Iowa. Ronald Reagan was a famed radio broadcaster, first for WOC in Davenport in 1932, the first commercial radio station west of the Mississippi River. His inaugural assignment was to broadcast the University of Iowa's homecoming game against Minnesota, which he did for $5 and bus fare. Although not a native Iowan, his years in Iowa radio likely influenced his transformation into an avuncular president during the 1980s.

Reagan gained national exposure when WOC consolidated with WHO, an NBC affiliate. His salary skyrocketed to $100 a week, an extraordinary sum for the 22-year-old. Reagan displayed his improvisational talent on air, recreating Chicago Cubs baseball games from the studio, using nothing but simple game statistics coming off the wire, creating "play-by-play" broadcasts that he never witnessed. In one episode in 1934, the wire went dead during the ninth inning of a Cubs-Cardinals game. He had the players continue to foul off pitches continuously – to the point that Billy Jurges was nearing a record for successive foul balls – until the line was restored. Reagan was the most popular radio personality in the state. He became a huge celebrity, so much so that WHO broadcasted his farewell party when he left Iowa to move to California and begin his acting career.

Iowa no longer dominates the silver screen or television set the way it did decades ago, but many influential actors and actresses still come from the state. Notable examples include Ashton Kutcher, a Cedar Rapids native who attended the University of Iowa for one year. Kutcher spent nearly a decade on *That 70s Show*, then jumped to the producer and host of MTV's *Punk'd*, then a slew of low-budget comedies before joining the cast of *Two and a Half Men* in 2011, following Charlie Sheen's Fukushima-level public meltdown. He tested his dramatic chops with the Steve Jobs biopic *Jobs*, which proved to Hollywood that casting an actor based purely on his physical resemblance to a real person is never a good operating procedure.

Other Iowans have literally saved the world. Brandon Routh, the star of the 2006 film *Superman Returns*, hailed from Iowa. He was the last Superman able to save Metropolis without simultaneously destroying it, unlike Henry Cavill's most recent incarnation of Kal-El in the 2013 reboot *Man of Steel*. Another famous Iowan is Victor native Elijah Wood. While he may not have saved our world, he can be credited for his character Frodo Baggins preventing Sauron from recovering the One Ring and overrun Middle Earth in the *Lord of the Rings* trilogy.

IOWAN ENGLISH'S DOMINANCE AND ITS DISCONTENTS

Not to say that there aren't Iowans who don't speak with some type of accent, particularly those who live in rural areas. Many speak with a casual patois. My father, who grew up in Deep River (population 279) prefers to say "warsh" instead of "wash" or "crick" instead of "creek." If he were experiencing terrible heat on a summer day, he might decide to go "warsh" in the "crick."

These discrepancies are ignored because there is a level of social conditioning among Midwesterners that their accent is perfect. Teachers do not correct students' normal pronunciation, and speech therapists do not offer any accent-reduction lessons, as they might in other corners of the country.

Other scholars have contested that Midwesterners do not speak with a neutral accent. Mathew J. Gordon, professor of English and linguistic researcher, published an article in 2002 that challenged this myth. Although he acknowledges that it is easy to imitate Southerns (y'all) or New Yorkers (fuhgedda-boudit) but not so simple with Midwesterners (uhhhh...... where's the corn?) this is not true.

Gordon's illusions were shattered in college when he discovered that words he had always pronounced as homonyms were supposed to be distinct. These included pairs such as *cot* and *caught* and *Don* and *dawn*. The vowel sound in the first of these pairs is supposed to be produced with the tongue low and back in the mouth and with the lips spread open, while the vowel of the second members of each pair involves a slightly higher tongue position and a rounding of the lips.

Most Midwesterners pronounce these the same, unaware that they are missing a vowel.

Regardless of the error, this mistake reinforces the dominance of Midwestern English rather than negates it. Nobody criticizes the cot/caught mistake, if they are even aware of it at all. Midwestern English, for all its faults and quirks, has become the default standard for correct speaking in the United States. Gordon argues that linguistic stereotypes have less to do with the actual speech of a region than with popular perceptions of the region's people. As long as the Midwest is considered by the nation at large as average, boring, neutral, or otherwise nondescript, its speech will be seen the same way.

The movement toward simplified English has had many critics over the century. Many are British, who resent that American communication forms are having an undue influence on their own language, watering down its intricacies for the sake of brute-force communication. The sharpest critic was George Orwell, who thought contemporary English of the mid-20th century to be "ugly and inaccurate." In his dystopian novel *1984*, he wrote of a totalitarian government that eliminated words in everyday speech, reducing "bad" to "ungood." By cauterizing the population's vocabulary, it worked to eliminate their ability to even produce the mental concept of these words, ultimately shutting down higher brain functions and making them ignorant and blindly submissive.

Despite criticisms of General American English, the dialect dominates the world today. It is the accent taught to people learning English as a second language across the globe, a number at least in the hundreds of millions, possibly over a billion. From packed schoolrooms of Chinese students to Korean businessmen to European doctors, all listen to the same language CDs teaching them the Iowan style of pronunciation.

The recordings nearly always feature these accents, even if they do not fit the material. My wife, an American, was asked to do a voice recording for an English instructional CD while we lived in Budapest, Hungary. The dialogue featured a British woman who had recently moved from London to her new home abroad. My wife asked the producer, "Does it matter if I am speaking with an American accent for this British character? Should I fake something?" He waved his hand – "No, no, don't worry about it. This is better."

Of course the Iowan accent can never be spoken correctly without a few extra requirements. Having straw in your mouth as you speak is the first. The second is to make innocuous and quaint comments about the weather ("reckon that storm will do a number on that unfinished 4H building at the fairground"). The third is to meet and greet people with equally folksy sayings ("weeeeelllll sir, reckon I better head back. You take care now.")

Learn these basic speaking patterns, and you will have mastered Iowan, the purest form of the English language, the apotheosis of American English.

CHAPTER FIVE

WHY IOWA CONTROLS YOUR POLITICAL DESTINY, WHEREVER YOU LIVE ON EARTH

In the throes of a harsh Iowa winter, a young mother in the small Iowa town called Pleasantville prepared to vote. She didn't have a ride to the voting station, but that didn't matter. She also didn't have a babysitter for her 2-year-old, but that didn't matter either. Republicans and Democrats had offered both of these, if only she would show up to cast her ballot on January 3.

She took advantage of the offers.

Pollsters, door-to-door campaigners, had harassed her and phone calls for months, she reasoned. Why not get something back? Besides, the army of politicos and reporters that had invaded her home state would be mostly gone by tomorrow. By next week it would be as if they had never heard of Iowa or its voters.

Iowa has by far the most disproportionate influence on who becomes president of the United States. Every four years Iowans get the chance to vote as the first state in the presidential nomination process. Any candidate who wins the Iowa caucuses usually wins presidency. As a result, each candidate spends months in the state.

The person who is vying to be the next American president, the person to control history's most powerful military juggernaut, one equipped with enough precision to kill a lone jihadist on the other side of the planet but enough firepower to blow up the planet twenty times over – this Seeker of Power must meet and greet and try to win over every last Iowan.

Because the American president is the leader of the free world and the most influential figure on the planet, pound for pound, vote for vote, Iowans have more political power than anyone else on earth.

Political campaigns realize this and allocate their resources accordingly. So many millions of dollars pour into Iowa for leaflets, campaign events, canvasser salaries, and rallies that the average vote of an Iowan costs over $200. (In contrast, candidates will spend less than a tenth of that amount wooing voters in other states).

Two years before an election takes place, both Democratic and Republican party candidates begin the grueling process of campaigning in Iowa. Some of them go so far as to make the state their de facto home. Campaigning means travel to every single one of the 99 counties, even counties with only 2,000 people, and attending six or seven campaign events a day to groups that often consist of fewer than 20-30 attendees.

Candidates are forced to attend the Iowa State Fair in the sweltering heat of August and munch on corn dogs or whatever else can be fried and put on a stick (which at the Iowa State Fair might include Snickers Bars and Chinese food). They have to greet residents on the town squares of tiny burgs and show up at meat packing plants at 6 a.m. And no matter the candidate's background, obligatory photo ops must include red barns, farm machinery, corn fields and livestock.

Relationships with local political power brokers are essential. A normally meaningless endorsement from the Chair of the Orange City Republican party is as coveted as a papal blessing. With enough of these endorsements, the reasoning goes, there is the possibility of winning the caucus. If they win Iowa, then they get an explosion of publicity to help fundraising and give momentum in other early-voting states. The White House, it appears, is just a few miles from Iowa.

Some politicians have tried to ignore this process, only to see their campaigns implode.

In 2007, Rudy Giuliani was the heavy favorite to win the Republican nomination for the 2008 presidential election. However, the former New York mayor bypassed Iowa and New Hampshire to focus on Florida, where many New Yorkers had retired.

Giuliani initially dominated the polls in Florida. But as the Iowa and New Hampshire contests pushed other candidates into the media spotlight, Giuliani began to lose traction while the media swarmed around John McCain and Mitt Romney. McCain won Florida and eventually the party nomination. Giuliani came away with a harsh reminder that hell hath no fury like an Iowa voter scorned.

Other politicians utilized the Iowa caucuses perfectly. Jimmy Carter finished first among named candidates in 1976 (although "Undecided" actually won in terms of total votes). This launched him on the road to the White House.

John Kerry and John Edwards finished first and second in the Iowa caucuses in 2004, giving their sputtering campaigns new life, and pushing them into the presidential and vice presidential nominee slots for the Democratic Party.

Barack Obama performed a major upset win over Hillary Clinton in the 2008 caucus. Obama was considered an outlier until he won the Iowa caucuses. But his win that led to a massive surge of volunteers and donations. He dubbed this triumph the beginning of his political revolution and perhaps even a new chapter for the nation. In his victory speech, Obama declared, "Years from now, you'll look back and you'll say that this was the moment, this was the place where America remembered what it means to hope."

THE CAUCUSES FROM AN INSIDER'S VIEW

I was a college student during the 2004 Iowa caucuses and worked for Iowa State University's student newspaper, the *Iowa State Daily*. I was given the political beat and reported on the caucuses in the months leading up to the vote. It was an exciting time to be a a rare opportunity to report on actual news, especially since assignments for student reporters more typically involved coverage of one of the campuses' hundreds of student groups holding a bake sale or some other nondescript event to "raise awareness."

The Iowa caucuses were a world away from those non-issues. Suddenly I was going to campaign events, rubbing elbows with reporters from the Associated Press or The New York Times, and interviewing the same presidential candidates that these national journalists were. It was like a kid suddenly being invited to the adults' table at Thanksgiving, then being asked my opinion on politics or the economy.

In November 2003 I attended a debate among the Democratic candidates in Des Moines. At a press event afterwards each of the candidates came backstage to talk to the media. I was given the chance to lob questions about foreign policy or whatever else to these politicians, which I did, of course, while trying desperately to sound intelligent.

Celebrities that aligned themselves with the Democratic Party were on hand, too, and I was ecstatic to see Rob Reiner, who directed *Spinal Tap*, one of my favorite films of all time.

As if I did this all the time, I casually walked up to him and said "Thanks for *Spinal Tap*."

"My pleasure," he responded.

Though that evening I rubbed elbows with more major political figures than I would again in my lifetime, this Rob Reiner moment definitely took the night.

Other chances to talk to important politicians included 30-minute phone interviews with then-candidates John Kerry and John Edwards. In no other state would these candidates give the time of day to a semi-coherent student reporter. But they knew that students read the *Iowa State Daily*, and each candidate was desperate for as many votes as possible.

Kerry, who is now Secretary of State, talked to me the same way he talks in every interview or press event: eloquent but long-winded and with a propensity to wander off from his main point. Edwards, who is now a disgraced former politician known best for cheating on his terminally ill wife and fathering a child with New Age video producer Rielle Hunter, also came off the same in a one-on-one interview as he did in the media. Edwards oozed smarminess and faux car-salesman charm, even over the phone.

Whatever opportunities I had to talk to these politicians, I was one of thousands of Iowans caught in the middle of a media circus. Iowans simply get used to seeing the national and global media on main streets in towns across the state. CNN satellite trucks are parked on small-town streets to cover debates between presidential candidates. Associated Press reporters show up at diners in places like Carlisle or Norwalk to ask residents their opinions of the flat tax or Mideast terrorism over coffee and scrambled eggs.

An endorsement to a candidate from The Des Moines Register means more than the favor of The Washington Post or The New York Times. When the Register unexpectedly endorsed Mitt Romney instead of Barack Obama in 2012, the endorsement itself ate up an entire national news cycle.

The only thing more plentiful than the media are the political campaigners themselves. Their TV commercials, radio ads, brochures, and phone calls seemed to be pumped into the state's air and water. Approximately $36 million is spent in advertisements. In the month before the caucuses, there are about nine hours of commercials every single day. There are Commercial breaks feature non-stop political announcements. As January 3 draws closer, pollsters or campaign volunteers call each house three or four times a night.

In 1972, Sen. George McGovern, who went on to be the Democratic candidate in the presidential election that year, explained the significance of Iowa with these words: "Iowa is terribly important. It's the first test in the nation, where we get any test at all."

His statement is only partly true.

There is another test that comes earlier, although it is far more informal and open to manipulation by the better-funded caucus campaigns. The first voting event in Iowa is the Ames Straw Poll, a presidential straw poll on the August of years in an election cycle. It is for Republican candidates only and is the first weather vane of popularity for the candidates.

A candidate can often win this contest by busing in his or her supporters, and artificially inflate the numbers. In 2003, Mitt Romney, who funded his campaign with his own personal wealth and those of his associates, put air conditioning in his campaign tent at the straw poll – a tempting lure to the undecided wanting to escape the stifling August heat. The straw poll also acts as the party's immune system, forcing out candidates that might have rabid supporters but are so fringe they might embarrass the party.

"The straw poll allows Republican contenders to strut their stuff, round up and bus in supporters, sponsor some music and food, and blare out their message," said Steffen Schmidt, an affable Iowa State political science professor known by his students and the media as "Dr. Politics."

"The results may serve as an early warning system for Iowa Republicans and the tens of thousands of caucus attendees as to what 'whacko bird,' as Senator McCain might call them, is on the hunt. The straw poll is like a food fair where the media can come and snack on the wares. Journalists go away reporting what's delicious and what's inedible. That spares the rest of the nation that distasteful job."

The real test of the Iowa caucuses is important for reasons that go beyond being the first voting contest in the nation. The level of support that candidates get from rank-and-file voters shows a good indication of how they will do with the rest of America. Iowans show close to the median of America in most categories: income, social views, military support, and tolerance of government intervention in daily life. The results from a campaign in Iowa serve as a microcosm of the rest of the nation and tell a candidate if his or her platform will gain traction elsewhere. If the message fails to affect voters in Iowa, it's probably not going to elsewhere.

The caucuses are also a good testing ground for a dark horse candidate to determine if he or she should bother with sticking through the entire campaign. Running in only one state is much simpler and cheaper than launching a nationwide campaign. Candidates can live off the land here and run their campaigns into near-bankruptcy, praying for a win or strong finish so that new supporters will come to their aid. For this reason, many second or third-tier candidates drop out of the race entirely if they do poorly in Iowa. To retire their debt, they offer their endorsement in a bidding war among top-tier candidates in return for a generous donation to the failed candidate.

Media attention swarms around the Iowa caucuses winner for two or three days; many start to consider his or her campaign to be viable. The winner also gets a fundraising explosion of several hundred thousand, if not millions, of dollars since many wealthy donors sit on the fence and wait to see who won before pulling out a checkbook. National party leaders will see the winner as a possible presidential candidate and start to warm up; they've shown their platform is desirable. Iowa is representative of Middle America and winning there proves that one is not an extremist and possibly has a shot at the national election.

VOTING FOR THE NEXT PRESIDENT IN YOUR NEIGHBOR'S LIVING ROOM

Explaining how the Iowa caucuses actually work is a four-year tradition that is as predictable in its coming as the voting process itself. Millions of Americans – and hundreds of millions more around the world – hear about the contest on the news for months, but they have no idea what it means, beyond a vague idea that it is a voting contest where somebody wins, and that winning is very important. Reporters alike are confused, as nobody but the veteran reporters have any idea how this voting process differs from regular voting. Don't voters just pull a lever or fill out a paper ballot, and the winner is the one who gets the most votes?

If only it were that simple.

The caucuses are run by the state Democratic and Republican Parties, not by the government. Approximately 1,781 caucuses take place around the state, where citizens gather in small community meetings to choose candidates and discuss local party business. These take place in meeting halls, church basements, municipal centers, and even living rooms. Perhaps the best explanation of the process comes from the *Economist*, a bit ironic considering it is a British publication. Here is a paraphrase of their take on the voting contest:

Caucuses are held precincts around the state. Representatives of each candidate speak before those attending mark their choice on a ballot. After a convoluted series of regional and statewide meetings, the candidates are awarded "delegates" in proportion to their share of the vote. The delegates, in turn, attend the national convention in August at which the party's presidential nominee is formally selected.

Iowa will send just 28 delegates to the convention, out of a nationwide total of 2,286. But because it is the first state to vote, its influence is completely out of proportion to its size. Candidates who do well in the caucuses gain momentum that can propel their campaigns forward; those that do poorly often find themselves starved of media attention, donations, and volunteers. The results from Iowa, along with those from New Hampshire and South Carolina, the next two states to vote, usually narrow the field down from nine candidates, leaving the rest of the country with just two or three options.

In the Republican caucuses, there is no opportunity to switch candidates after an initial tally, and no obligation to reveal your choice. But everybody votes at the same time and does so publicly. This open book process allows supporters of one candidate to exert pressure on their friends, neighbors and fellow parishioners.

The Democratic Party's caucus procedure is a more complicated. Everyone is in a big room, and participants show their support for a candidate by standing in a designated area of the caucus site. Democratic caucuses require more time and multiple candidate preferences from a participant. For 30 minutes, you can talk with your friend or neighbor, and try to convince them why you should vote for this or that candidate.

Some people in these groups will be deputized, and they go to other groups trying to pull in their support. After 30 minutes, supporters for each candidate are counted, and one has to meet a 15-percent threshold. If the group doesn't, they disperse and go join other candidate groups. Supporters of third-tier candidates that are unlikely to meet this threshold usually agree beforehand whom they will support. Then there's another 30 minutes of politicking where people try to convince one another. And when it's all over, the people in each camp are publicly counted and the results tabulated.

The turnout for the caucuses is low. Only 119,000 Republicans voted in 2008 to pick Mike Huckabee over Mitt Romney; just 88,000 were present in 2000 to choose George W. Bush over John McCain. That is a small fraction of the state's 645,000 registered Republicans, besides its 3 million residents. The caucus-goers tend to be older, whiter, and more religious than most Republicans, which is a party that is older, whiter and more religious than the nation as a whole.

That can lead to strong showings for candidates like Mike Huckabee, who was a former Baptist minister. It also diminishes the prospects of more moderate candidates, such as Romney, a former governor of Massachusetts. And the low turnout and the public element of the voting can favor candidates with dedicated ranks of volunteers, such as Ron Paul, a libertarian from Texas.

The Iowa caucuses already give outsized power to Iowa's 3 million residents; the nature of the caucuses amplifies this power by handing it to the 100,000 politically engaged citizens who actually show up. In sum, the future president is chosen by a population sample smaller in size than any of New York's five boroughs.

The voting procedure is also notoriously non-scientific. For the Republican Party caucus, each voter officially casts his or her own vote by secret ballot. Voters are presented blank sheets of paper with no candidates' names on them. Voters write down their choices, leave after they declare their preferences, and the Republican Party of Iowa tabulates the results.

This method has led to controversial snafus. In 2012, Mitt Romney was declared the winner by only eight votes. Three weeks later party members announced that Rick Santorum had actually won by eight votes. Analysts said that if the results had been correctly counted in the first place, Santorum would have got the party nomination, because he would have enjoyed the advantage of the press attention and donations that come from winning the Iowa caucuses. *Des Moines Register* senior political reporter Jennifer Jacobs wrote that such inaccuracies devalued its credibility in the eyes of the national media and both political party leaders.

Whatever the drawbacks to the Iowa caucuses, the entire process feels like a throwback to a Revolutionary-era America, where government policies were hammered out in raucous town hall meetings, with participants giving rousing soliloquies as they drank from their tankards of ale. It even evokes feelings of Athenian democracy, where any citizen can give a speech regardless of their knowledge – or lack of knowledge – on the topic at hand. The audience shouts praise or disagreement at their speech, creating a strong give-and-take dynamic.

Surprisingly, the national importance of the Iowa caucuses is a modern phenomenon. Drake University Professor Hugh Winebrenner documented it as a product of the TV and George McGovern Era in his study of the caucuses, "The Making of a Media Event." It began in 1972 when Democrats moved their caucus to January, giving the state its first-in-the-nation status. This status was then codified into law. According to Title II Chapter 43.4 of the Iowa Code, "the date shall be at least eight days earlier than the scheduled date for any meeting, caucus, or primary which constitutes the first determining stage of the presidential nominating process in any other state." Republicans followed suit by moving up their caucus in 1976.

That means that Iowa is legally obligated to stay in first place. It has been the epicenter of political and media attention ever since.

No state has ever put up an adequate fight to challenge Iowa's first-in-the-nation status. New Hampshire may harbor feelings of jealousy, as its primary only comes a few days after the Iowa caucuses. But New Hampshire has the first primary in the nation, giving the Granite State its own special status. Some campaigns have succeeded in the past by bypassing Iowa all together and focusing on New Hampshire instead. Two famous examples are John McCain's insurgent campaign against George W. Bush in 2000, where his win challenged the inevitability of Bush's nomination. Hillary Clinton also resurrected her campaign here in 2008 after a stunning loss to Barack Obama in the Iowa caucuses.

Whatever its quirks, the Iowa caucuses remain a treasured affair. Iowans consider it to be a pure form of democracy. Farmers and local professionals who engaged in the type of grassroots activism envisioned by the Founding Fathers passed it down. The caucuses are a break from the superficial sound bite culture of 21st-century politics, where complex positions on deficit reduction and nuclear proliferation are dumbed down to 30-second, focus group-tested statements. Caucuses allow for slower, in-depth discussion and honest exchanges between neighbors.

"It's magic to see people stand up and declare their support for a candidate, and it's a communal activity," said Gordon Fischer, a former chairman of the Iowa Democratic Party, to The New York Times in 2008. Iowans agree.

STRANGE HOPEFULS

Perhaps one of the most interesting effects of the Iowa caucuses is the strange characters that it brings to the state. Besides the

Democratic and Republican Party heavyweights are a slew of dozens of third-party contenders who flood the ballot every election but have no chance of winning. They spend months campaigning in Iowa, pushing as hard for their platform as do the legitimate candidates despite little attention except from those who share their eccentric views.

Some represent fringe beliefs such as fascism. Jackson Grimes was the 2004 front-running candidate for the United Fascist Union in 2004 and was an ardent follower of Italian leader Benito Mussolini. If elected, he promised to move politics toward astrology and paganism.

"I believe it is my destiny to become President," Grimes said on his Web site, www.ufu.gq.nu. "The stars and planets say it is time for the United Fascist Union to rule America, so that Pagan Rome can be back in the Physical World once more. It was written in the stars from the dawn of creation that Jack Grimes would become president."

If voters weren't excited about fascism, they could turn to the National Barking Spiders Resurgence Party, which promised lower crime, a cleaner environment and meatloaf on Wednesdays. "Today's National Barking Spider Resurgence Party is truly determined to renew America's most basic bargains: triple coupon Saturdays and ballots even a child can fathom," said candidate Michael Bay on his campaign web site.

Grimes and Bay were two of the many unknown figures running for president in 2004. A total of 178 people were registered to run for president, including 66 Democrats, 27 Republicans and 37 other political parties, including the Christian Falangist Party and the Turtle Political Party.

Robert Lowry, an associate professor of political science at Iowa State University, pointed out that off-key candidates have been a staple of every presidential election. Any American-born citizen with a few hundred dollars, several signatures and the right registration forms can campaign for the White House, and many do.

"There have always been these candidates running for president," he said. "Sometimes these people want to get their issue out. Other times they just want to get publicity."

Not all unlikely candidates exist under the radar. Ross Perot ran under the Reform Party in 1992 and 1996 and took more than 15 percent of the popular vote. In 2000, Ralph Nader was the Green Party alternative to traditional party candidates Bush and Al Gore.

However, the majority of third-party candidates are dismal failures. Prohibition party candidate Earl Dodge — whose main goal is reinstating the 1930s alcohol ban — has run three unsuccessful presidential campaigns. William Bryk, the Federalist Party candidate, represents a party that has been largely defunct since 1824.

Some candidates run despite being obviously ineligible. An example is Daniel Vovak, who ran for president in 2004. At the time he was a 31-year old Republican (U.S. presidents must be at least 35 years of age) who wore an American Revolution-era wig to his campaign events.

Vovak ran his campaign armed only with his colonial wig, a semi-reliable cell phone, and his truck, which he affectionately called "Air Ford One." He crisscrossed Iowa for several months prior to the 2004 caucuses. When voting results were tallied and Vovak sadly did not meet the minimum threshold, he dropped out of the race and become a waiter in Florida. But he was still proud of the ideals of his candidacy.

"I don't know the difference between Medicare and Medicaid," Vovak said in a 2003 article for *The Iowa State Daily*. "They both sound the same so I can't see why the government doesn't lump those two programs together." However, this lack of political acumen didn't stop his campaigning.

I had the chance to follow Daniel Vovak when he visited Iowa State campus. It was quite a sight to behold: an eccentric man in a fake powdered wig approaching students and telling them of his simple ambitions for the future."Hi," he'd begin, "I'm Daniel Vovak and I'm running for president."

Vovak wore the wig so voters would remember him. He claimed that he spent his time in small settings because he touted a platform called "Small Ideas for America." His three main platform ideas centered on tightening America's borders, controlling judges and lawsuits because they're "out of control," and canceling the White House copy of The New York Times because the president "should be reading about small- town America from small newspapers."

Vovak's enthusiasm was met with mixed reactions from students. Responses varied from confused laughter to questions like, "President of what?" But the laughter subsided when listeners realized that underneath the Revolution-era wig was a man completely devoted to winning the White House.

"At first I didn't believe he was running for president," said student Jennie Erwin. "It would be great to get somebody young elected. But the wig isn't helping him out."

The candidate disagreed. Vovak believed the wig was the key to giving him recognition as a candidate. It was a clever idea to help audiences remember him; it saved millions of dollars on advertising; and it evoked the Whig Party roots of the Republican Party and demonstrated his commitment to the fundamentals of the United States Constitution. "When I first arrived in Iowa in July on a Greyhound bus, they accidentally lost my luggage, which included my wig," he said. "When I lost my wig, I nearly lost my candidacy," he complained.

Vovak did get plenty of free publicity. He garnered interviews and feature stories in 52 newspapers and 6 television stations. Vovak's campaign strategy was to drop by the newspaper office when he first entered town. The editor would meet with him briefly, then run into the newsroom and say to a reporter, "You won't believe it. Some guy in a wig says he's running for president. Do you want to interview him?"

Reporters jumped at the chance. The wig-wearing candidate gave the small-town reporter a chance to write an amusing story about an eccentric figure, letting him or her break away from the tedium of reporting on high school basketball games, bake sales, grip-and-grin photos, and local charity auctions. As the reporter asked Vovak questions about his candidacy, in the back of his mind he or she was constructing anecdotes and clever quips about a vagrant trying to seek the White House. In return Vovak got the press attention he craved, so both won.

Vovak rightfully boasted of running his campaign on a shoestring budget. He slept in the back of his truck whenever he couldn't find someone willing to put him up for a few days. Indeed, when I interviewed him several years back, he didn't know where he would sleep that night. And he showed he understood the irony of this approach to campaigning. "A few months ago I met with [former Iowa Governor Tom] Vilsack and six hours later I was sleeping in the back of my truck. I'm showing people the humility of my campaign and that it's grassroots of the truest form."

It truly was grassroots. Vovak never had a permanent home during his campaign. When he politicked with locals and small town folk, he often asked them if he could stay on their couch for the night, right after articulating how he would be the best person to run the free world. And many, often pastors of small congregations, took him in.

Why would a well-spoken and seemingly intelligent man live for months in such an unpredictable, transient life for a stunt campaign? Was this a promotional scheme for some larger project? Was he secretly being filmed crashing formal events, similar to Sacha Baron Cohen's *Borat?*

It turns out that he had had a career as a comedy writer and had written a script for an unproduced film that satirized the Monica Lewinsky scandal. A former editor of newspapers in Ohio and Connecticut, Vovak had also ghostwritten a variety of novels. A book published under his own name initially opened the door for his presidential candidacy. The book, loosely based on Vovak's life, is about a young ideologue named Luke Vovak who is prompted to run for president. At the end of the book, the reader is left guessing as to whether Luke will run.

His actual campaign through Iowa was less storied. When he fired a question at the Iowa Governor during a press conference at the Iowa Press Convention, the governor waved away the question and called the wigged man an "invader from the east." On January 11, 2004, he was ejected from the audience of the final Democratic presidential debate because the event was invitation-only and not for Republicans.

In the end, he lost, of course, in the Iowa caucuses by then-president Bush.

However, Vovak was not finished with his political career. When Jack Ryan withdrew as the Republican Senate candidate for Illinois in 2004, Vovak sought the nomination against a young upstart named Barack Obama. The Illinois Republican State Central Committee even interviewed him to run. He showed up in his wig and did nothing to hide the facts that he was still living out of his truck and not even a resident of Illinois so they declined his candidacy.

Later in his life, Vovak spent time in legitimate politics. He was elected member of the Montgomery County Republican Central Committee, serving at-large in Maryland's largest county. Vovak died of cancer in 2011. His whimsical take on politics will be sorely missed in the Iowa caucuses, which can easily turn into a stuffy affair, regardless of its importance.

TOO WHITE, CONSERVATIVE, AND OLD?

Strange hopefuls aside, much criticism of the Iowa caucuses remains. We already mentioned that to a large degree, the most radical supporters participate in the caucus voting process. And typical voters are older, whiter, and more traditional than the average American. In the end, 100,000 people who don't represent a good cross section of the American public may well choose the next president. Thus the Iowa caucuses are at high risk of swaying elections in the wrong direction.

Critics complain that Iowa is too parochial, quaint, conservative, and out of touch with modern life in the United States to represent all people in America. The stereotype persists of farmers or small-town dwellers with social values two generations behind the mainstream, barely able to tolerate people of other races when most states have confronted these issues years ago.

Exhibit A offered to support this premise the argument is the outsized influence of Bob Vander Plaats. The three-time failed gubernatorial candidate has become a socially conservative power broker in Iowa and is courted by every Republican presidential hopeful. The lanky former high school principal rose to fame when he took on the Iowa Supreme Court's 2009 ruling that legalized same-sex marriage. Vander Plaats engineered a statewide campaign against three justices on the ballot in November 2010, leading to their crushing defeat. He hopes to eventually have the marriage law overturned.

Because of his position in Iowa, every prospective Republican candidate pays Vander Plaats a visit, and they typically must renounce abortion or same-sex marriage to have any hope of winning his support. If Vander Plaats is pleased with a candidate he will throw the support of his small and committed group of activists behind that person's election.

To outside analysts such as Steffen Schmidt, Vander Plaats is a "poodle trainer," who makes candidates "jump through hoops, threatens them, and makes them come to him if they want support. And he's been remarkably and frighteningly successful."

He has definitely been successful. Rick Santorum earned Vander Plaats's endorsement in 2012 and nearly won the Iowa caucuses as a result. Mike Huckabee won his support in 2008 and did win the Iowa caucuses.

Richard Cohen, a columnist for The Washington Post, blasted the entire Iowa voting contest for these reasons. In his column, "Iowa and New Hampshire, the GOP's Primary Problem," Cohen reacted to the Republican National Committee's "Growth and Opportunity Project" report this way:

> Missing from the report are any critical words about the Iowa caucuses or the New Hampshire primary. These are the early contests where, if past is prologue, the presidential candidates of the future will take positions pleasing to the ears of extraordinarily conservative and religious voters. They will call for a roundup of illegal Hispanic immigrants; condemn same-sex marriage; sing hosannas to local control of the schools; denounce the federal government in all its varied forms; promise to die for ethanol; lament the absence of God from the classroom; utter cockamamie warnings about vaccinations; vow to eradicate Planned Parenthood from planet Earth; rail against foreign aid, the United Nations, the mainstream press, the teaching of evolution and, for good measure, the mainstream press again. Whoever does this best might win the first two contests.

However, political analyst Steffen Schmidt answers these criticisms of Iowa's biases by countering that the true problem with Iowans having so much political power is not a problem with the voting system, but elitist columnists' *oikophobia*, or fear of the common man. Coastal elites worry that those knuckle draggers in the flyover state have too much electoral power. Imagine the horror that a New Yorker could ultimately be governed by a politician chosen by an Iowan.

New York Times columnist Frank Bruni expressed as much. He wrote that Ron Paul in 2012 trumpeted the endorsement of a pastor who spoke of executing homosexuals and Rick Perry pledged to use predator drones and thousands of troops to protect the U.S./Mexican border from illegal immigrants, using language often reserved for terrorists from Pakistan. They were only topped by Rick Santorum, who when bringing his "Faith, Family and Freedom" tour to eastern Iowa promised not to bend to secularists that believed a stable family did not require God-fearing parents. These candidates, Bruni wrote, all spoke to Iowa's shame:

> None of these three men is likely to win the Republican nomination. But before they exit stage right — stage far right, that is — they and a few of their similarly quixotic, similarly strident competitors will do no small measure of damage to the Republican Party and no great favors to the country as a whole. What happens in Iowa doesn't stay in Iowa: it befouls Republicans' image nationally, becomes a millstone around the eventual nominee's neck and legitimizes debate about some matters that shouldn't be debatable.

To Bruni, Iowa merely served as a theater of the absurd, underscoring "general nuttiness and moral extremism." The primaries served to bring out the extremism in candidates, when they tested statements that would resonate with a highly conservative audience. In Iowa, 100,000 of the most fervent voters, most of them white, coax out of the candidates a "Bible-thumping, border-militarizing harshness... that's a tonal turnoff to the swing voters who will probably decide the general election."

However, Schmidt argued that the Iowa caucuses are not as susceptible to the hijacking of "extremists" as its critics suggest. First of all, judging by how well the GOP has done winning statehouses and governorships, the Republican Party offers alternatives to Democrats' much more liberal positions. Regional and state races aren't won with just the Republican voters, since neither the GOP nor the Democrats have majorities. That means that Republicans in these 30 states have also attracted independent voters and probably also some "Reagan Democrats."

Second, Schmidt notes that while a "liberal like Cohen" may well see the Republican positions as sharply defined, extreme views are in reality Rush Limbaugh's and Michele Bachmann's positions. The Mitt Romney wing of the GOP was leading on the 2012 caucus night. The Romney wing takes a much more nuanced and sophisticated position on most of these issues. Furthermore, many Americans are, in fact, conservative in spite of changes in public opinion on issues such as same-sex marriage. In other words, Cohen seems to have missed the fact that some of these positions actually are the views of the vast majority of Republicans, and not just in Iowa.

Schmidt acknowledges that the Iowa caucuses are imperfect. But he defies anyone to come up with a better solution. After all, Iowa has a good track record of picking winners to run the state. Iowa and New Hampshire have very effectively picked winners in the past. Democrats Jimmy Carter, Walter Mondale, Bill Clinton, Al Gore, John Kerry and Barack Obama all won the Iowa caucuses and went on to get their party's nomination. Obviously, several of them also became president. On the Republican side, Gerald Ford, Ronald Reagan, George H.W. Bush, Bob Dole and George W. Bush won the Iowa caucuses and the nomination, and several of them went on to become president.

"We know that even final election results are imperfect," he wrote in a 2014 Des Moines Register opinion column. "While the vote counting can be improved, it's just silly to claim that this nullifies the very useful role Iowa plays in winnowing the field of candidates. After all, the 2012 caucuses produced three strong representatives of the three factions that are the Republican Party today. I'd say that Iowa voters have done their very best to take presidential candidate selection very seriously. They have never 'picked' the president, but they always have given people who think they could do the job a good looking over on behalf of the media and the American people. Iowa voters have then sent on their way three choices, one of which in all but one [election] year went on to become the candidate of their party."

AN IMPERFECT BUT SUCCESSFUL PROCESS

Not to say that other problems don't persist. Campaigns are willing to pay top dollar for Iowan politicians to join them and provide local expertise. This can result in bidding wars and even illegal, under-the-table payments for consultants to switch campaigns. The high dollar amounts are sore temptations to Iowa politicians, whose salaries rarely break out of the mid-five figures.

The Des Moines Register reported on the guilty verdict handed down to Kent Sorenson in 2014 for concealing payments he received from Ron Paul's presidential campaign. Sorenson, a Republican elected to the Iowa Senate in 2010, obstructed the investigation into the incident. He secretly negotiated with the Paul campaign to abandon Michelle Bachmann's sinking ship in 2012 and received $73,000 in secret payments to do so. One $25,000 check was given to Sorenson's wife by a company owned by a Paul campaign staffer's wife. Other monthly payments were routed through a film production company to avoid Federal Election Commission reporting requirements.

Iowa politicians moved into quick damage control to protect the status of the caucuses, their darling of civic democracy. After the verdict, Governor Terry Branstad said he believed the integrity of the caucuses remained intact. The Sorenson case, he said, was an isolated incident of wrongdoing. It was not like Illinois, whose Chicago style politics results in a revolving door between prisons and the Senate Chambers.

"This is the way we do things in Iowa," Branstad said. "When we find wrongdoing, we investigate it and we take action to see that justice is done. I think it is a tribute to the political system of our state and to the Senate itself."

In short, whatever the problems that surround the ballot-casting process of the caucuses, Iowa deserves its status as having the first-in-the-nation voting. It is a remedy to the problems that many Americans perceive as the sickness in our politics.

Analysts such as Glenn Reynolds have dubbed the current class of Congressional representatives as the worst in history. Many see these officials ignorant, uninformed, and controlled by lobbyists' cash.

In light of the foibles in America's national politics, there is something delightfully quirky about handing over so much power to run-of-the-mill Iowans. Yes, they are not fully representative of a democratic cross-sampling of every racial, ethnic, religious, and ideological group in America. Yes, it is mostly the party zealots who come out to vote. And yes, Iowa is a small farm state that looks nothing like California or New York.

But once every four years the American political system, so often dominated by powerful outside interests, corporations, and billion-dollar lobbying firms, is guided by something so small and understated as a quiet state in the center of the country. How right it seems, somehow.

CONCLUSION

IOWA AT THE CROSSROADS

Iowa could be called the small state that always punched above its weight. At its most densely populated time, only 3 million people lived here, and many people outside of Iowa would be hard-pressed to name any of its natives, except perhaps President Herbert Hoover, hardly an exemplary choice. But as this book has shown, it managed to change global agriculture, reform the world's university system, teach the world how to speak English, and provide plenty of multicultural fodder for the American dream.

Iowa is an underappreciated land with an outsized influence and a capacity to inspire extraordinary affection.

There is another place that has the same number of residents and also has a mighty reach despite its small size. That place is Jamaica, the Caribbean island known for reggae, dreadlocks, steel drums, and Olympic sprinters.

Roifield Brown is a British producer and digital media strategist of Jamaican background. Much like myself, he has worked to show how his homeland's deeds remain unsung. Also like myself, he wants to sing those songs and make them known. He has produced the podcast "How Jamaica Conquered the World," which was fully sanctioned by the Jamaican government. The end result is an oral history of the island from its Western colonization to the 50th anniversary of independence in 2012.

But has Jamaica really had that much influence, or is he merely a native son looking at his ancestral homeland through rose-colored glasses?

Brown argues the former.

Other countries of similar geographic size such as Qatar, Lebanon, and Gambia barely register on the global radar. Those with similar population sizes such as Armenia, Mongolia, and Kuwait are similarly non-descript. But Jamacia's Olympic athletes consistently overpower its American and Chinese competitors. Its accent is the lingua franca of the world's youth. And its music transformed the global record industry.

"Jamaica conquered the world primarily through music," Brown told me. "The one thing that anyone in the world will say about Jamaica if you ask them to name one thing is reggae. Then, they will say Bob Marley. And increasing in the last five years, they'd probably end up saying Usain Bolt. That in itself feels incredibly unremarkable. But if you are to put everything in context of other countries of a similar size or GDP, such as Cambodia, it is a country which has an incredibly rich history, but the average person couldn't say one thing about Cambodia. If Jamaican culture were 3,000 years old, there would be professors studying it like ancient Greece. It would be a serious topic for study and commentary."

To Brown, Jamaica is a global culture that is used to express everything from euphoric joy to rebellion. When the Arab Spring started in Tunisia in 2011, protestors were singing "Get Up, Stand Up" as they marched down the road. Slums in Kampala, Uganda feature images of Bob Marley as a symbol of fighting oppression. Puma, the official sponsor of the Jamaican Athletics Team, deliberately sponsored Jamaica because it has an attractiveness to Western youth and youth around the world.

But despite Iowa and Jamaica's similar outsized influence in the world, they have little culture in common. A white middle-aged farmer dressed in a flannel shirt and Carhartt jacket wouldn't have much to say to a dreadlocked Caribbean Rastafarian.

Sadly their homelands also face similar problems. Both have

struggled with long-term economic decline. In the American colonial period, Jamaica and the rest of the Caribbean were the wealthiest places to settle. Vast tracts of land for sugar cane production made its owners rich beyond belief. The earliest migrants to the mainland American South hailed from the Caribbean. Their new home was much poorer and more disease-ridden than their old home. Today, the relative wealth of the American South and Jamaica is completely reversed.

Iowa is experiencing similar hardship. It has watched its small towns die for decades. The farm crisis in the 1980s meant bankruptcy for thousands of farmers. Some switched careers to lower-paying jobs, but most left the state. Its population dropped by 5 percent, a loss of 150,000 citizens. Today, many small towns look like the ruins of a once-great civilization. Half of the businesses on the square are shuttered. The rest are filled with second-hand stores, church annexes, or pay-day loan centers.

Many small towns rely on an outdated economic model. They thrived in the 20th century when physical proximity to goods and services mattered. It no longer matters in the 21st century, when most Americans prefer to shop at big box retailers in large cities or on the Internet. Businesses closed and families left. In response, the state government has been consolidating resources for decades. Small-town schools close in favor of county-wide schools.

Global forces drive traditional manufacturing, commerce, and other businesses out of small towns. More people are living in urban areas than non-urban areas for the first time in history. The leaders of this drive are the college-educated, or those with highly developed vocational skills. As they leave, the professional resources and tax base leave with them. If too many people in a rural community only have high school diplomas, there will not be enough high-paying blue collar jobs to sustain them.

Keeping the smallest Iowan towns alive requires everyone's help. CNN reporters visited Lone Rock in 2012. The 146 neighbors in the town were close-knit and helped each other when a business or farm was floundering. In the past they joined forces to harvest a sick farmer's field or cook, clean, and operate the Chatterbox Cafe when its owner was ill. But the average age of Lone Rock is 57. Few young people remain and nobody relocates there.

Similar problems plague more than 500 other towns that can barely keep themselves financially solvent or maintain their infrastructure. The Department of Natural Resources says many of these towns are not in compliance with the Federal Clean Water Act due to their leaky septic systems. Fixing them would cost millions of dollars for a new sewage system. Lone Rock took out loans of more than $600,000. Others simply fold.

With the loss of taxes comes a small-town death spiral: the town can't fix its infrastructure, so businesses leave. Soon the population dwindles. Schools shut down. Then banks. Then diners. Then bars. Soon there is nothing but empty buildings, elderly couples in run-down houses, and potholed streets. It is Detroit writ small, surrounded by corn-fields.

This book has argued that Iowa has an under-appreciated legacy and outsized influence on the globe. But that does not change the fact that Iowa is a second-tier state with deep economic and social problems. And whatever impact Iowa had in the past, its influence today can never match that of the larger, wealthier parts of the nation. Rich foreigners buy property in Los Angeles, Miami, or New York, never Des Moines. It is not part of the tourist route of any overseas visitor. When an Iowan travels abroad and tells locals where they are from, as I have many times, the answer leaves them confused. When I say that it is near Chicago (as near as 300 miles can be), they respond with, "Oh, OK – Michael Jordan!" Will Iowa always be doomed to this second-class status?

There are certainly problems for it to tackle in the future. The first is brain drain. The state's smartest students never stay in Iowa if they can help it. Why work at a small investment firm in Des Moines and barely make six figures when the same job can net you millions in New York? Why stay in Iowa if you want to be an actor, doing little more than commercials for local pizza chains, when you can seek fame in Hollywood? Why be a computer programmer for an insurance company when you can go to Silicon Valley, design software, and have enough money after the IPO to buy an NBA team?

Many of the stories of famous Iowans in this book are about those who left the state, even if they managed to take their values with them. John Wayne changed America's accent, but only when he relocated to Hollywood to appear in its films. Robert Noyce changed technology

128

and American business, but only when he ran successful ventures in Silicon Valley. Even Norman Borlaug only revolutionized crop science when he did his doctoral studies in Minnesota and left the United States altogether.

A second problem is substance abuse. Drug problems that have plagued America's urban centers since the 1970s are also tearing apart the heartland. Iowa has among the highest rates of methamphetamine usage and production in the United States. Why Iowa? Any fan of *Breaking Bad* will know that methamphetamine production requires a serious amount of lab equipment and produces noxious fumes. It is not a process that lends itself well to cramped areas. Large, open spaces away from the eyes of the law are preferred. Plus it doesn't hurt to produce it in an area with central distribution for the rest of the United States. For these reasons, the Midwest is perfect.

Although meth production in Iowa has declined in recent years, addiction remains in its wake. Mexican drug cartels have entered the state with their own high-purity forms of the drug. To stop this drug flow, Iowa has passed meth precursor laws, which bans the possession of critical substances for meth that can be freely purchased, such as anhydrous ammonia and ethyl ether. The law has had the unintended consequence of encouraging more dangerous methods of making the drug. More explosive materials are used, resulting in more lab deaths. One out of every 10 cooks will accidentally set their labs on fire.

Even the future of farming is under threat in Iowa. The family farm was once the bedrock of the state's culture, but it has been diminishing for decades and is all but dead. Only 1-2 percent of the population is directly involved in agriculture. Those that are involved typically have massive plots of more than 1,000 acres and run it with minimal staff. Even 3,000 acres can be run with a handful of workers, something that would have required the labor of dozens two generations ago.

Farmers that have stayed in business and reaped the spoils of longevity have net worths up to millions of dollars. But it is not their entrepreneurship alone that makes them wealthy. The largest farmers take hundreds of millions of dollars in federal subsidies per year in the form of crop insurance. In 2013, Iowa farmers received $1.3 billion in subsidies from the U.S. Department of Agriculture, nearly 10 percent of all national subsidies. Supporters say this program keeps America on top of global agriculture. It helps stabilize food prices for consumers and protects farmers from weather-related losses. Without this insurance, financially-stricken farmers might take land out of production, causing food prices to sharply fluctuate.

"Would you rather pay a dime now or a dollar later?" asked Mark Kenney, 33, a farmer from Nevada, Iowa. He raises 3,000 acres of corn, oats, and soybeans. He believes crop insurance is the best hedge against risk, both for himself and the national economy. "Of all the industries to be involved in, the security of our food, fuel, and fiber is of the greatest importance."

But critics say that crop insurance has turned American farmers into fat cats at the expense of tax payers. Subsidies have mutated into welfare for farmers that almost completely removes risk from agriculture. In 2013, drought drove corn prices to record highs. But farmers with "harvest price option" policies were paid those same record prices for what didn't grow, giving them record earnings as well.

Since the Depression, federal crop insurance has incentivized farmers to gamble on risky plantings by providing them with income even if their harvest fails. In 2013, it insured $117 billion worth of crops, or all the corn, cotton, wheat, and soybeans grown in the U.S. The program even covers the bills if crop losses exceed a predetermined limit. The program has been marred with fraud, ballooning to $14 billion in insurance, more than seven times higher than it was in 2000. Direct farm aid payments are capped at $40,000, but there is no limit on crop insurance subsidies, and the names of those who receive them are not publicly disclosed. Politicians have called it crony capitalism and a way to secure votes and donations from the farm lobby. This lobby spent over $91 million on candidates in the 2012 election cycle. Congress is afraid to cut them off and is poised to give billions more to wealthy farmers.

"The crop insurance program is terrible budget policy," said William Frenzel, a former 10-term Republican representative from Minnesota who served on the House Budget Committee and now analyzes fiscal issues at the Brookings Institution. He spoke to Bloomberg News about the network of fraud connected to the program. Over $100 million was bilked in North Carolina alone over the course of a decade through a network of claims adjusters, insurance agents, and farmers. "It's the kind of congressional back-scratching that got us into our debt and deficit situation."

Despite crop insurance's longevity, some of these rich subsidies have become politically toxic and are on the budget chopping block. The most notorious program is the billions of dollars given to the production of ethanol, a corn-based biofuel. A 2007 federal mandate guaranteed corn's role in the U.S. fuel supply. Back then oil imports soared and gas prices skyrocketed. Many thought it would reduce U.S.-reliance on Mideast oil.

The actual result has been a spike in corn prices, which has trickled down to hikes in food prices, putting strain on lower and middle class family budgets. Even many environmentalists such as Al Gore, who once touted ethanol as green energy of the future, have abandoned it. They say it diverts millions of acres of farmland from producing foodstuffs into fuel that is inefficient and even increases carbon emissions.

"Corn ethanol's brand has been seriously dented in the last 18 months," said Craig Cox, director of the Ames office of the Environmental Working Group, to Politico. He opposes the mandate as it's now structured. "The industry is still very politically well-connected, especially in the Midwest... but it certainly doesn't occupy the same sort of pedestal that it occupied two years ago."

Nevertheless, the outcome of ethanol funding, which is part of a massive subsidy program to Iowa, could mean economic life or death for the state. There are currently 41 ethanol plants and 14 biodiesel plants in the state, plus several cellulosic operators set to open. All of them could close if politicians kill the mandate.

Even if the elimination of federal farm grants don't ruin Iowa's economy, the depletion of its own soil could. Wind, rainstorms, and poor irrigation in fields remove tons of fertile topsoil from the state's 88,000 farms each year. The result of economic loss tops $1 billion in yield, according to Iowa State University Agronomy Professor Rick Cruse.

Agriculture is responsible for 25 percent of Iowa's annual gross domestic product of $152.4 billion. If the soil isn't properly buffered, the results could be catastrophic for its long-term economy. Some crop scientists even think that the trend of erosion is accelerating. With the reduction of Iowa farms from half a million in 2007 to less than a hundred thousand today and farmers chasing higher corn and soybean prices, conservation takes a backseat to profit.

REASONS FOR OPTIMISM

Despite all these problems, Iowans have many reasons for optimism. Iowa boasts some of the best schools in the United States. Its high schoolers rank in the top tier in standardized testing. The low tax rate makes it attractive for relocating businesses. It has never suffered from urban crime epidemics sweeping nearby cities like Chicago or St. Louis.

Iowa is even tackling some of its persistent problems. The long, slow death of its small towns may be exaggerated. That's at least what Iowa State Professor Terry Besser said to Iowa Public Radio. Many towns have been able to keep themselves alive due to pride and "social capital" – the sense of belonging to a real community. People band together in ways that would be alien in larger cities.

One example Besser gives is Conrad. In the 1980s many realized that the grocery store was going to close. They were horrified, since this was considered an "anchor store" in smaller communities, and would seal the fate of the community if it shut down. The community held a town meeting and came together to keep it running. After many small fundraisers, community events, the business was saved. Conrad weathered the storm, and it lives on today.

Farmers are also adapting to the 21st century. While big farmers dominate, as do their dependance on federal subsidies, smaller farms are sprouting up in the cracks. One such innovation is for farmers to trade their corn for grapes and open wineries. A 2006 profile on the phenomena noted that in Iowa, a new winery had been licensed every two weeks for the past year with nearly 70 commercial wineries in operation. The state has even hired its first oenologist to guide the novice winemakers.

Newly developed cold-hardy grapes are thriving in the rich soil of the Midwest. Some young people who grew up on farms and went to college are returning to enter the wine industry. They are attracted by the potential profits. One acre of corn can only net $40, while an acre of grapes can net $1,500. Some have reported more profits off selling grapes from two acres than 1,000 acres of corn and 3,000 head of hogs.

The most unimaginable bit of good news about Iowa, though, is that some hipsters are actually starting to consider Des Moines cool. In October 2014, The National Journal ran an article headlined "Do the Most Hipster Thing Possible – Move to Des Moines." Forget Brooklyn or Tacoma – Des Moines is the real place to be, due to its blossoming culture scene, urban beauty, and thriving start-ups. The article appears at first to be a bit of kitsch-loving hipster irony. After all, wouldn't a sub-culture whose entire wardrobe is ironic clothing want to live in the most ironically "cool" place on earth?

It turns out authors Matt Vasilogambros and Mauro Whiteman are dead serious. They write that ambitious minds are in the process of building a new Des Moines, a "tech hub in Silicon Prairie, an artistic center in the heartland, a destination for people who want to create something meaningful outside of the limits imposed by an over-saturated city like Chicago or New York."

Some of the new residents of Des Moines embrace these authentic virtues of the city and its kitsch value at the same time. Former Brooklynite Zachary Mannheimer moved here seven years ago to found the Social Club, a non-profit center for the arts. The 36-year-old had launched theater projects and restaurants in New York, but he wanted to find a place where he could revitalize a backwards urban community.

After visiting nearly two dozen cities, Mannheimer settled on Des Moines and founded the Social Club. It is lodged in a former firehouse built in 1937 and has bars, an art gallery, a theater, classrooms, and a restaurant. Over 20,000 visitors come through every month. Building such a center in Brooklyn would have cost over $300 million. The same facility in Des Moines cost $12 million. Similar cost savings affected his living quarters – trading a microscopic New York flat for lush digs in Des Moines.

"How much are you working every day? How much are you being paid? How much is your cost of living?" Mannheimer said to National Journal. "What if I told you we have per capita the same amount of cultural amenities here that you do in New York? Get over your, 'How do we even pronounce Des Moines?' and 'Where is it?' and 'Why should I even care about it?' Get over it, and come out here and visit."

Many young transplants to Iowa who have heeded his call work in start-up spaces. Gravitate, founded by Geoff Wood, inhabits 6,000 square feet of office space in the heart of downtown Des Moines for tech start-ups. The 12-story building houses multiple businesses on five floors. Over 40 entrepreneurs inhabit it, decked out with its artsy furniture, hardwood floors, desks, and open spaces. The number will soon rise to 100. These developers benefit from the lower costs in Iowa, which make them highly competitive with Californian developers.

The example of Wood and Mannheimer shows that the dream of Iowa still exists. People still come from across the nation to inhabit a place with open spaces, low prices, and the opportunity to create something new. The cost of living is six percentage points below the national average, job growth is 2.9 percent, unemployment has always been several points below the national average, and millennials are coming to the city in droves. In the fall of 2014, Forbes listed it as the best city for young professionals.

Iowa does not have the cultural flash of New York. It lacks the gorgeous landscape of California. But it has swaths of virgin soil – both literally and figuratively – where ideas, business, and social movements can be planted and take root. Unlike the coastal cities, nobody has to build on somebody else's foundation or depend on massive family fortunes. All it takes is vision and the hard work to make the dream a reality. The Midwestern blend of selflessness, ambition, and hard work still fuel new possibilities.

One last question remains in our discussion of Iowa.

If our beloved farm state has all these virtues and such a fantastic history, why doesn't anyone know about it? For anyone outside of the Midwest, it doesn't even register on their radar. If it does at all, a generic joke about its backwardness usually suffices to typify the state, even if the joke is better suited for somebody from West Virginia. A fast internet search of "jokes about Iowa" turned up some of these gems:

Q: Did you hear that the governor's mansion in Iowa burned down?
A: Almost took out the whole trailer park!

Perhaps my favorite gem is this:

Q: Why does all of the corn in Iowa lean to the east?

A: Because Nebraska blows and Illinois sucks!

The two jokes fail spectacularly. The first one looks like the handiwork of a third-rate stand-up comedian, doing the comedy club circuit and ending up in Des Moines without any new material, trying to rib the local audience with a generic zinger. The second joke has such a degree of Midwestern insider talk that it looks petty and quaint to an outsider. It would be as nerdy as a high school AV Club member insulting a marching band member's uniform.

Iowa does not register on the consciousness of outsiders because the identity of the state is the identity of its people writ large. Iowans are a humble people. Bragging of one's accomplishments, even if they are justified, comes across as pompous arrogance. A New Yorker might consider it a sign of confidence, but an Iowan thinks of it as grotesque flashiness, like wearing a designer coat on the farm while tending livestock at 5 am.

This is the true paradox of Iowa's greatness. Its people have accomplished much because of, not despite, their understated nature. Yes, it fed billions in the 20th century. Yes, it created the global education system. Yes, it provided the template for American English that is now being mimicked across the globe. Yes, it has more political power, vote-for-vote, than any place else on earth. Yes, it provides opportunities for those who want to create something from nothing.

Most importantly, it does all of these things without shouting its merits from the mountain tops. No state bumper stickers will say "Don't Mess With Iowa." Pop singers will never drone on endlessly about Iowa the way they do about California.

The wonder of Iowa is this – it is one of the most influential forces on earth. But if its citizens are doing their job correctly, you will never know it.

BIBLIOGRAPHY

"American Accent Schools Flourishing in Hong Kong." *Agence France-Presse in Hong Kong*, October 29, 2013.

Berlin, Leslie. *The Man Behind the Microchip: Robert Noyce and the Invention of Silicon Valley*. Oxford University Press, 2006.

Bloom, Stephen G. *Postville: A Clash of Cultures in Heartland America*. Reprint edition. New York: Mariner Books, 2001.

Bluth, Andrew. "Hot Spots – Silicorn Valley; Meditating For Fund And Profit." *New York Times* September 23, 1998.

Bouyerdene, Ahmet and Eric Geoffroy. *Emir Abd el-Kader: Hero and Saint of Islam*. World Wisdom, 2013.

Brilbeck, Aaron. "Illegal Immigrant Children Placed In Iowa." WHO TV, July 22, 2014.

Burton, Charlie. "The New Agricultural Revolution." *Wired*, November 17, 2010.

Camayd-Freixas, Erik. *US Immigration Reform and Its Global Impact: Lessons from the Postville Raid*. New York, NY: Palgrave Macmillan, 2013.

Chocano, Carina. "A Lotus Amid the Iowa Corn." *Los Angeles Times*, September 10, 2006.

Cook, Nancy. "What Goes On During the Iowa Caucuses, Anyway?" *NPR*. Accessed October 22, 2014.

Cooper, Christopher. "In This Farm Town, Gurus Transcend Party Politics." *Wall Street Journal*. January 8, 2008.

"Corn Ethanol Subsidies Are Alive and Well | Taxpayers for Common Sense." October 16, 2013.

Dillow, Clay. "Prospero The Swarming Farmbot Wants to Show

You The Future of Agriculture." *Popular Science.* June 15, 2012.

Edt, Erica Martinson. "Iowa Senate: Ethanol Fuels a Clash in Corn Country." *Politico*, July 31, 2014.

"Elkader: An Iowa Town Named After an Algerian, Muslim jihadist." *PRI's The World*, January 3, 2012.

Eller, Donnelle. "Erosion Estimated to Cost Iowa $1 Billion in Yield." *Des Moines Register*, May 3, 2014.

Fogarty, Robert S. *All Things New: American Commnies and Utopian Movements, 1860-1914.* Lexington Books, 2003.

Ford, George. "Iowa Farmers: $1.3 Billion in Subsidies: State Ranks Second in Nation." *The Gazette*, March 31, 2014.

Gillis, Justin. "Norman Borlaug, Plant Scientist Who Fought Famine, Dies at 95." *New York Times*, September 13, 2009.

Gladwell, Malcolm. *Outliers: The Story of Success.* Back Bay Books, 2008.

Goldsmith, Aaron, Michele Devlin, and Mark A. Grey. *Postville, U.S.A.: Surviving Diversity in Small-Town America.* GemmaMedia, 2009.

Gordon, Matthew J. "The Midwest Accent." *PBS: American Varieties.* Accessed October 31, 2014.

Green, Joshua. "The Iowa Caucus Kingmaker." *The Atlantic*, April 2, 2011.

Gross, Jan. "Celebrating a Muslim Hero, in Iowa." *Des Moines Register*, July 6, 2014.

Halstead, Alex. "One-On-One With Troy Davis, Illustrious Former ISU Running Back." *Iowa State Daily*, August 30, 2013.

Harsham, Philip. "Islam in Iowa." *Saudi Aramco World*, Nov./Dec. 1976.

Hartfield, Elizabeth. "Iowa Caucuses: The Historical Importance of Victory." *ABC News*. December 30, 2011.

Haygood, Wil. "Iowa Towns Dying Out As Farmers Quit Land." *Boston* Globe, May 8, 1986.

Herdt, Robert W. "The Life and Work of Norman Borlaug, Nobel Laureate." *Rockefeller Foundation*, January 14, 1998.

Hesser, Leon. *The Man Who Fed the World: Nobel Peace Prize Laureate Norman Borlaug and His Battle to End World Hunger.* 1st edition. Dallas, Texas: Durban House, 2006.

Holloway, Mark. *Heavens on Earth: Utopian Communities in America, 1680-1880.* Courier Dover Publications, 1966.

Hsu, Spencer. "Immigration Raid Jars a Small Town." *Washington Post*, May 18, 2008.

Jennings, Ken. "The Odd Story of How Elkader, Iowa Got Its Name." Conde Nast Traveler, September 15, 2014.

Jones, Maggie. "Postville, Iowa Is Up For Grabs." *New York Times*, July 11, 2012.

Karacay, Bahri. "Dünyayı Besleyen Adam: Norman Borlaug." TUBITAK *Bilim ve Teknik* 528 (Nov 2011): 60-67.

Kantor, Jodi. "Caucuses Empower Only Some Iowans." The New York Times, January 2, 2008.

Kovecses, Zoltan. *American English: An Introduction.* Broadview Press, 2000.

La Gresse, Bobby. "Football: The Legend That Almost Wasn't, How Troy Davis Overcame A Tough Freshman Year To Become An All-American." *Ames Tribune*, May 20, 2014.

Lull, Herbert Galen. The Manual Labor Movement in the United

States, 1914.

Lynch, David J., and Alan Bjerga. "Taxpayers Turn U.S. Farmers Into Fat Cats With Subsidies." Bloomberg, September 9, 2013.

Malcolm, Andrew H. "Iowa Town Contemplates Pitfalls of Being Mediators' Utopia." *New York Times*, January 1, 1984.

Mandelker, Ira L. *Religion, Society, and Utopia in Nineteenth-Century America*. University of Massachusetts Press, 2009.

Mastin, Luke. "The History of English – Late Modern English (c. 1800 – Present)." www.thehistoryofenglish.com. Accessed October 29, 2014.

Nebbe, Charity and Lindsey Moon. "Beating the Odds: How to Grow a Small Town." *Iowa Public Radio*, May 22, 2014.

Nienkamp, Paul. *A Culture of Technical Knowledge: Professionalizing Science and Engineering Education in Late-Nineteenth Century America*. PhD Dissertation:Iowa State University, 2008.

Noble, Jason. "Ex-lawmaker Pleads Guilty in Iowa Caucuses Case." *Des Moines Register*, August 27, 2014.

Paarlberg, Don and Philip Paarlberg. *The Agricultural Revolution of the 20th Century*. Wiley, 2001.

Peiser, Benny. "Happy Birthday Norman Borlaug: 100th Birthday of the Man Who Saved A Billion Lives." *Canada Free Press*, March 26, 2014.

Peterson, Anna L. *Seeds of the Kingdom: Utopian Communities in the Americas*. Oxford University Press: 2005.

Press, Robert M. "Borlaug: Sowing 'Green Revolution' Among African Leaders." *Christian Science Monitor*, June 29, 1994.

Rank, Scott. "Strange Hopefuls." *Iowa State Daily*, February 4, 2004.

----------. "Wig-wearing Candidate's Road to White House Runs through Ames." *Iowa State Daily*. October 9, 2003.

Roberts, Sam. "Unlearning to Tawk Like a New Yorker." *New York Times*, November 19, 2010.

Saulny, Susan. "Iowa Finds Itself Deep in Heart of Wine Country." *New York Times*, November 19, 2006.

Schmidt, Steffen. "Iowa Caucuses Still Useful For Both Parties." *Des Moines Register*, January 2, 2014.

----------. "Are Iowa And New Hampshire The Problem?" *Des Moines Register*. March 27, 2013.

----------. "Iowa Caucus Reforms 2014." *Insider Iowa*, January 31, 2014.

Schwieder, Dorothy. *Iowa: The Middle Land*. 1st edition. Ames: University Of Iowa Press, 1996.

Schwieder, Dorothy, Thomas Morain, and Lynn Nielsen. *Iowa Past to Present: The People and the Prairie*, Revised Third Edition. 1 edition. Iowa City: University Of Iowa Press, 2011.

"System Lets Iowans Redefine Gop Field." *Orlando Sentinel*, February 14, 1996.

Siegel, Fred. "Progressives Against Progress: The Rise of Environmentalism Poisoned Liberals' Historical Optimism." *City Journal*, Summer 2010.

Soniak, Matt. "When Did Americans Lose Their British Accents?" *Mental Floss*, January 17, 2012.

Sreenivasan, Jyotsna. *Utopias in American History*. ABC-CLIO, 2008.

Sutton, Robert P. *Les Icariens: The Utopian Dream in Europe and America*. University of Illinois Press, 1996.

"That Time Again: The Iowa Caucuses Explained." *The Economist,* January 2, 2012.

The Week. "Why The Iowa Caucuses Are So Important: 5 Theories." January 3, 2012.

Vasilogambros, Matt. "Midwest: A Victim of 'Rural Brain Drain.'" *Huffington Post,* March 2, 2011.

----------. "Do the Most Hipster Thing Possible: Move to Des Moines." *National Journal,* October 16, 2014.

"Yogic Flying Clubs for Students: Create World Peace and National Invincibility." *Yogic Flying Clubs,* www.yogicflyingclubs.org. Accessed November 5, 2014.

Winegar, Karin. "Iowa – Amana Colonies: Revisiting An Ideal That Really Worked." *Minneapolis-St. Paul Star Tribune,* February 7, 1993.

Wolfe, Tom. "Two Young Men Who Went West." In *Hooking Up,* 17-65. Picador, 2001.

Woodward, Billy. *Scientists Greater Than Einstein: The Biggest Lifesavers of the Twentieth Century.* Quill Driver Books, 2009.

ALSO BY MICHAEL RANK

SPIES, ESPIONAGE, AND COVERT OPERATIONS

FROM ANCIENT GREECE TO THE COLD WAR

BY MICHAEL RANK

TURN THE PAGE
TO READ AN EXCERPT

CHAPTER TEN

GEORGE KOVAL (1913-2006)
THE SOVIET SPY FROM SIOUX CITY, IOWA

Vladimir Putin, a former KGB officer who spent the 1980s in East Germany recruiting foreigners and sending them undercover to the United States, had a soft spot in his heart for sleeper agents. It was little surprise that on November 2, 2007, he honored a recently deceased Cold War deep-cover agent with a gold star, designating him a Hero of the Russian Federation, the nation's highest civilian honor. The ceremony introduced George Koval to the world.

But it was a great surprise to his friends and family. Russian acquaintances knew Koval as a physics professor, whose career was long and respectable but unremarkable. Americans knew him as a native Iowan – his actual birthplace – educated in Manhattan and a World War II veteran who loved baseball. He was affable, athletic, and a genius in technical studies. Once Vladimir Putin blew his cover – hidden for decades in old KGB files and only recently recovered by historians – both Russians and Americans learned his true identity as a man at the top of the pantheon of Soviet spies. His reconnaissance efforts were so far-reaching that they revised decades of the narrative of Cold War espionage.

George Koval worked at the Manhattan Project's laboratories in Oak Ridge, Tennessee, and Dayton, Ohio. He was the only Soviet agent to gain access to the top-secret project. Putin credited him with securing classified intelligence on the most crucial aspect of the atomic bomb, the device that initiates the nuclear reaction. The nuclear secrets he stole reduced by years the time it took for Russia to develop nuclear weapons, thus ensuring the preservation of its strategic parity with the United States, which it achieved in 1949. If not for him, four decades of the U.S.-Soviet arms race would have never happened.

Koval took these secrets to the grave, but bits of his legacy were first revealed in a 2002 book by Russian historian Vladimir Lota, entitled *The GRU and the Atom Bomb*. It recounts the activities of a Soviet spy code-named Delmar who, only with the exception of British scientist Klaus Fuchs, did more than anyone else in developing the Soviet atomic weapons program. His activities were so well hidden that Putin is thought to have only learned of them in 2006 when he saw Koval's portrait at a GRU museum and asked of the man's identity. The answer shocked the Russian premier.

George Abramovich Koval was born in Sioux City, Iowa, on Christmas Day in 1913. He was the second of three sons to a family of Jewish immigrants from Belarus, at the time part of the Russian Empire. The city had a large Jewish population and at least a half-dozen synagogues. At the turn of the century it appeared poised to become another Chicago, a Midwestern cultural and commercial hub that attracted immigrants from across the world. His parents came to Sioux City as part of a massive wave of Russian and Eastern European immigrants to the United States in the late nineteenth and early twentieth centuries, particularly its Jewish citizens, who suffered under Russia's pogroms. Many came to Iowa for its farms, meatpacking plants, and coal mines. The Koval family spoke Belarusian in the home, a language closely related to Russian, but Koval retained an American tinge in his fluent Russian for the rest of his life.

His father, Abraham, a carpenter, and his mother, Ethel, the daughter of a rabbi and former member of an underground Russian revolutionary socialist group, were ardent communists and supported the Bolshevik Revolution. They believed a new regime would right the wrongs of the anti-Semitic tsarist Russia and remained in contact with family members in the newly-formed Soviet Union. Abraham participated in local communist organizations, which flourished in pre-World War II America. In early 1914, the leftist Industrial Workers of the World organized a "free speech fight" in Sioux City to add industrial and agricultural laborers to their union. They found sympathy among newly arrived immigrants such as the Kovals, who were prone to exploitation by employers. In 1924, Abraham became the secretary of the Sioux City branch of ICOR (derived from the Yiddish name, "*Idishe Kolizatzie in Sovetn Farband*"), an organization that sought to establish a Jewish agricultural settlement in the Soviet Union. ICOR's goal was to construct the autonomous region in the Soviet Far Eastern province of Birobidzhan. The plans succeeded, and in 1934 it became the capital of the Jewish Autonomous Republic.

George Koval's Midwestern boyhood made him an ideal "sleeper" or deep-cover agent. By all appearances he was a typical American. Koval played baseball and spoke fluent American English, fully comfortable in the conservative social mores of early twentieth-century rural Iowa. Yet his bilingualism and biculturalism made him a spy in the classic mold of Jack Higgins's Kurt Steiner in *The Eagle Has Landed*, a novel about a German-English spy attempting to kidnap Winston Churchill during World War II. In the story, as Grosjean recounts, Steiner's father is a major general in the German army and his mother an American. The bicultural child becomes the leader of a German commando unit. Having been brought up in both England and Germany, he is the perfect candidate to abduct the prime minister.

Koval did not perform such daring feats in his spy career, but he came from a similar background. The youth was American by upbringing, Russian by family, and communist by indoctrination in his early years. He became involved in the communist cause, joining a local chapter of the Communist League, which in the years prior to the Cold War had not yet received pariah status. Classmates remembered Koval as being vocal about his communist beliefs. He was a delegate for the Young Communist League at the 1930 Communist Party in Iowa Convention when he was still sixteen. In 1931, he was arrested for occupying a municipal office and demanding shelter for two women evicted from their homes.

Koval was also exceptionally bright. He graduated from Central High School at age fifteen as a member of the Honor Society He enrolled in the University of Iowa to study electrical engineering for two and a half years.

According to his FBI file, he commented to his schoolmates that his family planned to return to Russia in 1932. ICOR facilitated their move to Birobidzhan in the midst of the Great Depression to work on a collective farm, a "utopia" that Russia was building for the Jews. The region was an isolated province in the Russian Far East near the

147

Chinese border. Stalin established it in the 1920s to integrate Jews into Soviet society and protect them from the anti-Semitism of the Russian gentile population while also creating a buffer against Chinese and Japanese expansion. To the Kovals, it was a new beginning for Russia, free from its tsarist past and Jewish pogroms. While on the farm, Koval improved his Russian enough to study chemical engineering in Moscow at the Mendeleev Institute of Chemical Technology. He met Lyudmila Ivanova while at the Institute, whom he married shortly after. He graduated in 1939 with honors and became a Soviet citizen.

It is unknown when Koval began to work for the Soviet secret service (GRU), but he was drafted into the army shortly after graduation. The GRU was likely scouting universities across the Soviet Union, looking for intelligent students with potential for a career in espionage. Several years of Stalin's purges depleted the ranks of the intelligence community, and there were many open positions. Koval was perfect for this role. He was raised as an American and could pass as one with little difficulty. He possessed a knowledge of science – a highly valued attribute at a time when Russia wanted to develop its military capabilities against increasing Nazi aggression – which made it possible for him to infiltrate laboratories in America. Yet he was a doctrinaire communist, a true believer in the cause, and would likely not defect to the West if embedded there, a perennial problem for the Soviet Union throughout the Cold War, when spies abandoned their posts for the greener pastures of Europe or America.

Koval was "drafted" into the Soviet Army in 1939 to cover up his disappearance from Moscow. Exactly how he was recruited is unclear, but Koval has written that he did not accept an offer of military training. He never wore a uniform nor was sworn into the armed forces. Rather, he was trained by the GRU to conduct espionage in the United States for an eight-year term, from 1940 to 1948.

Koval found it easy to sneak back into America even though his parents had relinquished their U.S. passports. In October 1940, he boarded a U.S.-bound tanker. Upon arrival in San Francisco, he simply walked across through border control with the ship's captain, his wife, and little daughter, who sailed together with him. He immediately went to New York. There he took command of the GRU station.

The Raven Electric Company, which supplied a number of U.S. firms such as General Electric, served as the station's cover. He created a cover story so bland that it would stifle the interest of any listener: He was an unmarried orphan raised by his aunt, and he never traveled.

Koval kept his political opinions to himself, never uttered a word about the Soviet Union, and established no contact with any communists outside of his handlers. It worked: After only a few months in the U.S., Koval registered for the draft. Raven secured for him a job deferment for a year because his Soviet handlers believed that his ability to steal information on chemical weapons would be compromised if he were drafted. They could not have been more wrong.

He joined the army on February 4, 1943. Koval received his basic training at Fort Dix before being sent to the Citadel in Charleston, South Carolina, to join the 3410th Specialized Training and Reassignment Unit. On August 11 he became a member of the Army Specialized Training Program (ASTP). This program gave talented enlisted men technical training at colleges and universities. Koval was enrolled in City College of New York (CCNY) to further develop his knowledge of electrical engineering. It was considered a Harvard for the poor and famous for brilliant students. He excelled there.

"He was very friendly, compassionate and very smart. He never did his homework," said Arnold Kramish, a retired physicist who studied with Koval at City College and later worked with him on the Manhattan Project, in an interview with *The New York Times* following Koval's death. "Of course, that was because he was already a college graduate back in Moscow, although we didn't know that at the time."

Koval's classmates thought it strange that he was a decade older than them. Although he fit in well with the group of student-soldiers, and he was something of a father figure, many aspects of him stood out. He smoked his cigarettes down to where they almost burned his fingers, which Kramish later learned was a distinctive Eastern European habit. He was quite a ladies' man, although his classmates didn't know that he had a wife in the Soviet Union. He had a casual manner, standing six feet tall, with a penetrating gaze.

The Army Specialized Training Program ended shortly after Koval enrolled due to the Allied need for more combat troops. Most program participants were transferred to the infantry. Koval, however, received a spy's chance of a lifetime. The Manhattan Project suffered manpower shortages and requested technically adept recruits from the Army. A colleague of his, Duane Weise, believed that Koval's high scores on the Army's intelligence test and his specialized training in handling radioactive materials caught their attention. Koval was sent to the blandly-named Special Engineer Detachment, which was actually a branch of the nuclear project.

The Manhattan Project was America's most secret military endeavor. In order to produce fissile materials, it grew during the war to employ more than 130,000 and cost over $2 billion ($26 billion in 2014). Los Alamos devised the bomb, but Koval was sent to the Oak Ridge laboratories, a critical research center where the bomb's parts and fuel were developed. It was considered the most difficult part of the atomic project.

His job in Oak Ridge couldn't have been better for his spy mission if his Soviet officers had wished it into existence. He was an army sergeant given the position of "health physics officer," requiring him to track radiation levels throughout the complex. Koval was given top-secret clearance and access to the entire facility. He drove from building to building, making sure stray radiation did not harm the workers. The Soviet Union now had a trained operative inside a secret center producing America's most closely guarded military technology. He was even given his own Jeep, which very few officers had.

"He didn't have a Russian accent. He spoke fluent English, American English. His credentials were perfect," said Steward Bloom, senior physicist at the Lawrence Livermore National Laboratory in California, who studied with Koval and called him a regular guy who "played baseball and played it well," usually as a shortstop.

"I saw him staring off in the distance and thinking about something else. Now I think I know what it was."

Koval's spy career spanned World War II and the Cold War, a period that ushered in the high-water mark of global espionage. All Cold War powers developed at least one government agency dedicated to intelligence gathering. The CIA was formed in 1947, and its goals were shaped at the outset by America's foreign policy challenges. It was authorized to conduct "secret operations against hostile foreign states or groups or in support of friendly foreign states or groups." In response, Russia formed the KGB in 1954, which acted as the internal security, intelligence, and secret police. Within U.S. borders, the FBI prosecuted spies, which it did with fervent zeal between 1935 and 1972 – the years of director J. Edgar Hoover, a fanatical anti-communist. It began investigating Soviet espionage in 1943 and doubled in size to 13,000 agents within two years. The agency scored many early victories against Soviet moles, particularly when it received information from Elizabeth Bentley, who prior to her capture passed on intelligence to Russia. She gave them a 112-page confession, naming 80 people as spies or paid informants.

Koval was aware of the growing paranoia of Soviet infiltration. He took many precautions, and sent information to his GRU handler through the use of couriers and the diplomatic pouch from the Soviet Embassy. He likely used other means that still remain unknown due to the limited number of extant sources that describe his manner of espionage.

Manhattan Project scientists developed two types of atomic bombs, one based on a relatively simple technology that required an enriched form of uranium, the other based on plutonium, which had not been isolated until 1941. Scientists at Oak Ridge discovered that in order to build a functional plutonium warhead, they required enriched uranium and the rare element polonium to initialize the chain reaction. Both materials produced lethal levels of radiation. Strict safety protocol was required, and Koval continually monitored radiation levels throughout the complex. He also kept inventory of experimental substances that were tested for their effectiveness as bomb fuels.

In his reports to Moscow, he described the Oak Ridge complex and its functions, the production of polonium and uranium, and the monthly volume of polonium. He notified them that polonium was being sent to Los Alamos. The Soviets already had a spy there, Klaus Fuchs, who gave the Soviets detailed information about the bombs. The information supplied by Fuchs and Koval on the importance of polonium allowed the Soviets to integrate the leaked scientific secrets coming from the two labs.

Koval was not the only agent who spied on the Manhattan Project for the Soviets. In recent years, as Russian archives have opened to historians and classified FBI files from decades back have been declassified, scholars and federal agents have identified at least a half-dozen Soviet spies involved in the project. They were mostly concentrated at Los Alamos. But all of these were "walk-ins," or spies who were ideological sympathizers but lacked rigorous training. Koval, in contrast, was an intelligence officer who had been groomed for his assignment in the Soviet Union for years and had wider access to America's atomic plants than any other mole.

On June 27, 1945, Koval was transferred to another secret lab in Dayton, Ohio, where the polonium initiator was being constructed and the polonium itself refined. The factories refined polonium 210, a highly radioactive material. It was crucial, as plutonium was considered too unstable to initiate a successful atomic reaction. Once again,

Koval's status as health physics officer gave him free rein throughout the installation. He was there to witness scientific breakthroughs and the ultimate triumph of a controlled nuclear explosion. The initiator was a success, and the first atomic bomb was detonated at Trinity in New Mexico on July 16 (the experiment in which Los Alamos director Robert Oppenheimer, watching the terrible mushroom cloud form, quoted the Bhagavad-Gita: "Now I am become death, the destroyer of worlds.") Three weeks later, in August 1945, two bombs, one uranium-based and the other plutonium-based, were detonated over Hiroshima and Nagasaki, forcing Japanese Emperor Hirohito to surrender.

After the detonation of the two bombs, the Soviet Union accelerated its nuclear program. The information provided by Koval and other spies pushed their program forward by years. They rapidly developed the polonium initiator for the plutonium bomb. This initiator was based on the information provided by the Soviet agent Delma– the code name for George Koval. In 1946, the CIA believed that the Soviets would not be able to successfully build an atomic bomb until 1950 at the earliest or 1953 at the latest. Their estimates tilted toward 1953. They were shocked when intelligence reports revealed that Soviets had tested a plutonium-based atomic bomb on August 29, 1949, at their Semipalatinsk Test Site in Kazakhstan.

In the run-up to the Soviet nuclear triumph, Koval was offered continued classified work in Dayton but began to fear his cover would be blown. Another GRU officer, Igor Gouzenko, had defected to Canada and revealed the extent of Soviet infiltration into the United States, even within the Manhattan Project. Another scientist, Alan Nunn May, was arrested in Britain as a result of Gouzenko's confession. At no point was Koval's cover in danger of falling apart; his alibi was airtight. But worries remained. Michael Sulick argues that he fled due to danger, because the Soviet Union would not have recalled him otherwise due to his excellent placement. The Soviets held on tenaciously to their spies; in the case of atomic spy David Greenglass, his handlers redirected him to the University of Chicago to target scientists working on classified military research even after he had been discharged from the U.S. Army and lost access. Therefore, Koval would not have left the United States unless capture was imminent.

Andrey Shitov, a Russian chronicler of Koval, writes that a Soviet defector told the FBI that an unknown GRU chief was based in New York and dealt electronic products. American counterintelligence agents found old Soviet literature that hailed the Koval family as happy immigrants from the United States. A pamphlet read that the Kovals came to the Soviet Union and "had exchanged the uncertainty of life as small storekeepers in Sioux City for a worry-free existence for themselves and their children." Intercepted Soviet intelligence cables had begun to implicate KGB-run spies such as Harry Dexter White, a senior Treasury Department official in the Roosevelt administration who died of a heart attack before being subpoenaed in 1948. Koval's old colleagues in Oak Ridge and Dayton confirmed that they had been interviewed by the FBI in 1949 and 1950. They were asked specifically about Koval, whom they learned at this time was not an orphan but an Iowan with communist parents. The FBI finally understood the full extent of their failure but swore his fellow scientists to secrecy. The U.S. Government refused to admit this failure, as it would have been highly embarrassing to have this divulged.

But they were too late for damage control. Koval had already left America, and his departure had been planned for years. Following the end of World War II, Koval received his honorable discharge from the army with reference to his "brilliant" work. He earned two medals, one "For Victory in World War II." Koval returned to New York, where he resumed his studies again at City College He completed his bachelor's degree on February 1, 1948, graduating *cum laude*. He then told his associates that he received a job offer to plan the construction of a power plant in Europe. Koval obtained a new U.S. passport for six months' travel and used a trading company, Atlas Trading, as a cover for his travel plans. He boarded the ocean liner *SS America* for Le Havre in October 1948, departing American shores. Koval never returned.

Meanwhile, the arms race between America and the Soviet Union that Koval launched began in earnest. As Michael Walsh recounts in *The Smithsonian*, when reports reached Harry Truman in 1949 that the Soviets had detonated a nuclear weapon, he apprised the American public of their test on September 24: "We have evidence that within recent weeks an atomic explosion occurred in the USSR. Ever since atomic energy was first released by man, the eventual development of this new force by other nations was to be expected. This probability has always been taken into account by us." But behind these resolute words, policy makers, government officials, and scientists debated whether to push for international arms control or produce the next generation of nuclear weapons. Truman made the decision when he authorized the development of the hydrogen bomb in 1950. Fears of nuclear annihilation between the world's superpowers were more real than ever.

Koval delivered intelligence to the Soviets that advanced their military technology by years, to the point that they were nipping at the heels of the United States in the decades-long arms race of the Cold War. Despite his achievements, Koval was not particularly well received in his adopted homeland. Whether due to Soviet embarrassment that they had to steal military secrets to develop their nuclear program rather than rely on their own scientific finesse, or worries that Koval could be an American double agent or mole, the intelligence establishment kept him at arm's length. He did not receive any high awards when he arrived, and his background as a spy in America negatively affected his life.

When he was discharged from the Soviet Army in 1949, he was given the rank of private and described as an untrained rifleman, despite nine years of service in the armed forces. This apparent poor performance in the army as well as Koval's academic and foreign background hindered his ability to find a job. He sought a position as a teacher or researcher but suspicions about him lingered. According to his CV, he spent 10 years, from 1939 to 1949, as an enlisted soldier but received no promotion despite his decade of service and higher education. Koval ended up having to beg the GRU to help him find a job.

He was only able to secure a position as a laboratory assistant at the Mendeleev Institute following Stalin's death in 1953, when his old superiors intervened with the Ministry of Higher Education. He earned his doctorate there and became a professor and prolific scientist, publishing over 100 scientific papers in the next four decades. His students thought him unexceptional, but they sometimes giggled when he pronounced the Russian words for technical terms such as "thermocouple" in an American accent. Koval worked as an instructor for the next 40 years. Rossiiskaia Gazeta said that he was a soccer fanatic even when elderly people at the stadium who knew of his secret past as a spy would quietly point him out.

Back in the United States, security tightened down and the Red Scare flared up. Accusations of Soviet espionage by former communist spies had been made public. These included testimonies by Elizabeth Bentley and Whittaker Chambers, a former Communist Party USA member and Soviet spy who later renounced communism and fiercely

154

criticized it. He testified before the House Committee on Un-American Activities (HUAC) in the perjury and espionage trial of Alger Hiss, an American government official accused of being a Soviet spy in 1948 and convicted of perjury in relation to this charge in 1950. American intelligence officials deciphered coded messages that unearthed an increasing number of Soviet spies. The FBI and CIA and its allies broke up Soviet spy rings in the years ahead, most notably the Cambridge Five. This ring consisted of British communists recruited during their education at Cambridge University in the 1930s. They passed on information to the Soviets during World War II and into the 1950s until fleeing Britain. The extent to which the establishment had been infiltrated was only now becoming apparent.

Koval lived for decades in obscurity, unknown in America or by his compatriots. Only in 2000 did the GRU recognize his accomplishments when it threw him a closed ceremony at its headquarters. He was awarded a medal for his service to military intelligence. The story of his exploits began leaking to the Russian media, but he was still only known by his code name. Koval himself preferred it this way. When Vladimir Lota interviewed him for his book, *The GRU and the Atom Bomb*, Lota wanted to identify Delmar by his true name, but the retired spy refused. He even kept his true identity from his family. They had vague knowledge that he worked for the GRU and that it was somehow related to the nuclear bomb, but for him it was a forbidden topic. Perhaps he was scared that he would be seen as a liability to the Soviets and shipped off to prison camp. "Maybe I should not complain (and I am not complaining – just describing how things were in the Soviet Union at the time) but be thankful I did not find myself in a Gulag, as might well have happened." Koval eventually changed his mind, but he died a month later on January 31, 2006, in Moscow at the age of 92.

In the decade before his death, Koval's old American army friend, Arnold Kramish, tried to reestablish contact with him, even after learning from an FBI interview that he had been a spy. As Walsh notes, Kramish came across some references to Koval and the Mendeleev Chemical institute in 2000 while at the National Archives. Kramish contacted the Moscow institute and was surprised to hear his old friend answer on the other end of the line. "It was an emotional moment for both of us," he said. Kramish and Koval began a letter correspondence that turned into swapping e-mails. Koval did not go into great details of his life, but he lamented that the Soviet Union did not offer him any high awards upon his return, especially amid "the terrible government-instigated-and-carried-out anti-Semitic campaign, which was at its peak in the early fifties."

Public appreciation only came posthumously, and even this came with an asterisk. First, Putin's acknowledgement in 2007 of Koval's contributions had less to do with honoring him and more to do with politics. The award ceremony came a month before Russian Parliamentary elections and coincided with Putin's promise to restore Russia's military might. Second, nations rarely bring public attention to their spies, even long after they have died, and particularly in the paranoid, secretive world of Russian espionage. It was likely to do with what Sulick describes in *Spying in America* as Putin touting the past achievements of the intelligence services as part of his nationalist agenda. As the former leader of the Federal Security Service (*Federalnaya Sluzhba Bezopasnosti*), he has significantly increased the authority, budget, and morale of Russia's intelligence services and grafted them into his personal power apparatus, blackmailing and spying on his political opponents.

Few spies have done so much for their homeland but received so little recognition. But in an odd twist, Koval's understated legacy is further credit to his ability as a spy. The American-born communist never sought out a career in espionage, he only saw it as the best means to support the communist cause. He never had any regrets and truly believed in the system. This is perhaps the greatest asset for a spy to have: to be content with a job well done, even if the public never knows of his accomplishments – as Joshua's spies realized over 3,000 years ago. After all, if his job is done correctly, they never will.

END OF THIS EXCERPT

ENJOYED THE PREVIEW?

BUY NOW

OTHER BOOKS BY MICHAEL RANK

Off the Edge of the Map: Marco Polo, Captain Cook, and 9 Other Travelers and Explorers That Pushed the Boundaries of the Known World

Lost Civilizations: 10 Societies that Vanished Without a Trace

The Most Powerful Women in the Middle Ages: Queens, Saints, and Viking Slayers: From Empress Theodora to Elizabeth of Tudor

History's Greatest Generals: 10 Commanders Who Conquered Empires, Revolutionized Warfare, and Changed History Forever

From Muhammad to Burj Khalifa: A Crash Course in 2,000 Years of Middle East History

History's Most Insane Rulers: Lunatics, Eccentrics, and Megalomaniacs from Emperor Caligula to Kim Jong-Il

The Crusades and the Soldiers of the Cross: The 10 Most Important Crusaders, From German Emperors to Charismatic Hermits and Warrior Lepers

Greek Gods and Goddesses Gone Wild: Bad Behavior and Divine Excess, From Zeus's Philandering to Dionysus's Benders

History's Worst Dictators: A Short Guide to the Most Brutal Rulers, From Emperor Nero to Ivan the Terrible

ABOUT THE AUTHOR

Michael Rank is a doctoral candidate in Middle East history. He has studied Turkish, Arabic, Persian, Armenian, and French but can still pull out a backwater Midwestern accent if need be. He also worked as a journalist in Istanbul for nearly a decade and reported on religion and human rights.

He is the author of the #1 Amazon best-seller "From Muhammed to Burj Khalifa: A Crash Course in 2,000 Years of Middle East History," and "History's Worst Dictators: A Short Guide to the Most Brutal Leaders, From Emperor Nero to Ivan the Terrible."

ONE LAST THING

If you enjoyed this book, I would be grateful if you leave a review on Amazon. Your feedback allows me to improve current and future projects.

To leave a review please go to the book's Amazon page. Thank you again for your support!

Made in the USA
San Bernardino, CA
01 March 2019